Examinati[...]
English [...]

Sr. Francis Mary

Successful Writing

A Rhetoric for Advanced Composition

Successful Writing

A Rhetoric
for Advanced
Composition

Maxine C. Hairston
THE UNIVERSITY OF TEXAS AT AUSTIN

W·W·Norton & Co.   New York   London

Library of Congress Cataloging in Publication Data

Hairston, Maxine C.
  Successful writing.

  1. English language—Rhetoric. I. Title.
PE1408.H297 1981   808′.042   80-24134
ISBN 0-393-95148-0

W. W. Norton & Company, Inc. 500 Fifth Avenue, New York, N.Y. 10110
W. W. Norton & Company Ltd. 25 New Street Square, London EC4A 3NT

3 4 5 6 7 8 9 0

Contents

Chapter 12: A Brief Review of Grammar 244

Guideline Questions for Students 272

A Glossary of Terms for Composition 273

Index 279

Preface

Successful Writing is a text for students who have mastered the basic writing skills and are now ready and motivated to learn more about the writing process. They want to know how to generate and organize ideas, how to adapt their writing to various audiences and purposes, and how to revise, edit, and polish their writing. They want to develop the skills they will need for writing in courses across the entire college curriculum and later for writing in their professions.

This book is designed to meet all these needs. It begins by defining good writing and explaining the principles underlying it. The second chapter analyzes the writing process, stressing that it is generative and recursive, and gives students a working model of the process that helps them to understand what happens when people write. The next two chapters suggest strategies for exploring writing options and making choices that are appropriate for audience and purpose, and also strategies for organizing and developing material. Chapter five focuses on linguistic and psychological techniques for interesting and holding the reader, and chapter six offers guidelines for making effective word choices. In chapters seven and eight, students learn what kinds of sentences and paragraphs work best for specific writing situations.

The chapter on revising, a special feature of this text, stresses that revising is an integral and ongoing part of the writing process, not a final stage in composing. The chapter not only gives specific strategies for revising, but it shows how to revise in stages and how to set priorities for revising. The final two chapters of the text stress varieties of working writing in order to give students practice in interdisciplinary academic writing and to prepare them to write case studies, grant proposals, abstracts, and other kinds of functional documents.

Several distinctive features of the book make it particularly useful for a variety of practical writing courses beyond the beginners' level. First, all student writing examples come from the papers of students in advanced courses. Second, suggested prewriting activities and writing assignments focus on pragmatic, real-life writing situations. Third, illustrative examples are taken from functional writing, not literary sources. Fourth, the book provides a comprehensive set of questions to help students evaluate their own written work and that of their peers. These questions will also increase their audience awareness and teach them how to become their own critics and editors. Finally, the advice about usage and conventions throughout the book is based on and supported by the results of a questionnaire that determined which lapses in usage professional people find most offensive. A summary of those results is included in the handbook section.

The underlying premises of the book are that writing is a dynamic process that can be taught and learned, and that people evolve as writers by writing and revising in a variety of situations. I believe these principles and the methods that grow out of them work for all kinds of expository writing.

Acknowledgments

I received encouragement, support, and valuable advice on this book from a number of colleagues and friends, but I want to express my special appreciation to Professor Michael Keene of Texas A & M University. His contribution to the book is major. He has been a perceptive and conscientious critic for every chapter in the book and has given me invaluable help on the sections on process, logic, and revision. I owe him a great deal.

I also want to express my thanks to the following people who made useful and enlightening suggestions at all stages of manuscript preparation: Edward P. J. Corbett of Ohio State University, Linda Cades of the University of Maryland, Joseph Trimmer of Ball State University, Andrea Lunsford of the University of British Columbia, Robert Rudolf of the University of Toledo, Susan Miller of the University of Wisconsin, William Harmon of the University of North Carolina, Amy Richards of Wayne State University, Douglas Atkins of the University of Kansas, John Walter of the University of Texas, E. D. Hirsch, Jr. of the University of Virginia, Paula Johnson of the University of Wyoming, Steven J. Vander Weele of Calvin College, and the late Gregory Cowan of Texas A & M University. And thanks go also to my efficient, prompt, and concerned typist, Nena Bentley.

To the Student

If you are a student using this book, presumably you are at least a functional writer, but you would like to become a competent and confident writer. You want to learn more about how good writers work, what skills they must have, and how those skills can be developed.

Such a goal is a reasonable one for a person motivated to learn how to write and willing to invest considerable time and energy to do it. Although undoubtedly the finest essay writers—people like Joan Didion or George Orwell—are blessed with special talents that the rest of us probably cannot acquire no matter how hard we might work, most people who write clear, effective prose are simply hard-working craftsmen who have mastered a set of skills. By study, trial and error, and a great deal of practice, they have developed the ability to communicate well in writing. That process is not a mystery; it is a tedious, slow, and often frustrating operation, but one that can be learned and taught.

As people work at their writing, they become more proficient and the words come faster and more readily, but I know of no one writing consistently who says that writing is easy. For most of us it continues to be hard work that we do because we need or want to say something and because we like the results. Being able to write well is immensely satisfying. It is also important.

Writing in College

Most college students know that the way they write is going to affect their grades in at least some of their courses, but they may believe that although writing skills are important in areas such as English, history, government, and journalism, they do not matter much in courses like engineering, accounting, or the health sciences where the subject matter is hard data, not ideas. Professors in those fields don't agree. They point out that data in any research study is seldom useful until it is analyzed, interpreted, and compiled into reports, and those reports must be clear, concise, and well documented. As activity in any field, either humanistic or technological, increases and the amount of information expands, the more important it becomes for people in that field to write. For this reason, an increasing number of departments and schools in universities are beginning to suggest that their students take sophomore or junior writing courses to help them develop the skills they must have when they begin practicing their professions.

Writing on the Job

Apparently almost all preprofessional students underestimate the amount of writing they will do when working in their field. In 1974 the University of Wisconsin at Milwaukee conducted a survey among retail, wholesale, and service organizations and among selected professional groups in Milwaukee. Respondents for the business organizations said that over 50 percent of their employees' time is spent writing reports, and that writing skill was a significant factor in promotion. On the average, lawyers spent 17.6 hours per workweek; engineers, 12; both social workers and architects, 10; doctors, 7; and dentists, 4.7.[1] Certainly nurses, bankers, salesmen, or research scientists must spend comparable amounts of their work time writing, and administrators in almost any organization—governmental, industrial, or academic— probably spend at least half their time writing.

These figures may surprise people who handle almost all of their personal communication by telephone, and who seldom *see* anybody writing. And with the advent of more electronic methods of communication such as long-distance conference phone calls, closed-circuit television, and direct phone selling, even some professionals in the field of communication such as Marshall McLuhan have said that writing is losing its importance in our society. But Professor Thomas Sawyer of the University of Michigan challenges this conclusion and argues that people put themselves at a serious disadvantage when they depend too heavily on getting a job done by speaking with people personally or on the telephone.[2] One major drawback of oral communication is that the audience cannot go back and review the message; thus speakers must repeat, illustrate, and restate their main ideas if an audience is to grasp them.

Sawyer also stresses that anyone who hopes to direct or coordinate any activity successfully *must* write; listeners simply cannot retain or follow oral instructions or directions of any complexity over any extended period of time. Those involved in spending either public or corporate money have an even greater need to write. No administrators accept oral proposals about how

1. Rhoda L. Sherwood, "A Survey of Undergraduate Reading and Writing Needs," *College Composition and Communication,* May 1977, p. 148.
2. Thomas Sawyer, "Why Speech Will Not Totally Replace Writing," *College Composition and Communication,* Feb. 1977, pp. 43–48.

money should be spent or oral explanations of how it has been spent. They require complete and explicit reports.

Indirect Effects of Knowing How to Write

Although an increasing number of people may realize that they must learn to write well if they are to function effectively in the business or professional world, many do not realize that how one writes can have consequences that one seldom hears mentioned. The first is that people who write poorly may never get a chance to demonstrate their intellectual abilities or professional competence because those who have authority and responsibility frequently use writing as a screening device. Applicants for a job, a scholarship, or admission into graduate or professional school are often asked to write a short essay; if that essay is marred by serious errors in mechanics or usage, or if its content is vague, pretentious, or badly organized, its author will not survive the first round of sifting.

Decision makers may also use writing as a screening device even though neither they nor the applicant fully realize what they are doing. In such cases an admissions officer or a personnel manager may react to a letter with errors in spelling or usage by assuming that the writer is careless or badly educated; that person will probably not get an interview. Applicants who write letters that are technically correct but wordy, vague, and difficult to follow may make an even worse first impression; those letters usually go straight to the wastebasket, and the dossiers are returned with a cordially phrased form rejection letter. The applicant may never know the real reason why he or she was turned down.

People who learn to write well, on the other hand, are not only able to open doors for themselves and enlarge their range of opportunities, but they substantially increase their chances of becoming leaders in whatever profession they choose. Almost by definition, leaders are people who can use language effectively to communicate and persuade. Learning how to write won't *make* you a leader; achieving that goal requires ambition, drive, and a number of other traits. You can be virtually sure, however, that you won't become a leader if you cannot write.

Powers Cameron, senior vice-president in Planmetrics, Inc., an industrial consulting firm based in Barrington, Illinois, says that the ability to express one's self concisely and effectively is a key element for success in the corporate world. One of his firm's major goals is helping executives to improve their writing. He believes that those people who do well after they finish an executive training program are those who know how to write.

But what is good writing? Business people or journalists or professors who complain about how badly people write sometimes give the impression that their chief concerns are poor spelling, faulty punctuation, and nonstandard usage. Those matters are important, as the summary of survey responses on p. 244 shows, and careful writers take care to see that these surface features of their writing meet traditional standards. But as we shall see good writing is much more than correct writing. Chapter 1 focuses on defining good writing.

Successful Writing

A Rhetoric for Advanced Composition

1 What Is Good Writing?

People who write do so for a variety of audiences and purposes. At times they may be writing for themselves in order to discover ideas or to express their emotions or to do exploratory, problem-solving writing that no one else will read. Most of the time, however, writers do expository writing to inform, entertain, or persuade other people. Writing which serves that purpose is the kind of writing I will be discussing in this book.

Because there are many kinds of writing, there are many kinds of good writing; it can be simple and terse or elegant and complex. Nevertheless, most people who talk about quality in expository writing agree that the key element of good writing is that it communicates effectively and efficiently with the audience for which it is intended.

The phrase "with the audience for which it is intended" is crucial because good writers never write in a vacuum. They adapt every element of their writing—tone, method, vocabulary, and choice of supporting material—to the people they are addressing, and they give careful thought to that audience both before and as they write because they know that writing that works well with one audience may not work well with a different one. But regardless of the concessions and adjustments that writers make for specific audiences, almost all good writers would agree that certain qualities are common to all effective nonfiction prose. Those qualities are significance, clarity, unity, economy, and acceptable usage. Another quality that is desirable, although not absolutely essential for communication, is vigor or energy. Writers who can produce prose that has all these qualities stand a good chance of enlightening, persuading, and pleasing their readers; those who cannot are apt to confuse, bore, or alienate readers.

Since most writers are also readers, you have probably already intuitively adopted these standards for the material you read. You know instinctively that you find writing most instructive and enjoyable when it says something that is interesting and informative, uses language you can understand, flows smoothly, and doesn't waste your time. That kind of writing communicates effectively. It works; therefore it is good.

Of course none of us should be so impatient or smug as to decide that anything we find hard reading must be badly written. The author may be dealing with a concept or situation too complex to explain in simple terms and sentences, and you must be willing to dig out the meaning, rereading and looking up words if necessary. Nevertheless, if intelligent readers who are willing to work at understanding a piece of writing have trouble following or comprehending it, then they are justified in suspecting that the selection may be poorly written.

The Problem of Models

Unfortunately, amateur writers frequently pattern their own writing after poor models. Rather than being annoyed or disgusted by wordy writing that is full of unfamiliar words and specialized terminology, they are impressed and try to imitate it. They think that writing must be good if it appears in a textbook or an official publication or report, or if it appears under the name of a well-known person. For example, here is a paragraph, written by the famous behavioral psychologist, B. F. Skinner, which many readers might find intimidating.

> The struggle for freedom and dignity has been formulated as a defense of autonomous man rather than as a revision of the contingencies of reinforcement under which people live. A technology of behavior is available which would more successfully reduce the aversive consequences of behavior, proximate or deferred, and maximize the achievements of which the human organism is capable, but the defenders of freedom oppose its use.[1]

One reason these sentences are confusing is that they have no personal or visual words; every word refers to an abstraction that cannot be grasped by the senses. Another reason is that phrases such as "contingencies of reinforcement" and "the aversive consequences of behavior, proximate or deferred" are psychological jargon that is unfamiliar to us. Yet in his novel *Walden II*, Skinner vividly dramatized the same principles of behavioral psychology he sets forth in the book quoted here. The topic itself is not difficult; it only appears to be because of Skinner's prose style when he discusses it in *Beyond Freedom and Dignity*.

Here is another example of obscure, inflated writing that might awe a reader because the language sounds impressive. Ironically, it comes from a pamphlet inviting people to submit grant proposals for ways to improve the teaching of writing.

---

1. B. F. Skinner, *Beyond Freedom and Dignity* (New York: Alfred A. Knopf, 1971), p. 125.

Studies here should concentrate on the links between the learning of classroom discourse rules and cognitive achievement through such mediating factors as social and referential understandings and the teacher's differential distribution of information due to varying expectations of student abilities.[2]

This sentence is unclear. After reading it seven or eight times, I still cannot figure out what the phrases "such mediating factors as social and referential understandings" and "differential distribution of information" mean. This is the kind of writing that at first glance seems scholarly and profound, but upon analyzing you find that the words may look impressive, but they don't communicate.

This kind of language that looks awesome at first, but really does more to confuse than enlighten, is like the emperor's new clothes in the old Hans Christian Andersen fairy tale. You remember the story about the emperor who allowed two confidence men to sell him some nonexistent clothes, which they claimed were made from cloth so fragile and precious that it was visible only to people of wisdom and high position. When the emperor put on his "new clothes" and appeared in public, the people who saw him nodded and exclaimed how lovely his robes were because everyone feared that he or she was the only one who didn't see the clothes. The onlookers didn't dare to point out that the emperor was naked for fear that other people would think them stupid and inferior. The crafty salesmen got away with their fraud because the spectators were so unsure of themselves that they didn't trust what their senses told them.

In the same way, intimidated readers often pretend to understand obscure and confusing writing for fear that if they ask, "What does this mean?" other people will think they are stupid or uneducated. Thus they tolerate writing that is evasive, pretentious, and pompous, and sometimes even try to write that way themselves in order to impress others. The farce ends only when someone, like the child in Andersen's fairy tale, has the courage to say, "But the emperor doesn't have on any clothes." In the world of working writing, an editor or boss who cannot understand a report is apt to say it rather quickly.

In official or academic prose one often encounters another kind of poor writing, which, though not always difficult to understand, communicates poorly because it is dreary and flat. Frequently such sentences are weighted down with abstract terms, long plodding sentences, strung-out noun clauses, and passive or linking verbs that convey no sense of movement or action. Here is an example from an education textbook.

In the first place, most classroom learning tasks are potentially meaningful; that is, they are related on a nonarbitrary, substantive basis to a previously learned background of meaningful ideas and information. Rotely learned materials, on the other

2. *Basic Skills Research Grants Announcement*, The National Institute of Education, Summer, 1977, p. 5.

hand, are discrete and relatively isolated entities which are only relatable to cognitive structure in an arbitrary, verbatim fashion. Second, because they cannot be anchored to existing ideational systems in the learner's cognitive structure, rotely learned materials are much more vulnerable to forgetting.[3]

The author is simply saying that students learn best when they can connect what they do in the classroom to their everyday experiences, but that students tend to forget material memorized for its own sake. The author could quickly have made that not very complex point if he had used plain language and given an example or two; instead he has forced the reader to wade through a thicket of abstract terms to track down the meaning.

Standards for Readable Prose

On the other hand, here is an example of clear writing about a theoretical topic.

> The most obvious examples of scientific revolutions are those famous episodes in scientific development that have often been labeled revolutions before. . . . Each of them necessitated the community's rejection of one time-honored scientific theory in favor of another incompatible with it. Each produced a consequent shift in the problems available for scientific scrutiny and in the standards by which the profession determined what should count as an admissible problem or as a legitimate problem-solution. And each transformed the scientific imagination in ways that we shall ultimately need to describe as a transformation of the world within which scientific work was done. Such changes, together with the controversies that almost always accompany them, are the defining characteristics of scientific revolutions.[4]

While the writing is not concrete, it is specific. Kuhn has used almost no ambiguous or fuzzy terms. He has used strong verbs like ''produced'' and ''transformed,'' and although his sentences are long, he makes them easy to follow by using parallel structure.

In other words, writers usually communicate best if their writing does not put an excessive strain on the reader's attention or capacity to absorb meaning. As one theorist puts it, the more time and effort a reader must invest in deciphering a writer's language, the less time and energy that reader will have left to absorb meaning.[5] If you have to fight your way through a piece of prose, trying to translate phrases, sift through excess words, and dig for the

3. David P. Ausubel, ''A Cognitive-Structure Theory of School Learning,'' in *Instruction: Some Contemporary Viewpoints*, ed. L. Siegel (San Francisco: Chandler, 1967), p. 209.
4. Thomas S. Kuhn, *The Structure of Scientific Revolutions*, 2d ed., International Encyclopedia of Unified Science, Vol. 2, No. 2 (Chicago: University of Chicago Press, 1962), p. 6.
5. E. D. Hirsch, *The Philosophy of Composition* (Chicago: University of Chicago Press, 1977), p. 77.

main points, you will not learn from it as quickly or as well as you would if the writing were clear, specific, and economical. Of course this doesn't mean that a writer should always try to make everything so simple that an average reader can grasp it with very little effort. Nevertheless, though writers can certainly expect their readers to work at understanding their writing, they should not make that writing any more difficult than they have to, given the subject matter.

When readers have to go back and reread, they are less efficient readers. Thus if you can make your writing so clear and so tightly organized that the reader can always move forward, you're writing well. Most of us are not good enough writers to do that all the time, but the goal is worth striving for.

What Is Significant Writing?

Good writers say something significant; that is, their writing informs, entertains, enlightens, persuades, or stimulates the reader to action or further thought. It pleases readers by telling them something of interest or value that they didn't know before.

You may think this part of the definition of good writing puts impossible demands on a novice writer. You may also find it confusing, saying to yourself, "That isn't very helpful—what is interesting or significant to one reader may be useless and boring to another. How am I supposed to know?"

You are right, of course. You will have to analyze how much your audience already knows on a topic and what will interest them before you can decide what writing will be significant for that audience. Making such an analysis and then deciding how to approach your topic is a complex process that we will be studying throughout this book. But the basic requirement is simple and obvious: good writing should say something of some consequence to someone. It need not be earthshaking, profound, or original; most writing isn't. It should, however, have some "surprise value."[6] It should be more than a collection of obvious statements, generalizations, or trivial observations. Here, for example, is a student paragraph that is not significant because it has no surprise value.

The idea that a candidate elected to public office should owe favors or special treatment to those special interests which helped to finance or support his campaign goes against the concept of representative government. Each citizen has a right to be represented, and an elected official has an obligation to represent all his constituents equally. The elected official should owe no more to special interest groups which supported his campaign than he owes to every citizen he represents. Special interests

6. James Kinneavy, *A Theory of Discourse* (Englewood Cliffs, N.J.: Prentice-Hall, 1971), p. 93.

should be given no more weight than the interests of any other group, and the public interest should be paramount.

This is the kind of safe, slick paragraph that many writers can turn out with little thought or effort. It is correct, it is smooth, it is literate; but it is not good writing. It is canned discourse that serves no purpose in the world of real writing.

Some kinds of writing—for instance, papers done for some college courses—do not necessarily have to have surprise value, but there are ways to make such writing significant even if it does not tell the reader something new. Later I will suggest specific approaches and techniques to use in those circumstances.

What Is Unified Writing?

Writing is unified when it is so well held together by transitional devices or by a pattern of development that readers are not likely to lose their way as they read through it. In a unified paragraph every sentence develops or supports the main idea, and in a unified essay, every paragraph connects with those before and after it. No sentences go off in irrelevant directions, and no unexpected topics crop up in the middle of a section. The writing is tight; it sticks together.

Here is a unified paragraph from a student paper.

Ilie Nastase. You may love him or you may hate him, but either way you've got to admit that he's interesting. Nastase, affectionately known as "Nasty," is easily one of tennis's most controversial players. Nastase is famous for prancing the court mischievously like a grown-up Dennis the Menace, occasionally hitting tennis balls at linesmen and fans, sporting obscene gestures to the fans, and always being totally unpredictable. Who else but our loveable Rumanian would show up for an important tennis match wearing polka-dot pajamas? No one else would pull such a stunt for a measly fifty dollars, but "Nasty" did in the 1965 Macon International. Yes, even in the 60s the bad boy of tennis had the reputation of being a troublemaker. He hit tennis balls at linesmen so often that manager Bill Riordan had to work out a system for fining him. Nastase was fined fifty dollars if he hit the linesman, twenty-five if he missed.

This is a tight, carefully developed paragraph that holds together because every sentence grows out of the opening sentence, and each sentence hooks into the next one.

In contrast, here is a poorly unified student paragraph.

Another big chunk of the union man's wage pays for medical and dental care. The health benefits paid out to auto workers cost more than the steel used to manufacture the cars they are assembling. How dangerous can throwing cars together be when those meddling sissies from OSHA practically make it a felony to allow a man to scrape his knuckles on the assembly line? Where can the money be going? The doctors and dentists profiting from these costs understand better than anyone what a poor value these add-on costs make American products. When they go shopping for a new car, they frequently choose a Mercedes or BMW.

This paragraph falls apart because the writer starts off talking about the high cost of union medical benefits, gets sidetracked into talking about safety in the auto plants, and winds up talking about doctors buying foreign cars. The reader gets the feeling that there is no plan behind the writing, no real point being made.

What Is Acceptable Usage?

For our purposes in this book, we can define acceptable English usage as the kind of language that most educated people use and expect others to use in formal or informal communication. It is the level of usage that you encounter in a magazine or newspaper and hear people speak at conferences, in serious conversations, or in public speeches. For the most part, that language conforms to the rules of usage you spent three or four years learing in high school and may have reviewed in college. But the phrase "for the most part" is important. Anyone who knows all the fine distinctions that one finds in a complete handbook of English usage also knows that many successful and influential people do not always speak absolutely "correct" English. Many fail to distinguish between "who" and "whom,"; they frequently split infinitives and sometimes they use effective sentence fragments. But their audiences usually don't even notice these deviations from standard usage because such lapses are so minor and so common, even among extremely articulate and well-educated people, that they don't matter. In other words, these people's usage is acceptable. They don't make the kind of blunder that distracts the audience's attention from *what* they are saying or writing to *how* they are saying or writing it.

At the beginning of the handbook section to this book you will find a list of those specific deviations from standard English usage that seem particularly serious to a representative group of professional people, and therefore should be avoided by a writer who wants to make a good impression on that audience. You will also find a review of the standard conventions of usage and punctuation. For now, however, you should get along fairly well if you remember these major guidelines.

1. Most sentences should have verbs; if you omit the verb, do it deliberately and for a specific reason.

2. Subject and verb must agree in person and number.
3. Pronouns should agree in number, gender, and person with the nouns they refer to.
4. Use correct verb forms; if you have trouble with the forms of irregular verbs—for instance, *go, bring, know*—get a handbook and memorize them.
5. Avoid double negatives.
6. Use commas to set off items in a sentence that should be separated or to mark natural pauses. (For discussion of when to use commas, see the grammar review.)
7. Use the objective form of a pronoun after a preposition.
8. Use the correct adjective and adverb forms.
9. Keep parallel structure when you have two or more clauses or phrases in a sentence.
10. Check to see that modifying words and phrases cannot be matched with the wrong term, especially in the introductory portion of the sentence.

If you are using this book, you probably already follow most of these conventions naturally without even thinking about it. But many students who speak and write quite acceptable English worry far too much about making "mistakes in grammar" when they write. That anxiety is understandable because writing does lead readers to make judgments about the writer. But remember two things. First, usually your audience doesn't care about every last grammatical detail being correct; what they want is smooth, clear prose free from distracting blunders and obvious misspellings. Second, if you proofread and edit your writing carefully on the second or third draft, you should be able to clean it up to a level that is acceptable to your audience. If, however, you get overly concerned about correct forms and punctuation when you are trying to develop and organize your ideas into a first draft, you may get so tense and scared that you will not write nearly as well as you are capable of writing.

Correct spelling, however, seems to be very important. Although the correct spelling of English words has become standardized only in the last 100 years, today most educated readers notice misspellings and condemn them. In fact, many administrators or business people quickly reject any application or report with several misspelled words, particularly common or important words. While these readers may not claim that a poor speller is unqualified for a job or a place in a professional program, they usually do conclude that the person is careless or indifferent to the opinion of others.

By this stage in your life, you should know whether you are either a fairly good speller or a poor one. If you are a poor speller—and many bright and capable people are—do something about it. Get a dictionary and use it consistently. One professional writer I know says he has already worn out two dictionaries because he has to look up dozens of words every time he writes a column—but he does it. You can also develop ingenious strategies that will help you; for example, remembering that "stationary" with an "a" is an *ad*jective, but "stationery" with an "e" is the kind that comes with *e*nvelopes. One poor speller I know sometimes looks in the Yellow Pages of the telephone book to find words she needs; she looks under Italian Restaurants to find "lasagna" or under Physicians to find "orthopedic."

If you want to improve your spelling so that you won't have to resort to such measures, take a crash spelling course if one is available or buy a programmed spelling text. Or finally, find a friend or colleague who can spell and get that person to check over your paper or report before you turn it in. And even if you are a fairly good speller, check your own paper and look up any words you have the least doubt about.

With most educated audiences you just cannot afford glaring spelling errors. They simply cost too much. So whatever the reasons for correct spelling being so important—and they are probably more psychological than rational—writers who want to make a good impression on their audiences are meticulous about their spelling. I would make one important exception to that generalization: most professors do not expect flawless spelling in essay exams or papers written in class. Nevertheless, careful students at least memorize key words and names in the material they are going to write about. You can at least do that much to convince your audience that you care about the impression you are making.

These guidelines have not told you everything you need to know about what makes writing work, what makes it effective and readable, but by now you should feel that you have at least some workable criteria for distinguishing good writing from bad. I will be adding to and elaborating on those criteria throughout the book.

EXERCISES / *Prewriting Activities*

1 Rank each of the following four paragraphs on a scale of one to ten (*one* = excellent, *ten* = terrible), using as your criteria the qualities significance, clarity, unity, economy, acceptable usage, and vigor. Give the reasons for your rankings.

Airbags are thought by many to be a miracle device which would tend to give many drivers a false sense of security against injury. This would tend to make them less alert and therefore less competent drivers. There are today already far too many incompetent drivers on the road, and a false sense of security would tend to make the situation even worse. It is far safer to have a good driver who can avoid accidents than a bad driver who will cause accidents, but has equipment which will hopefully save him from serious injury or death. Another safety problem with airbags is that in tests, for one reason or another, they have been known to inflate when there was no collision. It is impossible to control a car with an inflated airbag in it, so this would likely cause a collision.   Student paragraph

Ronnie Prado graduated from high school two years ago and went to work for a small construction company. His weekly paycheck of $180 seemed like a lot of money. He bought a new color television set and a stereo on credit. The monthly payments were only $65—chicken feed. With all the money he had saved during school, he bought a good used truck. Nice apartment, some new clothes—everything fell into place. In November Ronnie had an accident with his truck. He hadn't insured it against collision, so it cost him a month's pay just to get it running again. The new year brought an increase in his rent of $40 a month. His grocery bill had jumped another $20 a month in the past year. Gasoline was half again as much as it was when he bought the truck, and he often had to drive fifteen or twenty miles to a construction site. By March the Friendly Finance Company had repossessed his television and stereo. The rent was ten days past due, he had no money in the bank, and his girlfriend was talking about marriage. His credit rating was shot. So Ronnie sold the truck, married the girl, and now lives with her parents.   Student paragraph

One holds the knife as one holds the bow of a cello or a tulip—by the stem. Not palmed nor gripped nor grasped, but lightly, with the tips of the fingers. The knife is not for pressing. It is for drawing across the field of skin. Like a slender fish, it waits, at the ready, then go! It darts, followed by a fine wake of red. Even now, after so many times, I still marvel at its power—cold, gleaming, silent. More, I am still struck with a kind of dread that it is I in whose hand the blade travels, that my hand is its vehicle, that yet again the terrible steel-bellied thing and I have conspired for a most unnatural purpose, the laying open of the body of a human being.

Richard Selzer[7]

Such possibilities may not redeem society, but they might help make life in society more bearable for those who see its contradictions and feel that the situation is too hopeless to warrant surrendering one's own development for dreams of revolution. The resulting possibilities might remain abstract—both in content and in their isolation from social praxis—but they are preferable to self-delusion or to paralyzing self-consciousness. Despite their experience of the limits of discourse, the modernists have recovered the two basic values inherent in the humanities: an active sensibility able to participate sympathetically in the manifold particularity that constitutes empirical reality and the possibility of realizing aspects of consciousness shared by all men and offering an enlarged sense of one's own identity. Beyond that, at their most triumphant moments, the modernists have

---

7. Richard Selzer, "The Knife," *Mortal Lessons* (New York: Simon and Schuster, 1976), p. 92.

glimpsed a vision in which the structures of consciousness and the diversity of experience seem dialectically related.   Charles Altieri[8]

2   How comparatively readable are these examples from advanced writing students' papers?

Recently the President of the University proposed to the Board of Regents that student counseling services be discontinued because of a lack of funds. We students, as a body, need to express our concern over this important development. Throughout our lives we have had and will have need for counseling of some sort. Parents raised us as children, guidance counselors listened to us in high school, and friends will help us as we get older. College is a phase in which we have certain needs. Counseling is one of them. We must all become aware of how vital this service is for us here at school.

As more and more land is used for construction sites, no appreciable efforts are being made to acquire additional land to compensate for this loss in parking spaces. The main reason for this inactiveness is the lack of available funds. It has been suggested that we draw upon the Available University Fund. This fund, however, has been committed to vital academic projects and is already tentatively budgeted for future appropriations. Thus the university has been unable to allocate funds to alleviate this problem.

The most substantial tennis equipment investment you make should be for shoes. Don't cut corners here. If your feet don't feel comfortable when you are playing tennis, it is very difficult to get into the proper position to hit the ball. For $30 you can get a fine pair of lightweight durable tennis shoes that feel so good you'll be itching to get out on the courts. Be sure to get the kind with a basically flat, no-skid tread pattern. These will be fine for whatever surface you play on: cement, asphalt, or clay. Ridged-soled jogging shoes just won't do. You'll end up slipping to a hard fall more often than not. Check the toe for a hard rubber finish. This will come in handy if you drag your back foot on serves as many people do. By the way, there's nothing wrong with that; most professionals do it.

3   Clip a short article or newspaper column that you think is clearly written. Analyze it for the features that you think make it clear.

4   Analyze the writer's word choices in this opening paragraph from a student paper; then try to rewrite it to make it more vigorous.

8. Charles Altieri, "Objective Image and Act of Mind in Modern Poetry," *PMLA*, 91, No. 1 (January 1976), p. 113.

The rush hour traffic is heavy. Beginning at about 6:00 P.M., the narrow lanes are crowded to capacity with an array of various individuals jockeying for position. No, this description is not of a crowded street in a business district; it is of the running path which encircles Town Lake in Austin or any of the similar public running facilities in most American cities. Competitive races like the Boston Marathon have attracted record numbers of participants each year since 1973. Austin's own race, the Capitol Ten Thousand, is now so large that the sponsors are considering limiting the field.

Suggested Writing Assignments

1 An eminent Shakespeare scholar once said that writing clear directions is far more difficult than writing literary criticism. Write directions that would enable your reader to accomplish one of the following operations. Before you begin to write, analyze your reader. What is his or her age, educational level, and degree of sophistication or experience?

A.   Pick up a rental car at the airport and get to a meeting at a hotel in the center of your city.

B.   Travel from a major city to a small city, changing planes at large terminals and then taking a commuter flight to the final destination. For example, travel from El Paso to Dallas on one airline, change at the Dallas–Fort Worth Airport to another airline, fly to Dulles Airport in Washington, and take another flight to Newport News, Virginia. Or fly from Urbana, Illinois to O'Hare Airport in Chicago on one airline, change airlines and fly to Kennedy Airport in New York, then take a different plane to Ithaca, New York.

C.   Groom an animal for the show ring.

2 Write a job description of a job you have or have had in the past. Assume that the reader for this description is the personnel director in a company; that the person needs to know not only what the responsibilities of the jobs are, but what skills it requires and what kind of person would work most effectively in it.

3 If you live in or near a major city, go to the museum shop of your local art museum and study the reproductions and prints they have on sale. Then select three items and write descriptions of them, averaging about 50 words per item, that could be used in a mail-order catalog that such museums send to members and patrons.

CHAPTER 2

What Happens When People Write?

People who are not writers often assume that the writing process is a mystery, not subject to analysis, and that people who do write well do so because they possess the magic combination of talent and inspiration. Such a belief is partly justified. One cannot write a detailed and objective account of all the steps a writer goes through to produce an article or book just as one cannot describe precisely the motions that good tennis players go through as they perform. And certainly the best writers are people with talent just like the best performers in any other field. But the qualification does not mean that most working writers possess special secrets and powers that are beyond the reach of the average literate person any more than it means that only a few gifted people can play a good game of tennis. Tennis coaches know differently. By paying close attention to the way superior tennis players perform, and by analyzing their own games, those coaches devise guidelines and techniques that will help novice players improve.

In the past few years, composition specialists have been using similar techniques to find out more about what both professional writers and competent amateur writers do when they write. By combining these new insights with the classical rhetorical principles, they have developed some generalizations and guidelines about writing to help people who want to improve their writing. They certainly have not devised a foolproof system for teaching writing, nor even one that will help everyone; one cannot, after all, draw a blueprint for creative activity. Nevertheless, working from what we now know about how people write, we can draw useful conclusions about the writing process.

I should specify that I am talking here about expository writing; that is, writing to get a job done. One could also call it task writing, problem-solving writing, or working writing. It is not what is usually called "creative writing," that is, fiction, poetry, or drama. Of course, expository writing is also creative, and the way people do it is not radically different from the way people write novels, stories, or plays. A major difference, however, is that people usually do expository writing only when they take on or are assigned some specific writing job. They write because they need to explain, persuade, inform, or report. They have a problem; they write to solve it.

Student writers in composition courses often have trouble writing because the problems they choose or are given to write about don't seem real or important enough to warrant their putting out the effort required to produce a creditable piece of writing. You can overcome that obstacle by trying from the start to pick topics that are fresh and interesting to you. If you consistently try to play it safe by writing routine papers on familiar and easy topics, you are going to be bored. And it is much harder to write well when you are bored—not impossible, just more difficult. Obviously, people who must do a lot of job-related writing are sometimes bored, but they do a competent job anyway. For now, though, you shouldn't impose any more unnecessary handicaps on yourself, so try to find or work out with your instructor some topic that interests you enough to make research and inquiry about it a pleasure, not a chore.

When you do have to write on an assigned topic—for example, one professor might ask you to write about the Hudson River school of painters in nineteenth-century America and another might assign a paper about the conflict between the antitrust division of the government and the big oil companies—you are likely to enjoy writing your paper more if you dig out some concrete material from original sources rather than using information from your text. If several people are working on one topic, you might have a brainstorming session to help you generate ideas. And whenever you can, work in your own experiences and conclusions to give your paper an individualistic flavor.

The ideal would be a real writing assignment, one you have to do for your job or for another course. Lacking such an assignment, you can invent one of the kind you expect to encounter in your profession or personal life. In other words, engage in the kind of game simulation that students might do in a business management course.

To demonstrate this kind of simulation and illustrate the stages of the writing process, I have chosen a model topic, one that comes from my own interest in the problems of career women and my experience on a college campus.

MODEL TOPIC: A proposal to establish a first-rate day-care center on campus for the children of students, staff, and faculty.

This is an idea that I have thought and talked about a good deal, but have never written about. But because I care about the issue and because I am an experienced writer, I am sure I can write a convincing proposal. As I work it out, I'll try to explain what I am doing. My method won't be the only way or perhaps not even the best way to proceed, but it will illustrate one workable approach to carrying out a writing task from problem to solution.

Writing as Creative Problem Solving

First we need to backtrack a little and see how the writing process fits into the larger context of general creative and problem-solving activity. A writer's attempts to organize ideas and express them in words have much in common with the efforts of scientists to understand and draw conclusions from their

Table 1 / Hypothetical Diagram of the Writing Process

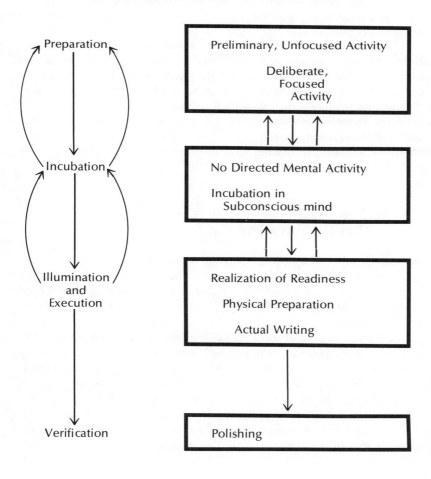

data and artists' struggles to capture their visions. Understanding this will help you to tolerate and work through your frustrations, blocks and false starts much better. There *does* seem to be a predictable sequence of events, a pattern that underlies the creative process. True, that pattern is messy and changeable, not precise, and sometimes one works through it and finds a dead end rather than a solution. Nevertheless, knowing about the pattern can be illuminating and comforting to would-be writers.

People who have investigated how creative persons go about getting from the problem to the solution agree that there seem to be four stages to the creative process: preparation; incubation; illumination and execution; and verification. During the preparation stage, the writer is gathering material and tools, defining the problem, thinking about various ways to approach it, making preliminary sketches or notes, perhaps conferring with or reviewing the work of other people in the field, and probably deciding where to start. He or she may even start working on the problem or the project to get an idea how it is going to develop.

Sometimes a creative person seems to spend very little time on the incubation stage, and appears to go from preparation directly to execution and finally to verification. Usually, however, the person struggling with an idea or a problem finds it productive to stop thinking about it directly for a while. Then when the mind goes back to work it is fresher and more selective, ready for insights. In the illumination and execution stage, the person working on a problem finds a solution, develops it, and writes it out. In the final stage, verification, the writer trims, touches up, checks for accuracy, and ties up loose ends.

The Preparation Stage

Especially for new writers, the preparation stage may be the most important stage. This preparation stage has two parts. The first covers all those years you spent gathering the experiences you bring to your writing. The second stage begins when you start to think about a specific writing task. This state of the writing process is called "prewriting" or "invention."

The writer can control and direct this second stage of preparation. The preliminary stage, however, is largely set by the time you receive a writing task because it includes virtually everything that you have previously experienced, read, or thought about. During that time your mind has been acting like a giant computer that gathers and stores information from books, television, movies, work, social encounters, political activities, personal relationships—everything and anything. The important point for writers to remember is that they have tremendous reserves to draw on for examples, supporting evidence, anecdotes, analogies—all of this material is there stored in this subconscious data bank ready to be tapped. But techniques must be developed for getting to it.

Within this broad and general store of material, you can focus in on specific background information and experience that relate directly to the problem you want to solve. Koestler and others who write about the creative process continually stress that moments of insight and discovery come most often to people who are well prepared. Thus if you intend to do a lot of writing in a specific area—film criticism, for example—the more films you see, and the more you know about the history and technology of film making, the better able you will be to write good film criticism. Having an abundance of background material at your fingertips helps you to generate ideas. And the beginning writer who has to choose a topic should, whenever possible, pick one on which he or she already has some expertise.

MODEL TOPIC: *Day-Care Center*

Background information, general.

Personal experience as a working mother. Knowledge about the poor quality and high cost of most day-care centers around campus. Information about day-care programs in other counties. Information about employee-support programs in industry. Information about college efforts to recruit women faculty. Statistics on number of women returning to school.

Background information, specific.

Friendship with faculty women who feel that they have to choose between having a career and having children. Discussion with women students who have small children. Experience as faculty sponsor of campus women's center.

Direct Prewriting.

The actual prewriting stage for a paper begins when writers find their tasks. That task may be as general as writing a 10-page paper for a professional meeting or as specific as writing instructions for rigging the sail of a Sunfish. For a general topic, the first job is to limit the topic as much as possible. One writing teacher gives the only partly cynical advice, "Always choose the smallest possible topic out of which you can squeeze the requisite number of words." What he means is that the shorter a piece of writing is going to be, the less material you should try to cover in it.

If, for instance, I were asked to give a 20-minute talk to a group of composition teachers, I know that I should write no more than 10 pages. With that limitation I would be in trouble if I tried to talk in general about the problem of teaching composition. All I could do would be to put together a collection of generalizations, few of which would be news to my audience. What I would do instead is focus on one specific problem and deal with it in detail. A good motto for any writer, then, is to try to write more about less. Almost invariably you will produce a better paper than if you try to talk about the Big Picture.

Once you know your topic, you are ready to ask the two crucial prewriting questions: Who is my audience? What is my purpose? To complicate matters, although they are two quite distinct questions that require separate answers, they are nevertheless so interdependent that they can't be considered separately because the answer you give to either one nearly always controls the answer to the other. Let me illustrate.

Suppose your topic is the Law School Admissions Test (the LSAT), which you have just taken and which strikes you as a poor instrument on which to base decisions about who gets admitted into law schools. But what is your purpose in writing about it? Do you want to get the test changed, do you want to persuade the law schools to abandon its use, do you want to explain what you suspect is your own poor performance on it, or do you want to warn other applicants about what they should expect on the test? Each of these purposes suggests a different audience.

Purpose	Audience
Change the test	Directors of Educational Testing Service
Persuade law schools to stop using test	Faculty and admission board of law schools
Explain performance on test	Parents or admissions board of specific law school
Inform other applicants	Pre-law students

Probably you could get some overlapping here, or an additional audience for some of the purposes; nevertheless, when you focus on a specific purpose, you should realize that you immediately sharply limit your audience. Also your writing task becomes more manageable.

If your audience is already identified, then you need to adjust your purpose to the audience. For example, if the pre-law association on campus were to ask you to speak to them about the test, you might begin by saying that you think it should be changed, but you would be wasting your time and theirs to focus primarily on that issue. That audience cannot do anything about the LSAT, and what they want from you is advice, not complaints.

Learning to keep one's audience constantly in mind may be the single most important ability any writer needs to develop. Writers' purposes sometimes change as they generate new ideas in the process of writing, but seldom can they change their audience. Good writers adapt to it, and make their choices about vocabulary, tone, style, content—everything—with that audience in mind. Often the chief stumbling block for unsuccessful writers who work hard but show little improvement is that they don't seem to be able to shape their writing with someone in mind. As long as their audience is general, their writing is also apt to be general, lacking the precision, focus, and concrete details that a specific audience would require.

MODEL TOPIC: *Audience and purpose*

AUDIENCE: President and regents of the university, the people who make the decisions about what facilities the school will provide and decide how university money will be spent.

PURPOSE: To convince the regents and president that a good day-care center for the children of faculty and students would be in the best interests of the university.

Discovering What You Know.

Unquestionably, many writers, working from trained intuition, trial and error, or some private method, manage to produce a great deal of writing without consciously going through any kind of organized preparatory activity. Most inexperienced writers, however, find that when they try to sit down and just start writing, hoping that the ideas will come, they get nowhere. That is when instructors get the complaint, "But I don't have anything to write about." That complaint is seldom true, but many would-be writers need help to get at the stock of material they have stored. They need some method of discovery that they can apply every time they have to write, some reliable techniques for tapping their own resources.

One such method of discovery is commonly called "brainstorming"; policy makers in many different fields use it frequently in problem-solving and idea-generating sessions because it quickly produces a body of material to examine, sift, and evaluate. You can brainstorm by yourself or with one or more people working on the same problem. If several of you work together, you can pool your ideas.

The technique for brainstorming is simple. Using a typewriter, pencil, or tape recorder, concentrate on the topic you want to develop, and start writing down everything that comes into your head, no matter how extravagant or irrelevant it may seem. You can get your ideas down in sentences, words, symbols—any way that they come to you. Don't worry about correct spelling, grammar, quoting accurately, or any of the niceties; just get down as much as you can. Try to keep writing or talking for at least 20 or 30 minutes and at the end of that time you should have a lot of material, some of which you will probably be able to use in developing your paper. But the most important thing that happens in brainstorming is that you begin to generate intellectual energy and in doing so you start a flow of ideas going. The writing process is under way.

MODEL TOPIC: *Brainstorming*

kibbutzes in Israel / cost of special sports center / cost of maternity leaves / returning women students / decline in 18-year-old students / women's movement / divorce rate / Texas Instrument's physical-fitness program / equal opportunity legislation / advantages of breast feeding / effect of anxiety on studying.

Another reliable discovery technique is to ask the questions that news reporters often rely on: Who? What? Why? Where? When? Often it is a good idea to add How?, particularly for a persuasive paper. If you consider your topic with these questions in mind and write out fairly explicit answers, you may find that you have a framework of assertions that can be expanded into a paper.

Notice how this question approach could work with the proposed paper on the Law School Admissions Test.

WHO: Faculty and admissions board of university law school.
WHAT: Do away with the LSAT as the chief determiner of who gets into law school.

MODEL TOPIC: *Using reporters' questions*

Who: University president and board of regents.
What: Establish a quality day-care center on campus for children of faculty and students.
Why: Increase enrollment, attract better faculty, improve student and faculty productivity.
When: As soon as possible.
Where: Local university.
How: Appoint a director to start the center and appropriate $1.2 million to finance it.

WHY: LSAT rewards a narrow, unimaginative kind of intelligence, sometimes discriminates against minorities, and cannot measure motivation or creativity.

WHEN: As soon as possible.

WHERE: University law school.

HOW: Appoint a committee to work out an admissions plan that will screen
people for the qualities that characterize successful lawyers.

Although a critical reader would quickly realize that this kind of inquiry often
yields oversimplified answers, the process can provide the take-off points
needed for research or more focused and intensive thinking.

Another way of focusing your thinking in getting started is to put your
chief points in capsule form. Try imagining how the paper you are going to
write would be described in a summary of 50 words or less. Theoretically, if
you are clear about your proposal or argument, this capsuling should be easy
to do, but you should be surprised at how tough it can be. It is an excellent intellectual exercise in forcing you to say what you mean.

MODEL TOPIC: *Capsuling*

Many young married women who want to go to college or become
teachers at a college are handicapped because they have young children. The university should show its commitment to equal opportunity for women by establishing a quality, low-cost day-care center on
campus for the benefit of these women.

Gathering Material.

By this time you should have a fairly good idea of where you are going,
and you will be ready to start gathering specific material. This can be done
randomly by looking through available sources such as magazines articles,
recent newspaper stories, statistics, textbooks or course material, the card file
in the library, and thinking about personal experience, anecdotes, conversations, observations—just about anything. As you gather your ideas, don't try
yet to do much sorting or sifting; just get a stack of notecards or pieces of
scratch paper and start making notes. Accumulate as much as you can because, as the writer and teacher Donald Murray says, the good writer writes
from abundance.[1]

Ideally you should have so much material that you can select only the

---

1. Donald Murray, *A Writer Teaches Writing* (Boston: Houghton Mifflin Co., 1968), p. 11.

best. What you discard is not necessarily wasted. It becomes a backlog, a reserve of material that you may be able to use later for some other piece. So save your notes and never discard an idea.

As you are making your notes, keep reminding yourself that for expository writing that is intended to explain or persuade, you need facts, evidence, specific cases, and experiences. Most alert audiences are willing to read, learn, and be persuaded if you give them data, not opinions and theories—or at the least, they want your opinions and theories supported by solid evidence. As the successful author and economist John Kenneth Galbraith puts it:

> Nothing is so hard to come by as a new and interesting fact. Nothing is so easy . . . as a generalization. . . . My advice to young writers is to stick to research and reporting with only a minimum of interpretation.[2]

So dig especially hard for concrete material; you'll need more of it than you do theory.

Organizing Material.

After you have collected as many notes as you have the time and energy to gather, spread them out on a large table and begin to sort, sift, and organize. Arrange them in categories, grouping together points that seem related. For example, if you have accumulated a stack of notes to write the paper criticizing the LSAT exam, in reading over them you might find that a number of them point up ways in which the test could be called discriminatory. Another group might list ways in which the material on the test seems to have little relationship to the skills that a lawyer needs. A third group might list important qualities that the test cannot test for, such as motivation, self-discipline, and ambition. A fourth category might raise issues about the reliability and fairness of machine-scored tests. And while you are doing this reading and sorting, be sure to have extra note cards handy to jot down the additional ideas that will almost surely come to you as you work.

When you have finished this review and classification of your raw material, you should have a good idea of the options that are available to you and be ready to make important prewriting decisions. You can tell by looking at your stacks of notes which facet of the topic has generated the most material; that is probably the subtopic on which you can write most effectively. Set aside the other piles of notes, keeping in mind that you might be able to use some of them, and rough out some plan for organizing and developing your ideas.

2. John Kenneth Galbraith, "Writing, Typing and Economics," *The Atlantic*, March 1978, p. 104.

Organizational Plans.

I say "some plan" because almost all writers agree that they have some kind of plan in mind when they begin to write. They don't just begin writing and depend on inspiration or divine guidance to help them order their thoughts as they go along. Those plans, however, are as individualistic as the authors themselves, and it seems evident that one can no more prescribe how a writer should organize his or her writing than one can give writers a formula for making their word choices. All one can do is describe some methods of organization that seem to be useful to many writers.

THE TRADITIONAL OUTLINE.   One method is the traditional outline. Writers who favor this method divide the main topic into a number of subtopics, write a heading or main assertion for each of the subtopics, and then fill in a number of subheadings or subordinate assertions for each subtopic. Model outlines in textbooks usually show assertions stated in full sentences, at least two subdivisions under each topic, and all headings and subheadings in parallel form.

MODEL TOPIC: *Traditional outline*

I. Introduction: the growing number of women faculty and women students at universities raises the issue of day-care facilities on campuses.
   A. Returning women students often cannot afford to come to school full time if they have children.
   B. Women faculty with children cannot teach and do research if they do not have good and cheap care for their children.
II. This situation is harmful to the university.
   A. It loses potential students.
   B. Women students are distracted from their studies.
   C. Women faculty may leave the profession.
      1. They will have to have to choose between family and career.
      2. They will not get tenure if they do not have time for scholarship.
III. The university could take steps to remedy this situation.
   A. They could provide good child-care facilities at no cost to parents.
   B. They could subsidize off-campus child care for students and faculty.
IV. Conclusion: The university would improve its image and the quality of its faculty and student body by solving the problem of child care on campus.
   A. Industry has benefited from similar plans.
   B. The university would help women to achieve.

Some people work well from this kind of outline. It helps them to marshall their thoughts and keep track of the main points they want to make. If they spend a good deal of time on the outline and include supporting detail, they find that writing becomes easier. B. F. Skinner, for example, says:

> When I begin to think of a developed paper or a book, I turn almost immediately to outlines. These grow in detail, almost to the point of producing the final prose.[3]

If you are the kind of person who functions better on a job when you make thorough and meticulous plans ahead of time, then this prewriting approach is certainly worth trying. Also, remember any outline can be changed. You do not have to follow it slavishly if new ideas come to you.

THE ROUGH OUTLINE OR LIST.   Other writers, however, not only dislike making formal outlines, but actually find them a handicap in writing. For example, Jacques Barzun says, "For my taste, outlines are useless, fettering, imbecile."[4] Barzun favors instead what he calls "a memorandum listing haphazardly what belongs to a particular project." And most writers do seem to write some kind of memos to themselves in order to keep track of the main points they intend to make and establish at least a tentative sequence for making those points. One kind of memo is the informal, rough outline that includes topics and subtopics but is not written in complete sentences or parallel form. Another kind of working memo is an open-ended list similar to the list that people make when packing for a trip or moving to another city. Such a list would have the main categories and some of the items to be included under each of those categories. But the list would leave room for new categories or additional items under the existing categories. The advantage of this kind of plan is that it provides one with a working scheme, but is loose and flexible enough to allow for change and expansion as one writes and generates new ideas. As one writer puts it:

> The rough scheme [his form of plan] is a map to the territory of my thoughts. The map is never precise, first because the territory has not been thoroughly explored and second because writing is in itself the discovery of new territory. I usually anticipate discovery in the act of composition.[5]

His point is crucial. Writing *is* an act of discovery, a dynamic process in which the stages mingle, overlap, and interact. For that reason it is often a mistake for writers to try to draw a complete blueprint of the finished product ahead of time. They might find that rigid specifications shut off their creative

---

3. Quoted in Janet Emig, "The Composing Processes of Twelfth Graders," NCTE Research Report no. 13 (1971), p. 23.
4. Jacques Barzun, *Writing, Editing, and Publishing* (Chicago: University of Chicago Press, 1971), p. 11.
5. Max Bluestone, quoted in Emig, "The Composing Processes of Twelfth Graders," p. 24.

abilities. So while careful planning is sometimes useful, particularly for certain kinds of writing tasks that we will be discussing later, "hang loose" can also be a good motto at this early stage.

MODEL TOPIC: *Alternate plan of organization*

Need for day-care center on campus:
  Increasing number of young women returning to school.
  Students don't have the money for maids or sitters.
  Poor quality of care in commercial centers.
  Discrimination against women faculty.
  Equal opportunity laws (?).

Why university should sponsor center:
  Can afford it.
  Would bring in students.
  Good will.
  Other reasons? No paid maternity leave?

Analogies from other groups:
  Physical fitness programs in industry help morale.
  Socialist countries—Sweden, Israel, Russia

Examples to use:
  Personal experience.
  Statistics from *Chronicle of Higher Education*.

TITLE AND THESIS SENTENCE.   Finally, you can help yourself organize and plan your paper by making use of two tools that are simple but sometimes effective: a title and a thesis sentence. At this preliminary stage, any title you choose will necessarily be a tentative one, but nevertheless a working title for your piece can serve as both a focusing device and as an anchor. Just trying to select a title will help you focus for if you discover that the only title you can think of is vague and extremely broad, you will be forced to realize either that the paper you plan is far too ambitious or that you haven't done enough preliminary work to clarify in your own mind just what it is you want to do. For instance, if the only title you could think of for the paper on the Law School Admission Test was "You and the LSAT Exam," you probably haven't sorted out the issues well enough to start writing.

A working title can anchor your paper by constantly reminding you of the promise you are making to your audience. A title is, after all, an announcement; by making it you raise expectations that you must then fulfill, and just having the title there to refer to as you work will help you to stay on the topic. If as your paper develops, you realize that you are not sticking with your title, you will also realize that your paper is developing in a way you hadn't anticipated, and that you are going to have to change your title.

Although we will be taking up the matter of titles again in connection with introductions and abstracts, some preview about the kinds of titles you might use could be helpful now. Here is a classification of titles that Professor Harry Crosby has made.

1. Titles which announce the general subject; for example, *The Joy of Sex* or *The Age of Affluence*.
2. Titles which indicate a specific topic; for example, "Teaching Yourself to Relax" or "The Improbable Rise of Red Neck Rock."
3. Titles which indicate the controlling question; for example, "Is Exercise Worth Your Time?" and "Why Can't Johnny Write?"
4. Titles which announce the thesis; for example, "How Further Education Helps You Get Ahead" or "Small Towns Aren't Really Good for Children."
5. Titles which bid for attention; for example, "Tube or Not Tube?" and "Death in Disneyland."[6]

As Crosby explains in his article, thinking about and trying out various titles before you begin to write helps you to generate ideas for your paper and to control the paper. Those that fall into categories two, three, and four can be especially useful at the planning stage.

MODEL TOPIC: *Possible titles*

Type 1. Day-care centers on campus.
Type 2. The benefits of a low-cost day-care center on campus.
Type 3. Why should the university finance a day-care center on campus?
Type 4. Low-cost child care and high-quality education.
Type 5. Toddlers on campus.

Finally, you may find that that old reliable organizing device, the thesis sentence, works well for you. A good thesis sentence summarizes the main points of your paper concisely and specifically, and provides a kind of working generalization from which you can generate supporting material. To be useful, however, it must be rather long and inclusive; simply a brief statement of your topic such as, "The LSAT is a poor test," or "The admissions policy of the university law school is unfair," will not take you far in the prewriting process. A good one, however, could provide a framework for your paper.

---

6. Harry H. Crosby, "Titles, A Treatise On," in *The Shape of Thought*, ed. Bond and Crosby (New York: Harper and Row, 1978), pp. 161–67.

Table 2 / Hypothetical Diagram of the Writing Process: Preparation Stage

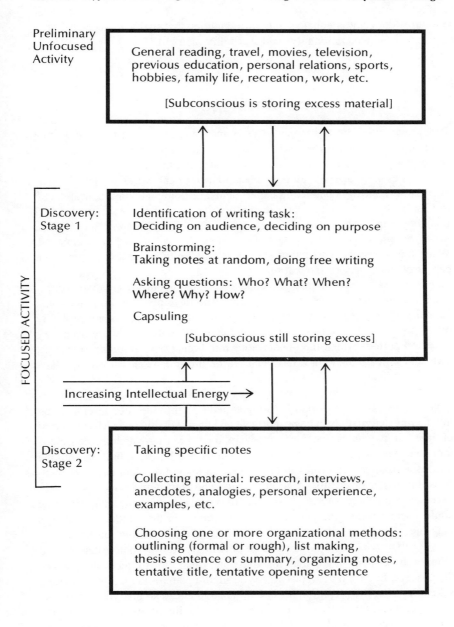

Preliminary
Unfocused
Activity

General reading, travel, movies, television,
previous education, personal relations, sports,
hobbies, family life, recreation, work, etc.

[Subconscious is storing excess material]

FOCUSED ACTIVITY

Discovery:
Stage 1

Identification of writing task:
Deciding on audience, deciding on purpose

Brainstorming:
Taking notes at random, doing free writing

Asking questions: Who? What? When?
Where? Why? How?

Capsuling

[Subconscious still storing excess]

Increasing Intellectual Energy →

Discovery:
Stage 2

Taking specific notes

Collecting material: research, interviews,
anecdotes, analogies, personal experience,
examples, etc.

Choosing one or more organizational methods:
outlining (formal or rough), list making,
thesis sentence or summary, organizing notes,
tentative title, tentative opening sentence

For example, "The Law School Admissions Test, which puts a premium on correct English usage, a good memory, and the ability to work fast under pressure, does not adequately measure qualities that make a successful lawyer: perseverence, rationality, and flexibility of mind."

The Incubation Stage

People who put a lot of time and energy into the preparation stage of writing frequently find that they are exhausted at the end of it. They have been going through a period of intensive and concentrated thinking, and thinking is hard work. They may also have done substantial physical work: going to the library, interviewing, conducting experiments, or doing a computer search. So ironically, by the time they feel ready to write the paper, they may also find that they can't seem to get started on it. If they try to force themselves, nothing comes, or anything that does come seems clumsy or hackneyed. When this happens, it's time to stop, shut off the mind, and let it go into a period of dormancy or incubation.

People who have investigated and speculated about the creative process believe that those periods in which people who have been working hard on a mental project suddenly find that they are making no progress are probably really not periods of idleness or digression at all. Rather they are necessary gestation periods which the unconscious mind must have in order to absorb, sort, and process the data it has been fed before it can select from that data those items that best suit its purpose.

We don't really know what happens at this stage, but apparently the creative faculty goes on a kind of fishing expedition into the subconscious, and that fishing activity has to be be a private and unsystematic one. After a period of time—it may be twelve hours or several days—during which the conscious mind has been looking the other way, the hook that has been probing into the unconscious suddenly brings to the surface an insight or illumination that enables the writer or creator to go into action and start putting his or her ideas together into coherent form. This cycle of preparing, stopping, and restarting could occur several times for a writer, especially in the course of writing a long piece, but each time it occurs, it usually yields valuable material.

Incubation is so important and so potentially fruitful that writers should think of these spells of apparent inactivity and frustration as necessary parts of the process. In fact, if at all possible, you should plan for them in your writing schedule. Start the preparation stage far enough ahead so that you can stop at some point and either switch your attention to a quite different kind of mental effort, or, better yet, do something physical or nonintellectual. Swim, run, play tennis, cook, clean the house, or even sleep.

Table 3 / Hypothetical Diagram of the Writing Process: Incubation Stage

No Directed Mental Activity:

Exercise, recreation, sleep, pursuing hobby, physical activity, unrelated thinking, etc.

Getting ready for illumination

Subconscious is busy:
Sorting, scanning, evaluating

12–48 hours of inactivity

I find my insights come most often when I am moving: walking, swimming, bicycling, driving the car. Other people find listening to music, cooking, knitting, or gardening most productive. But whatever your form of diversion is, you should not feel guilty because you are not working on the job you have to do. You are working; it just doesn't feel like it for the moment.

But now, having assured you that idleness is not necessarily laziness, I will add two important cautions. First, while you are relaxing from the period of preparation and waiting for the subconscious to do its work, keep some portion of your mind alert and ready to go into action when the moment of insight strikes. You can't know whether the incubation period is going to be a few hours or two or three days, and when the insight or idea surfaces you need to seize it and write it down as soon as possible. If you don't, it can vanish almost as quickly as it came. In fact, it is a good idea to keep notecards or a pad of paper close by all the time in which you seem not to be thinking about your topic.

Second, don't wait indefinitely for an idea to strike. If after a reasonable length of time your subconscious still stubbornly refuses to produce what you need, put your conscious mind back on the job and try to start writing. Review your notes or your outline and run through in your mind what some of your options might be for getting started. Consciously try some of the techniques for development (see Chapter 4) or just try to get out two or three paragraphs even if you are not very happy with them. The chances are good that the ideas that have been germinating beneath the surface will start to emerge and you can start actually writing on your assignment.

Illumination and Execution

Now comes the hard part. You have decided on your audience and analyzed it, you know what your purpose is in writing, and you have generated several good ideas and have a fairly clear sense of how the piece is going to develop. But the writing itself remains to be done. No one can tell you how you should shape your sentences or choose your words. But knowing something about how consistent and successful writers operate and what procedures and rituals seem to work for them can help you develop your own effective writing methods.

Creating a Writing Environment.

First, choosing a congenial physical setting, a specified time to write, and tools and equipment that are right for you seems to be important. Many writers insist that they can write only in certain places; some at a desk, others in a certain chair, some in bed, some at home, others in their office or in a cubicle in the library. Almost all think they write best at a particular time, and, when they are involved in a project, begin writing at that time every day and write for a regular number of hours. They religiously use certain tools; some believe they can compose only on typewriters, while others must work in pencil on yellow legal pads.

The fetishes and idiosyncracies of professional writers are legendary. As Jacques Barzun says,

> We know that Mark Twain liked to write lying in or on a bed; we know that Schiller needed the smell of apples rotting in his desk. Some like cubicles, others vasty halls. 'Writers' requisites,' if a Fifth Avenue shop kept them, would astound and demoralize the laity. Historically, they have included silk dresssing gowns, cats, horses, pipes, mistresses, particular knickknacks, exotic headgear, currycombs, whips, beverages and drugs, porcelain stoves, and hair shirts.[7]

Others have to have a certain kind and color of paper, and panic if it is not available. Some have to go through certain rituals before they begin to write. One writer I know says that before he begins to write his weekly column, he must trim his fingernails; he has done this every week for 25 years.

Such eccentricities may seem like frivolous indulgences or simply dis-

7. Barzun, *Writing, Editing, and Publishing,* p. 12.

Table 4 / Hypothetical Diagram of the Writing Process: Illumination and Execution (part one)

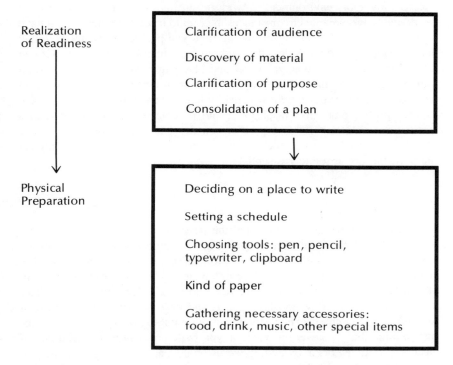

Realization of Readiness

Clarification of audience

Discovery of material

Clarification of purpose

Consolidation of a plan

Physical Preparation

Deciding on a place to write

Setting a schedule

Choosing tools: pen, pencil, typewriter, clipboard

Kind of paper

Gathering necessary accessories: food, drink, music, other special items

plays of "artistic temperament." Logically, that may be true, but at that critical point when one is trying to discipline one's self into starting to write, logic alone is usually not sufficient. Writers who are tempted to use any excuse they can find for not getting to work can partially counteract those temptations by creating the most advantageous possible physical environment for working. If blue paper helps you to write, buy a ream of it; if you enjoy being able to look out the window while you compose, arrange your desk so you can do it; if music seems to help, put on the right records. Lay in a supply of chewing gum, peppermints, number two pencils, sticks of incense, or whatever props you think you have to have. Don't feel silly about it because the props can definitely help.

Apparently what you are doing when you surround yourself with the right combination of external aids is giving your subconscious the signal to start writing. The visual stimulus of the blue paper and the hum of the typewriter or the feel of the pencil help to shut out distractions and put the intellectual processes in motion. So why not indulge your whims if you can? When you are writing, you need all the help you can get.

I should add a caution, however. Even though I believe that most writers do best when they write on schedule, and that whenever possible they should create a favorable environment to work in, at times almost all of us have to work under unfavorable circumstances in order to meet deadlines. If you have to take a child to the doctor during the time you planned to write, you may have to skip your cooking class that night in order to finish a paper. And if you don't have access to your typewriter and blue paper, you may have to do a rough draft in pencil in a spiral notebook. For instance, I prefer to write in complete isolation, using yellow paper and an electric typewriter, but I have written professional talks in airports, and I wrote my master's thesis in a parked car with a portable typewriter on my lap. The writer who has to produce can't afford to be too rigidly tied to rituals and routines. They are helpful, but not absolutely essential.

Getting Started.

Even after writers have created the best possible conditions for themselves, most of them still admit that they have trouble getting started. Getting down a title and an opening generalization helps, as I mentioned earlier, but actually writing the first paragraph or first page can be agonizing, particularly if you take it too seriously and think it has to be just right. It doesn't. There may be many good ways to start a paper, and we'll be considering a number of them in a later chapter. For now, the important thing is to get started, keeping in mind that whatever introduction you write now can be changed later if necessary. So just begin by getting words on the paper, writing anything that bears on the topic. Put down something to get the juices flowing; you'll probably throw it away later anyway.

What you should *not* do is wait for inspiration to strike. When you have set your task, done your preparation, allowed whatever time you can afford for incubation, set your time and place and start writing. If you wait until you "feel" like writing, you may never start. As Galbraith has written,

All writers know that on some golden mornings they are touched by the wand— are on intimate terms with poetry and cosmic truth. I have experienced those moments myself. Their lesson is simple: It's a total illusion. And the danger in the illusion is that you will wait for those moments. Such is the horror of having to face the typewriter that you will spend all your time waiting. I am persuaded that most writers, like most shoemakers, are about as good one day as the next . . . , hangovers apart. The difference is the result of euphoria, alcohol, or imagination. The meaning is that one had better go to his or her typewriter every morning and stay there regardless of the seeming result. It will be much the same.[8]

8. Galbraith, "Writing, Typing, and Economics," p. 103.

Even if you do have to discard all or part of what you write in those uninspired moments, that portion of your writing is not necessarily wasted. You may have had to work your way through that intellectual underbrush in order to get to the substance.

If you are writing a paper over a period of several days and have many interruptions or have to stop to do other things, temporary paralysis is apt to set in again each time you have to start over. And the longer you are away from your writing, the harder it will be to start again. When that problem arises, try going back and rereading what you have already written or even rewriting the last page you did in the previous session. As one composition theorist, James Britton, puts it, reviewing what you have just written is like "running along the tracks we have already laid down." It gives you the momentum to move ahead.

Once they have actually started writing their first drafts writers work at different paces. Some write their first draft rapidly, getting the whole piece down in rough form at one sitting. I call these writers "sprinters." They think of this draft as only a tentative effort, a discovery draft. They plan on doing several more drafts so they don't worry too much about details in the first one. Writers who work this way often write much more than they need because they plan to cut and condense the second or third time around. Apparently writers like this need to get down all their ideas in a burst of energy before they stop. If you use this kind of nonstop approach for other tasks, such as learning a piece of music or building a fence, it might work well in your writing. But you must have the self-discipline to do those second, third, and fourth drafts.

Other writers work much more slowly at a first draft. They coax the phrases and sentences out painfully, one at a time, stopping frequently to delete words, insert phrases, cross out whole sentences and rewrite them, and they spend a great deal of time staring at their typewriters or chewing their pencils trying to think of the phrase or example they want to use. They reread almost every sentence they write two or three times, and they make many major changes *as* they write. They also pace, chew gum, eat, get drinks of water, and worry. I call these "plodders."

This kind of writer may take two or three hours to turn out one or two pages, but usually makes many fewer changes on the second draft because so much effort has gone into the first one. While the plodder does not regard the result of these tedious writing sessions as a finished product, he or she knows the hardest part of the job is usually over when that first draft is finished. One can generally revise this kind of draft fairly quickly, while the person who writes in a rush and then revises probably takes much longer to do the second and third versions.

Finally, there are the kind of writers that are called "bleeders." This type has to do everything right the first time, think out every phrase, every sentence, completely before putting anything down on paper. They cannot leave any blanks, and cannot go on with a new paragraph until they are completely satisfied with the one they have just written. These writers are the slowest and they are also, according to what Malcolm Cowley says in the first volume of the *Paris Review* Writers at Work series, the ones who suffer most when they write, but when they finally produce that first draft the job is over.

Although amateurs who are trying to master the craft of writing will have to experiment to find the pace at which they are most comfortable, I would suggest that you start out by trying to write the first draft rather quickly, making some changes as you go, but planning to do a lot of rearranging and substituting in the second draft. The advantage to this method is that getting your words together on paper will give you a sense of accomplishment and you will have a body of material to work with. And even though the first draft needs a lot of work, writing the second version will probably be easier, and you will have a better sense of what you want to say. The trouble with writing the first draft slowly but carefully is that progress seems discouragingly slow. Still, it seems to be the only way that some of us can write, and in the long run constructing the first draft slowly may not be more time-consuming than writing several drafts.

I would not recommend to any writer trying to find the best rhythms for writing that he or she emulate the "bleeders" and strive for perfection in the first draft. For one reason, one can get totally bogged down. Furthermore, one can seldom make a final judgment about a sentence or paragraph at the time it is written. At the distance of a few hours or a day, it could seem either better or worse than it did when it was written, and the original agony about getting it perfect may turn out to have been wasted. And people who worry about mechanical and grammatical perfection in the first draft can become so tense that their creative juices dry up, or so anxious that instead of trying to communicate their ideas, they limit themselves to words they can spell and sentences they can punctuate, no matter how dull or hackneyed.

But perhaps the most important reason that you should try to keep the flow of writing going rather than worrying about polishing each individual sentence as you go along is that writing is a generative process. The very act of writing helps us to think through what we want to say and stimulates fresh intellectual activity. Stopping too long to put one idea into precise form may make you lose the next idea; it can evaporate while you are still fussing over the one that triggered it.

Writing as Discovery.

One point is so important that I am going to repeat it: *Writing is a generative process.* Just as talking about a problem helps us to understand it better and can give us fresh ways to look at it, writing on a subject helps us to discover knowledge and perceptions that we didn't know we had until we began to write. It is as if by writing about ideas at the conscious level, we set off vibrations that stir up the subconscious. When we do, bits and pieces of a sharper, more accurate vision begin to rise to a level where we can grasp them. As we pull on them by the fragile thread of conscious searching, insights and hints of new truths begin to emerge. Sometimes the line snaps and we lose the revelation; sometimes it brings up rubbish instead of treasure; but sometimes the bits we capture are fresh and valuable, and we can put together a picture that we didn't know existed when we started.

At another time one might be writing from a title, a thesis sentence, and a list or rough outline, intending to cover the points systematically to arrive at a predetermined conclusion. But a third or half of the way through the paper, having stopped to check a reference or find an example, the writer may accidentally find new information that alters the thesis or changes the entire emphasis of the paper. Much of the outline may have to be discarded but the new version will be far more effective than the one that was originally planned. The writer has become a discoverer along the way.

Another way in which writers discover their content during the process of writing is by talking to other people about their work. As you are working, you may stop to discuss or explain some point you are making with your spouse, a classmate, or a colleague. That person's comments or questions can act as an important stimulus to developing your ideas or to helping you view your topic in a new way. If it is possible to do this kind of mid-process brainstorming with other people who are interested in your writing, seek them out. Professionals do.

The point is that writers almost never know exactly what they are going to say when they start writing even though they may plan ahead quite carefully. They count on material coming to them as they write, and so should you. Don't assume that when you have finished brainstorming, taking notes, capsuling your ideas, and making your outline that the prewriting and discovery stage of the process is over. Rather you should expect fresh discoveries as you work, and anticipate that some of them will cause you to alter or add to your plan. In fact, throughout the writing process there is constant movement back and forth between planning and execution, between discovery and explanation, between formulation and revision. The act of writing is dynamic, creative, and messy, not orderly and predictable.

It is as if you started off on a back-packing trip across country. Your goal is to reach Yosemite National Park. One way to do that would be to get out a road map and just walk along the shoulder of a well-marked thoroughfare, looking straight ahead of you. You would get there, but you wouldn't learn much along the way and other people wouldn't be much interested in your account of your trip. If, however, you took a less-traveled road in the same direction, and while you walked steadily toward your destination, kept looking

Table 5 / Hypothetical Diagram of the Writing Process: Illumination and Execution (part two)

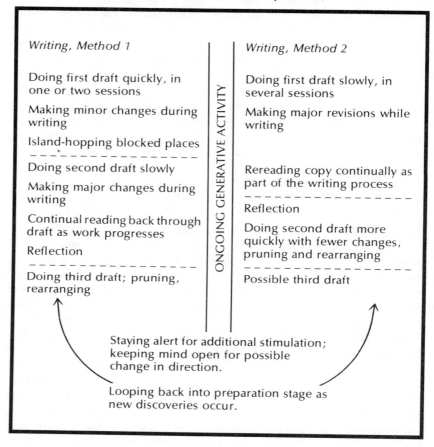

Writing, Method 1	ONGOING GENERATIVE ACTIVITY	Writing, Method 2
Doing first draft quickly, in one or two sessions		Doing first draft slowly, in several sessions
Making minor changes during writing		Making major revisions while writing
Island-hopping blocked places		
Doing second draft slowly		Rereading copy continually as part of the writing process
Making major changes during writing		
Continual reading back through draft as work progresses		Reflection
Reflection		Doing second draft more quickly with fewer changes, pruning and rearranging
Doing third draft; pruning, rearranging		Possible third draft

Staying alert for additional stimulation; keeping mind open for possible change in direction.

Looping back into preparation stage as new discoveries occur.

from side to side as well as straight ahead, you might have a very different trip. For one thing, you could learn so much about the country that surrounds Yosemite that the park itself would take on new significance by the time you got there. Or by taking a side road, you might find a much better way to get to Yosemite than by the usual route. Or you might, by looking on the side, discover new and more interesting territory that you wanted to explore.

Similarly, in writing you should start out with a goal in mind, but not focus on that goal so single-mindedly that you are blind to new ideas or unexpected insights that might be hovering at the periphery of your mind. Keep your side vision operating and your mind open to stimuli from new sources. Be alert for signals from your subconscious so that if a new path opens up you notice it.

And when you write it is especially important to keep reviewing where you have already been in order to determine where you want to go. In recent years research has confirmed what practiced writers have long known; writing is *recursive*. As effective writers work, they continually reread, looping back through the previous material to check on how their pattern of thought is developing and to get new ideas to push them further along.

With most writers, this need to spiral back through what they have already written in order to move forward seems to be so strong that they cannot go on writing if they are prevented from rereading.[9] Research also shows that the best writers are those who consciously stop at frequent intervals to reread and reflect on what they have written.[10] And inexperienced writers will also find that they can improve their writing by using this apparently time-consuming technique.

Revision

Just as you should think of the planning and execution stages of writing a paper as activities that merge and interact, you should also think of revision as an ongoing process. It is not merely a mopping-up or proofreading operation. For most professional writers revision begins almost as soon as they start writing and may continue until the moment they turn their work over to a typist or editor. They rearrange, add, delete, and substitute as they work, seeing revision as an essential part of the creative process. They find out what they want to say and how they want to say it by trying out their options and making changes as the piece develops.

Then, when they have a complete document that they can call a first draft, they engage in *re-vision*.[11] They put their work aside for a day, two days, a week—however long they can afford—so that they can achieve psychological distance from it and view it with some detachment. Sometimes they get a perceptive friend to read it and give suggestions. This way they are able to get a fresh look at what they have written and see what changes they need to make to improve it. They can then start revising, adding, deleting, and rewriting to make the finished product correspond more closely to the original version they had in mind when they started to work.

Writers who set out to do this kind of creative revising must keep a number of concerns in mind as they work, so many that they can scarcely pay attention to all of them at one reading. Probably, then, they can work most ef-

9. James Britton, "The Composing Processes and the Functions of Writing," in *Research on Composing,* ed. Charles Cooper and Lee Odell (Urbana, Ill.: NCTE, 1978), p. 13.
10. Sharon Pianko, "Reflection: A Critical Component of the Composing Process," *College Composition and Communication,* October, 1978, pp. 275–78.
11. Donald Murray, "Internal Revision," in *Research on Composing,* ed Charles Cooper and Lee Odell (Urbana, Ill.: NCTE, 1978), p. 143.

ficiently by revising in stages, focusing on a limited number of problems at each stage. In Chapter 9 I suggest a plan for doing this kind of revising and discuss specific procedures.

Verification

The final stage in writing is verification, or checking for major or minor defects or omissions. At this point, reread your manuscript meticulously to check spelling, punctuation, subject-verb agreement, transitions, clear pronoun reference, correct verb forms—the multitude of mainly external features that affect the appearance of your writing and the first impression it may have on your audience. Although these elements in your writing may not have any bearing on *what* you are saying, they are important, very important, and you cannot afford to neglect them. So finish your job by careful proofreading and editing.

Table 6 / Hypothetical Diagram of the Writing Process: Verification Stage

Polishing final draft

Making minor word changes

Rewriting introduction if necessary

Rewriting title if necessary

Checking for lapses in usage

Checking for transitions

Checking for spelling errors

Preparing clean copy

Proofreading

Proposal for a University Day-Care Center

I believe that the regents of the university should consider the advantages to the university of establishing an on-campus day-care center for the children of university students and faculty. Such a center would benefit the university in several ways.

First, it would provide good child—care facilities for many young mothers who would like to return to college full—time but are not able to do so because they cannot make adequate provisions for their preschool children. According to The Chronicle of Higher Education, the largest increases in college enrollment in the next ten years will come from women in the 25–34 age group; these are the young mothers who need day care for their children. If the university would provide such care, it could count on several hundred of those young mothers in this area enrolling in classes.

Second, a good child—care facility on campus would help to recruit young faculty members who give family-related fringe benefits a high priority when they choose their jobs. A 1979 Ladd—Lipset survey of recent Ph.D. graduates showed that 43 percent of them are in two-career marriages. The university will not be able to compete for the best of these new graduates unless it can assure them that having young families will not put them at a disadvantage. Young women faculty members, in particular, need to know that high quality and convenient care is available so that they will be able to continue their work even if they have children. Universities in Sweden and Australia, where such on—campus child—care centers are found on virtually every campus, report that the scholarly productivity of their women professors under the age of 35 is 27 percent higher than it is for comparable women in the United States.

Third, students and faculty now at the university would benefit significantly from having a good day—care center on campus. Many married couples, both students and faculty, have major problems planning their academic schedules because both husband and wife work, and children must be taken to baby—sitters or nursery schools; often those facilities are 10 miles or more from campus. Students like these are often forced to reduce the number of hours they can take, and the difficult child-care arrangements cause physical stress and mental anxiety that affect their health and their academic performance. Faculty who have the same kind of problems cannot give their full attention to their teaching and research.

A fourth reason that the University should establish

a day-care center is that doing so would help it to meet its Affirmative Action and Equal Opportunity obligations. Since our university does not provide paid maternity benefits or parent leave for its faculty, it is vulnerable to charges that it is not aggressively trying to hire and retain women faculty members. Providing good child care for faculty women would prove the university's good faith in this area.

If the regents were to act now, the day-care center could be opened by the fall of 1981. The center could be housed in the old Littlefield Mansion, a building on the northeast corner of campus that will soon be vacated by the University Stenographic Bureau. The building is outmoded as office space, but it could be converted into a child-care center at relatively low cost. When converted, it would provide attractive and roomy facilities for at least 250 children. At present construction costs, adding the necessary bathroom and kitchen facilities and repainting the rooms would cost about $110,000. Equipment and fencing for the playground would cost another $20,000. The cost for full-time, professional staff for the first year would be approximately $85,000 and for part-time workers and student interns, about $36,000. So the total budget for the first year would come to $250,000.

Probably these first-year building costs would have to come from the university's construction fund, and the cost for personnel would have to come from, at least partially, the special services budget. Once the center was established, however, parents could pay fees on a sliding scale adjusted to their income. Two-income faculty families could pay fees comparable to those charged in high-quality private day-care centers, $35 to $40 a week, and low-income students could pay as little as $5 a week. Even if most of the 250 users paid no more than $15 a week, the gross income per week would be over $3,000; over the long 39-week term, the center would collect at least $136,000. That sum would allow the center to hire three or four trained specialists, enable it to hire a health professional, and to serve nutritious noonday meals. Probably after the first year, university money would be needed only to pay the semiskilled workers and student interns who would have to be hired to provide the low

child–adult ration that good child care requires. That
should come to no more than $55,000 or $60,000 a year.

I believe this modest initial investment and continuing subsidy would be more than repaid by increased
university enrollment, increased recruitment of quality faculty, higher academic and scholarly productivity, and greatly improved morale for students and faculty.

E X E R C I S E S / *Prewriting Activities*

1   List the various writing tasks that people in the following professions
must do.

>   engineering   diplomatic service
>   nursing   college teaching
>   banking   business management

2   List all the experiences you have had that you might find useful in writing a paper on one of the following topics. Include experiences such
as seeing movies and television shows, reading books, or hearing
someone speak on the subject.

>   What it means to be a pre-med student.
>   The hazards involved in running.
>   The great health-club boom.
>   The growth of the fast-food industry.

3   Explore a possible topic for a paper—for example, "The Joys of Scuba
Diving" or "The Ballet Boom in the Eighties"—by asking these questions about the topic and writing out the answers.

>   Who? What kind of people are participating?
>   What? What is involved in the activity?
>   Why? Why do they participate?
>   When? When did the activity start, or when does it occur?
>   Where? Where does the activity take place?
>   How? How is the activity carried out, or how do the people
>   involved act?

4   Write a 100-word summary of the main ideas you would include in a
paper on one of these topics.

>   Designing a Personal Exercise Program.
>   The Art of Buying at Discount.

Picking the Right Graduate School.
Preparing to Take the Law School Admissions Test.

If you prefer to work from an outline instead of a summary, make an outline for the same topic.

5 Get together a group of three or four people and brainstorm for 20 minutes on one of these topics. Ask one person to be the recorder and write down every idea or suggestion that the group mentions.

jet lag	the Sunbelt
microwave ovens	defensive driving
junk food	crash diets

Suggested Writing Assignments

1 The free magazines put out by airlines publish a wide variety of articles on almost every subject imaginable; for example, the psychology of wearing a tie, the art of tipping, part-time careers, coping with stress, and so on. They frequently feature articles about cities or resorts to which their airlines fly. An enterprising free-lance writer might be able to use a personal interest or hobby as the basis of a salable article for one of these magazines. Some topics are suggested below, but you could get additional ideas by thumbing through a magazine next time you fly. Your article should probably be no longer than 1,000 words unless you and your instructor decide ahead of time that you will need more to do a good job.

Before you begin to write the paper, write an analysis of what kind of people you think might read your article and what they would probably expect to get from it. Then write out your purpose in writing: What do you expect to do for the reader? Include a descriptive title.

TOPICS:
Eating Seafood in New Orleans (or in Boston).
Shopping in London (or Hong Kong, Paris, or Honolulu).
Finding the Best Skiing in the West (or the East).
Tips for Business Women Who Travel Alone.
Planning a Fly-Drive Trip through the Pacific Northwest.

2 Using one of the sets of data given below, write a paper in which you analyze the meaning of the figures and hypothesize about projections one might make on the basis of the data. For instance, in considering the data about the cost of housing, you might write a paper speculating about what such figures might mean for new starts in the housing industry or how they might affect the decisions young people make

about their future. There are many other possibilities, including papers about building methods of the future, about the rate of inflation, or about possible changes in the patterns of American cities. In considering the figures on distribution of income and income taxes in the United States, you might write a paper pointing out the weaknesses in the "soak-the-rich" school of thought about taxation or on the fairness or unfairness of our tax system. Be sure to narrow your topic sufficiently and limit yourself to making one or two specific points.

Before you begin your paper, write out an analysis of your audience. Who would be interested in reading your paper, where might it be published, and what would your readers expect to find out by reading it? Be as specific as possible. Also write out a statement of purpose. Why are you writing the article? If you want to inform your readers, what information do you want them to have and why? If you want to entertain your readers, what response do you hope to get? If you want to persuade them, what action do you want them to take?

DATA 1:
A chart showing the average cost of new homes from 1963 to 1979 looks like this:

1963	$18,000
1976	$44,200
1978	$55,600
1979	$62,400

DATA 2:
The Internal Revenue Service published these figures about income taxes paid in 1975:

Taxable Income	Percentage of Population	Percentage of Total U.S. Taxes Paid
Below $5,000	31	1
$5,000 to $10,000	24	9
$10,000 to $15,000	18	16
$15,000 to $20,000	12	17
$20,000 to $30,000	10	22
$30,000 to $50,000	5	35
More than $50,000	1	9

3   Write a review of a book, a movie, or a television program that could be published in your local student or city newspaper. Clip from the paper the kind of review that you want to write and tape it to a sheet that you turn in with your paper.

Before you begin to write, define and analyze your audience. Who reads this kind of review, why do you think they read it, and what would they want to get from it? Then write your specific purpose. What is the main point you want to make in the review and how do you want your audience to react? Write a headline for your review.

CHAPTER 3

The Writing Situation

Every time you begin a writing task, you are working in a specific situation. You have a topic you are going to write about, you have a person or persons who will read or listen to what you have written, and you have a reason for writing. You are not operating in a vacuum; you are trying to communicate something to someone for some purpose.

I find it useful to think of the writing situation in terms of a communication square with its sides labeled Audience, Purpose, Persona, and Message.

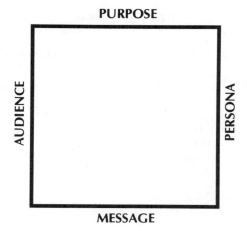

The term *persona* (per-sō-na, from the Latin, meaning an actor's mask or the character being acted) may be puzzling here, but I am using it rather than *writer* to convey the idea that the effective writer adapts his or her tone and approach to the audience being addressed.

You can use the communication square as a focusing and discovery device during the prewriting process. First, sketch out a square. Label the sides of your square with the answers to the following questions, writing them on the appropriate side. (Make your answers as specific as you can at this stage of your task even though later you will probably need to make each answer still more precise.)

Question 1: Who is my audience?
Question 2: What is my purpose?
Question 3: What is my persona or role as a writer?
Question 4: What is my message or thesis?

As you construct your square, try to keep in mind the interdependence of all the sides: the answer that you fill in on one side affects the answers for all the other sides. If one side changes, another one can also change.

Here is how the communication square might look for the model topic from the previous chapter.

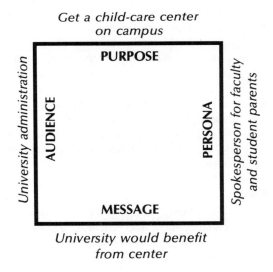

Notice that here the purpose and the message are not exactly the same. Often they are not, and it is because writers sometimes need to clarify that difference in their own minds that drawing and labeling a communication square can be useful.

Audience

If one had to pick out the piece of advice that recurs most often in books and articles about practical writing in nonschool situations, it would be *remember your audience.* The people who teach professional writing for business, in-dustry, and government hammer constantly at the theme ''Know your audi-ence, understand your audience, and write for your audience.'' Yet if I were to pick out the most common defect in the writing of nonprofessional writers, it would be their failure to identify a real audience and write to it. Most student writers have difficulty imagining any audience other than the instruc-tor who will read their papers, and as a result their writing is often drab and stuffy.

And though most academic writing situations are contrived, the papers that students write for courses are important in that they provide an opportu-nity for students to analyze and evaluate the material they are studying and then demonstrate to the teacher that they have mastered it. Writing about a subject is an important way of learning about it. But writing a paper that will be read only by an instructor does not help the aspiring writer develop a sense of audience. The student takes it for granted that a teacher will read the paper all the way to the end. So why bother to try to entertain or inform teachers? Why worry about wasting their time? If the teacher is bored, that's unfortu-nate, but not your problem; if the teacher is confused, that's more serious, but still not critical since he or she will probably try to figure out what you mean. You assume that your only obligation is to put down accurate information in standard written English.

When you face a real, nonacademic, writing task, however, you can no longer afford this attitude. Most of the time people don't have to read what you write. They are reading for entertainment or information—perhaps both—and if they find they are getting neither, they will quit reading. If you bore them, confuse them, overtax their reading abilities, or take up too much of their time, they will also quit reading. This audience is not being paid to read what you write.

Even if your reader is being paid to read your writing—a supervisor, ex-ecutive, personnel manager, admissions officer, or a person in charge of mak-ing grants, for example—you still cannot afford to bore or confuse that person or to waste his or her time. If you do, the reader may just drop your writing in the wastebasket. And those readers that do wade through to the end of a piece of stodgy and inflated prose might well become so annoyed at having to read it that they will reject whatever proposal or request you are making. You can't afford that kind of reaction either.

It is crucial then, that you start trying to write for real audiences and train yourself to focus consciously on your audience both before and as you write. Once an audience begins to seem real, you will probably find that analyzing it is not as hard as you thought, because actually you have done this in previous situations when it was important for you to do so. For instance, if you were writing to Mastercharge to point out a mistake in your statement, you would write a direct, businesslike letter explaining the error and giving them all the specific information they need to correct the problem. If you leave a note for your ten-year-old son giving him directions for cleaning the house while you are gone, you don't use big words or spend time on a long introduction. And when you write to your mother, you probably don't use obscene language even though you may sometimes sprinkle it liberally through your conversation.

We make such adjustments naturally when we know precisely who our audience is and when we care about communicating with it. We know that we should not anger, bore, or confuse people if we want them to pay attention to what we are saying; in this sense we are all communication experts. And what we do intuitively in personal and specific situations, we can learn to do rationally and systematically in broader and more impersonal situations.

You can train yourself to construct an explicit and detailed description of your audience by getting in the habit of asking yourself a series of questions. At first you will need to write out the answers to these questions in detail because such an exercise will force you to think systematically and thoroughly about your unseen readers. With practice, however, most successful writers develop a kind of built-in audience monitor that helps them stay on target as they write. They are still keenly aware of audience, but they no longer have to consciously define it for themselves.

Here are the questions that you need to ask about your audience before you start to write.

I. Who are my readers?
   A. Do I actually have two readers, one my broad audience, the other a specific person who acts as a censor or judge and decides whether my writing gets to the intended audience? For instance, an editor who decides whether a news release or article will be printed would be this kind of judge.

   B. Am I really writing for an audience other than the one I seem to be addressing? In writing a television speech for a candidate or about a bond issue, for instance, the real audience would be the unseen viewing audience, not the person who might be on the program to present the other side of the question.

   C. What is the educational level of the audience? How well do they read?

   D. What is important to the audience?

   E. How busy is my audience? How much time can they invest in reading what I am going to write?

You need to answer all these questions as specifically as possible in order to get your audience fixed clearly in your mind. A vague description such as ''Any reader who might be interested in my topic'' is not sufficient.

II. What does my audience want to get from the piece I am writing?
   A. Are they reading for information, instruction, entertainment, or guidance? What do they expect?
   B. Do they actually need to read what I am going to write?
   C. What will keep them reading?
   D. What will make them stop reading?
III. How much does my audience already know about my topic?
   A. Do I need to write in general layman's language, or can I use specialized terminology?
   B. Will detailed explanation be useful or boring?
   C. How many examples and illustrations do I need to get my point across?
IV. Will my audience be sympathetic, hostile, or neutral toward my subject?

The methodical and patient writer who carefully answers all these questions before beginning to write will collect a valuable body of material to refer to as he or she writes. If, however, you are not the kind of person who likes to solve problems systematically, you can go about developing audience awareness in another way. Imagine that your reader is an important guest, someone whom you would like to please and impress, someone whose needs and wishes you want to fulfill. Then as you write for that reader, keep in mind these rules of courtesy and hospitality.

- Don't bore your readers. Don't write dull, formal prose in an attempt to sound impressive.
- Don't waste their time by telling them more than they want or need to know.
- Don't confuse your readers. Give them frequent signals and cues to keep them on the right track, organize your writing in patterns that they can follow, and explain and illustrate difficult points. (More about ways to do all this in a later chapter.)
- Don't intimidate your readers. Don't make them feel inferior by using a specialized language and references that they don't understand.
- Don't threaten your readers. Don't attack their beliefs or suggest that they are stupid or immoral if they don't agree with you.
- Don't disappoint your readers. Give them what you led them to expect in your title, abstract, or opening paragraphs; make them feel satisfied when they finish reading your writing.
- Always assume your audience is intelligent, even if they are uninformed.
- Finally, be sure that you are not writing for that easiest of all audiences, yourself. Faced with a writing task that they do not find interesting or challenging, many student writers just begin expressing their opinions or repeating standard arguments. They don't stop to think whether anyone

would be interested in what they are writing or why anyone would want to read it. They are writing "teacher papers," so they forget about their audience, and write something that requires little effort from them and sounds good enough to get by.

Try not to let yourself slip into this habit, one that is especially tempting to competent writers who may have been getting rewarded for smoothly written papers with practically no content. If you are going to the trouble to write a paper, make it worth reading. Ask yourself these two questions: Would these comments really be useful or interesting to someone who doesn't have to read my writing? And, am I telling my readers something they don't already know? If your honest answer to these questions is no, then you are probably writing a "teacher paper" and doing little to improve your writing skills.

Another easy audience is one who already agrees with you, who shares your prejudices or attitudes, and is not likely to challenge you or make you prove your case. With an audience like this it is tempting to slip into clichés or restate points that have already been made dozens of times. This kind of writing might serve a purpose if you were giving a speech at a political fund-raising dinner or at a football rally, but it's more ceremonial than productive. Some people call such writing "preaching to the choir" or "cheerleading." You might enjoy doing it but you shouldn't confuse it with working writing that must convince or inform.

Purpose

You are not likely to take the easy way out by writing to yourself if, before you start, you have a clear sense of your purpose in writing. But just as student writers find it hard to realize that they need to think beyond the captive audience of the instructor, they also find it hard to think seriously about what purpose they might have other than pleasing that instructor. There are at least two ways to overcome this kind of handicap. One is to write on a topic that really means something to you; for example, pick out the television commercial you most despise and fire off a protest letter to the sponsoring company or write to your congressman urging him or her to draft legislation on some issue that concerns you. Such writing is good practice, and you might do some good with it.

But another way to move beyond the writing-to-please-the-teacher-approach is to use the simulation techniques people employ in other learning situations. For instance, people training to be emergency medical technicians can't wait for accidents to happen before they learn to treat shock or stop hemorrhaging, so they practice on each other, having one trainee play the role of a heart-attack victim, another that of someone who has been stabbed in the leg, and so on. Similarly, those in charge of training soldiers or marines play war games in which they create and minutely describe an imaginary enemy, specifying that enemy's position, equipment, numerical strength, and the kinds of strategies they are apt to use. Football coaches use the same techniques; so do law professors.

Participants in these games take them seriously because it is important for them to develop the skills to cope with a challenge before they actually face the real thing. In some instances, their survival could depend on how well they have practiced; in a less dramatic way, so could the welfare of a person who had been assigned an important writing task.

Once you have pinpointed your audience as specifically as possible, ask yourself two questions: Why would I be writing for such an audience? What would that audience want from me? Your answer to the first question is probably one of these: to inform, to persuade, or to entertain. If you want to inform your audience you should focus on giving facts and relating events; you would carefully avoid making judgments or adding personal comments. If you wanted to persuade your audience, you would probably make claims, support them with evidence, and try to convince your audience with reasoning. For other kinds of persuasive writing tasks—drafting a political press release or a fund-raising brochure—you would not only make claims, but inject vivid language and emotional appeals into your writing. And if you are writing about antics like chili-eating contests, you are interested mainly in entertaining your readers.

Of course such convenient pigeonholing of the purposes one might have for writing is too neat and simple to be realistic. Frequently we have mixed or overlapping purposes when we write. For instance, the corporation vice-president writing the annual report wants not only to give his reader the facts, but to persuade them that the company is doing well. The chemist who applies for a grant wants to persuade, but she is also going to have to inform her readers. Nevertheless, in any piece of task writing one usually has a main purpose, and that is the one to concentrate on. You may distract and confuse your reader if you attempt to do too much in one essay or report. Only skilled writers can handle trying to entertain their readers while they also inform or persuade them.

You should also remember not to get too ambitious. Don't carve out for yourself a task that is too large to handle effectively in the space and time limits you are working within. If as a community doctor you were asked to write a 500-word comment on the reasons for escalating medical costs in your city, and you tried to discuss all the contributing factors, your comments would have to be so general that they wouldn't be helpful or enlightening. If, however, you focused on one problem, for example, the cost of operating intensive-care units, you might give your audience some useful information. If you do face a substantial and complex writing task in which you must do several things, break your writing into several units and decide what your specific subpurpose for each unit will be. And outlining those subpurposes before you start will help immeasurably.

Once you have clarified in your own mind why *you* are writing, reverse your point of view and ask yourself "Why is my audience reading? What do *they* want from me?" Keeping that question in mind will help you to stay on course. If you remind yourself that they principally want information, you will avoid straying into opinion and judgment. If you are aware that they are reading mostly for entertainment, you will avoid giving them more information and details than they want to deal with. And always remember that there is something your audience almost certainly does *not* want: that is, to be told what it already knows. Only in some academic writing situations will you face that task; a future chapter will suggest some good ways to handle that challenge.

Persona

Only when you know your audience and understand why you are writing for it can you begin to think about your relationship to that audience and how you want to approach it. As you develop a feeling for what you are trying to accomplish, you should also develop a sense of your role in the situation you are getting ready to create. For each communication situation is a kind of drama which requires that you behave in a particular way in order to get your message across.

Thus when you write you create an identity for yourself. Using only words—no make-up, no costumes, no scenery, no music—you have to present yourself to an audience and get its attention and its confidence. And sometimes you have to do it in such a way that the audience is not even directly conscious of you. No wonder writing to an audience is so much more difficult than speaking! We are getting no cues or feedback from our readers and cannot even read their body language to help us adapt our presentation as we go along.

You can, however, by using imagination and trying to develop a sense of tone, learn to present yourself in various ways, to take on different roles according to the circumstances. In each case you are choosing what is appropriate to the situation; you are being flexible. For that is what choosing a persona involves; being flexible, but not radically changing your personality.

Here is how it works. Suppose you are writing the proposal for a campus day-care center, the model topic in the last chapter. Your audience is the board of regents, people who you assume are intelligent, dedicated to the welfare of the university, but fiscally and socially conservative. That is, they are reluctant to spend the university's money on a project that might be impractical or damaging to family life. Your purpose is to convince them that the day-care center will be a good investment for the university and will help both the children and parents of the families who use it. To achieve that purpose, you are going to want to come across as a knowledgeable, sensible person who understands that the university must run on a limited budget, but also believes that faculty and students should have reliable and professional child-care facilities for their children at a cost they can afford. You want to seem confident that the regents will listen to you, and competent to explain and defend your project.

As you do this kind of analysis, you are creating a character for yourself. Then you ask, "How can I use language to make my audience believe in this character?" Immediately you should sense that you should not criticize the university or sound angry. Pointing out that they just spent six million dollars adding on to the football stadium, and therefore should feel morally obligated to subsidize a day-care center probably won't help your case. Neither would suggesting that regents are too prosperous to understand the problems of students and young faculty. Although those two points might be the first ones that come to your mind, stressing either one could give your audience the impression that you are a discontented student who doesn't appreciate the problems of running a university.

If, however, you start your proposal with figures about how many married students and faculty at the university have preschool children, the average cost of child care at facilities close to campus, how many young married women are on the faculty, and an estimate of what it could cost to build and operate a good day-care center, you show that you are a reliable person who does your homework. If you also suggest that student and faculty activity fees might be raised to help pay for the center, you show that you are practical and responsible.

What you are doing above all by making this kind of factual and rational argument is selling yourself, establishing your credibility and reliability. The fact that you went to the trouble to research your project often pleases your audience more than the actual data you use; the reasonable attitude you show by suggesting that students and faculty help pay for the project can be more impressive than the amount of money involved. This kind of persuasive technique that is built chiefly on the character of the writer or speaker was defined by classical rhetoricians as the *ethical appeal*. They believed that the greatest asset a person arguing a case could have was his or her own good reputation. And there is still no stronger appeal. You convince people when they believe in you; that is why it is so important for a writer to create an effective persona.

In other kinds of writing situations, you would want to create an entirely different character for yourself. For instance, if you were writing a review of the performance of a jazz ensemble that had just opened at a local night club, you would assume a more relaxed role, talking candidly about what you did and didn't like about the group, and feeling no pressure to give data on jazz groups or support all your assertions. You might lapse into slang, and use specialized terms that only you and other jazz fans would understand.

If, on the other hand, you were writing the 600-word essay required of applicants for the $2,500 Harry S. Truman scholarship awarded each year to a college junior who wants to study international politics, you would want to convince your audience that you are a serious and ambitious young person who has the talent and drive to make good use of the scholarship. You would instinctively choose your language carefully, thinking about what kinds of personal statements you could make that would present you favorably without sounding like bragging.

In a period of a few months, you might have to do a wide variety of writing tasks, each requiring that you present yourself to an audience in a different way. If you were speaking with these audiences face to face, you would probably not have much trouble adapting your voice and persona to each individual situation because your audience would be helping you find the appropriate role through cues and feedback. When you are writing, however, you have to use your imagination and ingenuity to work out a persona suitable to your task. But you do not really create a role each time, in the same way that a dramatist creates a character; rather you select components already present in your self and manipulate and rearrange them to get the effect that you want. One time you might combine your zest for and knowledge of country-western music with your habit of remembering the details of conversations you overhear to write an entertaining account of country-western night-spots for the campus entertainment guide. At another time you might make use of your research skills and the knowledge of tax law to write a report for a company president on the effect that new tax regulations will have on the company's bookkeeping system.

Writers who go through this kind of role shifting in moving from one writing task to another are not taking on false identities. They are learning to identify and use their own resources and skills. In the process of writing, they are exploring and developing their versatility. The experience is often one of self-discovery for both experienced and inexperienced writers. All of us discover much about ourselves when we write.

Developing a credible persona and building a reputation as a trustworthy, reliable writer or speaker takes a long time. Columnists like Ellen Goodman, economists like John Kenneth Galbraith, and broadcasters like Walter Cronkite are read and listened to because over the years they have proved that they are competent, fair, and reasonable people. But even inexperienced writers can learn to use techniques that will make a good impression on people. These are the principal ones:

- *Do your research.* Take the trouble to find figures and evidence to support and illustrate your points. Show that you know the background of the issue you are writing about and be able to cite your sources.
- *Show that you are aware of the other side of the issue.* Acknowledge that the proposal you are making might raise some problems, or that other people have different views. You do not always have to offer solutions or suggest compromises, but you do want to indicate that you are not narrow-minded.
- *Don't overstate your case.* Avoid extreme language and highly emotional statements. Be especially careful about using the words *never* and *always;* instead, form the habit of inserting prudent qualifiers. Be careful not to draw broad generalizations from scanty evidence.
- *Don't oversimplify.* Demonstrate your maturity by indicating that you realize that serious problems seldom have simple solutions.
- *Show confidence.* Take a positive tone and don't make negative or apologetic statements about yourself. If you can find a way to do so, cite the qualifications and experience you have for writing on your topic.

A writer can control the degree to which an audience will be aware of the persona created in a piece of writing. At times the persona should virtually disappear, be so unobtrusive that the reader never thinks about the writer behind the material. For instance, if you are writing a technical or business report, a set of directions, a straight news story, or a scientific analysis you should strive to be invisible. Your writing would focus on the information you want to communicate rather than on the audience or yourself. You would use impersonal and objective language and avoid interpreting or giving your opinion although those restrictions do not mean that your language has to be dull, passive, or excessively technical. Nor does it mean that you have to completely avoid the use of *I,* especially if doing so means you have to resort to such phrases as ''the author of this report.'' In explanatory or exploratory reports in which you are describing your discoveries, the pronoun *I* is quite appropriate.

You are not really absent from either kind of report. You are responsible for the information in it—your name might be on it—and the impression it makes on the reader, for better or worse, is the impression that you have created.

In writing that is primarily persuasive, the writer's persona is usually easy to discern. Even though the writer does not speak directly to the reader or write anything that specifically establishes his or her identity, by making assertions, giving opinions, and using colorful language and striking images, the author creates a distinct personality. The way readers respond to that personality at least partially determines how easily they will be persuaded. And skillful persuasive writers are always thinking of audience; their writing is *audience-centered*.

Some prose is what one might call *writer-centered*. Although the author does keep the audience in mind, he or she focuses on personal experience. The purpose of the writing may be to inform, entertain, or even persuade, but it achieves that purpose by using narrative and anecdotes and expressing personal feelings and reactions. In this kind of writing, in which authors deliberately seek to get the audience involved with them personally, creating an attractive and credible persona is especially important.

Whatever kind of writing you are doing, and whatever kind of persona you want to project to your audience, you need always to keep in mind one hard fact about task writing: acceptable usage and spelling matter. Although grammatical errors and misspelled words are external features of written prose, they make a lasting negative impression on most readers. Your attitude about usage and mechanics is part of your persona.

Message

So far this chapter has been largely preparatory, a kind of setting the stage for the actual writing production. But as important as these concerns are, they are not the center of communication. The center is the message, the content of your writing. You now have to concentrate on what you are going to say, what the reader will actually encounter on the page.

While it is true that because writing is a creative and generative act, you may discover or alter some parts of your message as you write, nevertheless you need to have a clear idea of your intended message. Ask yourself the specific question, "What is it I want to say?" and force yourself to give a specific answer. That answer should be direct and limited. For example, in the article about your visit to the local country and western night club, your message would be: "The Broken Spoke is a good place to go if you want to hear authentic country-western music and meet real cowboy types doing 'kicker' dancing." In the report on new tax laws, your message would be: "Under the new tax provisions, Lone Star Industries, Incorporated, can save $45,000 next year by going to a cash-accrual bookkeeping system." In the model proposal on the campus day-care center, your message would be: "The university can increase student enrollment and attract more qualified young faculty if it establishes a low-cost day-care center on campus."

Writing your message down before you start will help you to focus your attention on it, and help you to write the important opening paragraph. Incorporating that message into a tentative title for your piece will also help you to control your writing as you work. And it helps to have repeated references to your intended message in the working notes or outline you prepare before you start to write. In short, do everything you can at the preparation stage to insure that your message will come through your writing clearly.

Finding the best ways to organize and develop that message and putting it into words effectively will be the subject of the next several chapters.

EXERCISES / *Prewriting Activities*

1   Here is a sample showing how one might go about analyzing the audience for a specific writing situation.

The writing situation: a young person applying to the board of elders of a church for a tuition scholarship to a college affiliated with that church.

Audience analysis: group of mature men and women who want to spend their church's limited resources wisely. They want to be sure that the person who gets the scholarship is an active church member who has a good academic record and can demonstrate that he or she needs financial help to go to college. They would also like to know whether the applicant plans to work while in school and what career plans he or she has.

Write a similar analysis for the audience for these writing situations:

A.   A patient complaining to the county medical society about a doctor who performed an unnecessary hysterectomy.

B.   A citizen petition to the city council for a zoning change that would prohibit apartment houses in a new subdivision that is being opened.

C.   A government pamphlet on nutrition designed especially for low-income families.

D.   A fund-raising brochure to raise $100,000 for new instruments for the college band.

2   Here is a sample showing how one might analyze a reader's reasons for reading a particular piece of writing.

An article on buying antique clocks: The readers for this article would read it to find out where to shop for such clocks, how to tell if they were genuine, what features to look for in good antique clocks, and how much they might have to pay for the clock that they might want to buy.

Write a similar analysis of readers' reasons for reading the following:

A.   An article on how to buy ski gear.

B.   An article on reading levels of students in the city's public schools.

C.   A political advertisement for a candidate for state judge.

3   Here is an example of the way one might analyze a writer's purpose in a specific writing situation.

An article on white water canoeing: The writer of this piece would probably want to let readers know that white water canoeing offers to people interested in outdoor activities, what kinds of skills it requires, where one might go to participate in the sport, and how much it costs.

Make the same kind of analysis of writer's purpose for the following writing situations:

A.   An article for parents on the effects of television watching on preschool children.

B.   A report on a new brand of microwave oven for a consumer magazine.

C.   A brochure on the benefits of exercise to be distributed to company employees.

4   Here is an example showing how one might analyze the persona he or she wanted to create for a writing situation.

Driver writing to a judge to appeal a six-month suspension of a driver's license: The writer wants to communicate the image of a sober, industrious person who will no longer speed and who must be able to drive in order to keep working.

Analyze the persona a writer might want to create in these writing situations:

A.   A lawyer is writing to a school board to explain why they cannot fire a teacher who has a worn a bikini in a bathing beauty contest.

B.   An official of a drug company is writing an article to explain the side effects of a new tranquilizer to physicians.

C.   A student is writing a professor to ask for a letter of recommendation to graduate school.

Suggested Writing Assignments

As a part of each assignment, write a one-paragraph analysis of your audience, including a statement about where your paper would be published and what your readers would want to know, a one-paragraph analysis of your purpose in writing, and a two or three sentence analysis of the persona you want to project in your writing.

TOPIC 1:
Write a news release to announce a seminar of one of the following issues. Include a headline. Remember that you have *two* audiences: the editor who

decides whether your release is worth publishing and potential readers who have an interest in your topic and want to know what the seminar has to offer them.

Issues:

> Survival strategies for the families of alcoholics.
> Guidelines for the small investor.
> Résumé writing for women reentering the job market.
> Learning how to trace your family's roots.

TOPIC 2:

Some law schools ask their applicants to submit an essay responding to this question: "Why do you think your application to our law school should be looked upon with favor?" In no more than 600 words, write such an essay.

TOPIC 3:

You are an aide for a state senator who is going to introduce one of the following bills to the legislature. Because the bill is going to be controversial, the senator has asked you to draft an explanatory letter to be sent to all political supporters in the district before the bill is announced to the public.

A bill to legalize gambling in your state.
A bill to increase aid-to-dependent children payments by 50 percent.
A bill to require chiropractors to have a medical degree.
A bill to raise tuition at the state universities by 100 percent.

TOPIC 4:

Do any of the writing assignments suggested in the prewriting exercises in analysis of audience, purpose, or persona.

4 *Starting to Write*

Most working writers agree that the hardest part of any writing task is getting started, actually putting down on paper those first sentences. Even though the would-be-writer has identified the audience, settled on a purpose, done all the necessary research, taken abundant notes, and decided on a tentative title, breaking through the inertia barrier can be a major problem. One is tempted to do more research, take more notes, wash the car, seize on any excuse to avoid writing that first sentence. And ironically, quite often the more we care about the writing task that faces us, the more difficult it is to get started.

Although there are undoubtedly a number of reasons for these temporary blockages that seem to affect so many of us when we start to write—reasons that range from a reluctance to make a commitment to plain laziness—probably the key reason is one so obvious that most writers have not thought of it. *It is hard to begin a new piece of writing because one has no previous writing to go back to for stimulation and impetus.* When writers can look back and reread and reflect on sentences and paragraphs they have already written, they are stimulated to go on writing. As already pointed out, beginning to write lays down tracks for us to move along. When we have to start without such tracks, our task is much more difficult.

The only way to get those tracks laid is to begin writing. Thus you should try to think of the first few sentences that you put down not as an introduction or formal opening, but as a beginning. It's a start, a place to move from; the real introduction can, if necessary, be written later. What you need now is to get something on paper to help you generate some intellectual action and begin writing.

Using Generative Sentences

One good way to start that process is to write down the main assertion or chief idea of your paper in what one team of authors call a "generative sentence."

By that term they mean a statement that generates or raises in the minds of the reader "certain questions that will be asked and should be answered."[1] For example, each of the following sentences is generative because it sets in motion a creative sequence by which several more sentences are generated.

Quality furniture has several distinctive characteristics.

With an increasing number of surgeons trained to do organ transplants, hospitals are experimenting with new ways to find donors.

Opponents of the Equal Rights Amendment claim that in many ways its passage would affect women adversely.

The recent discovery of huge oil reserves in Mexico is sending shock waves of change through that poverty-stricken nation.

Sentences like these serve a useful function for both the reader and the writer. For the reader, they act as a signal that supporting details are coming so the reader's mind is prepared to receive what follows. For the writer, they serve as a reminder that he or she has made a commitment to give explanatory or supporting examples, and the writer who is keeping the reader in mind immediately searches for ways to meet that commitment. For instance, after sentence number two a conscientious writer would list some of the programs hospitals have started to find organ donors, and after sentence four the writer would list ways in which the discovery of oil has affected Mexico.

As a writer you should recognize that when you write these kinds of thought-provoking sentences, you must not disappoint your reader. Each of them is the point of departure in what seems to be one of our natural thought patterns: *general to specific*. Each gets the writer started on a topic and suggests a pattern of organization for its development. More specific generating sentences can also be good organizing devices for paragraphs.

Working from Specific Detail

Sometimes, however, you can rack your brain and still not be able to come up with a generative sentence that will trigger thought processes and get the piece of writing started. In that case, some writers find they can break through the inertia barrier by starting to write about a specific incident or anecdote or example they have thought of in connection with the topic. This kind of focused and concrete writing can be particularly useful as a way of getting started because it allows the writer to begin with description or narration,

1. Harry H. Crosby and George F. Estey, *Just Rhetoric* (New York: Harper and Row, 1972), p. 30.

modes of writing that many people find easier than exposition or argument. Then, as you write about an isolated incident, more examples will come to mind and soon generalizations and comparisons begin to develop. So this method of beginning with the concrete is another way of getting the mind started on what seems to be another of our natural thought patterns: *specific to general*.

A number of professional writers make frequent and effective use of this technique. Alfred Kazin, a prominent critic and essayist, says "the detail is the clue" to finding a thesis. Whether Kazin is keeping a journal or writing history and essays, his work is rooted in the specific.[2] George Orwell worked in the same way. His essays against imperialism and exploitation of the poor focus first on specific details, and then move to generalizations. Joan Didion uses the same technique in writing about Hollywood and Las Vegas.

When the writing process has started, you may find that your writing will begin to fall into a pattern of organization without your having given any conscious thought to how you were going to order your ideas. Some people seem to be able to work out patterns that are natural for them as they write. If you are fortunate enough to be that kind of writer, it is probably best for you just to go ahead and write rather than to stop to analyze what you are doing. If necessary, you can trim, revise, and reorganize later.

Methods of Organization

Other writers, however, flounder around as they try to get started, and they need help in finding ways to organize their writing. As pointed out earlier, all writers need to impose some sense of order, some plan on their writing. When no plan comes to mind, many people find it useful to review what seem to be natural human patterns of thought: induction, claims and warrants, definition, cause and effect, comparison, narration, and process. Choosing one of them as an organizational tool for getting started can help a writer who is having trouble getting down those first tracks to get moving on. Later the writer can incorporate other patterns. Starting with a particular one doesn't mean you have to stay with it all the way.

Induction.

Induction is a pattern of reasoning by which a person makes observations about several specific examples and then draws a general conclusion about those examples. Thus people who choose this approach begin by gathering

2. Quoted in "An Interview with Alfred Kazin," *Composition and Teaching,* November 1978, p. 30.

evidence related to their topic. Such evidence can take the form of examples, statistical data, experiences, reports, or some combination of all of these. Writers gathering data may not know at the start exactly how they are going to use the material they are gathering, but usually they have in mind some hypothesis or claim that they want to demonstrate or support. That hypothesis guides them as they gather evidence and helps them focus their search.

Writers using the inductive approach to writing jot down relevant information as notes in rough draft form, and when they think they have sufficient evidence to support their hypothesis, they begin to draft their paper. (We will discuss shortly how one decides when the evidence is sufficient.) Two patterns are possible: the writer can give the evidence first and move to a generalization, or state the generalization at the beginning and then give the supporting evidence. The generalization doesn't have to be the central idea for the entire paper or report; it might only be the thesis for a section of it.

Here is an example of how you could base the major part of an argument on induction. Suppose you want to appeal to the county commissioners to close down a garbage dump half a mile from the residential development where you live. First, you need to think of what kind of reasonable claim you could advance in favor of such action; after all, the county has to have a garbage dump somewhere so a simple protest isn't going to be very persuasive. You decide that the hypothesis on which you will make the appeal is that the present location of the dump threatens the health and safety of people living in the development. You come up with these supporting facts.

1. At least once a week in the summer, spontaneous fires break out from the accumulation of methane gas at the dump.

    a. Twice last year high winds carried sparks from the fires into dry grass areas near the development and started fires that menaced several homes.

    b. Smoke from the dump fires frequently increases air pollution in your community above the permissible level.

2. In spite of fences and "No Trespassing" signs, children from your residential development continue to go into the dump. This is extremely dangerous.

    a. They are liable to be burned.
    b. They are liable to injure themselves on broken glass or sharp metal objects.
    c. They are liable to be bitten by the rats that overrun the dump.

3. Rats and other rodents from the dump are moving into the residential area.

Such evidence warrants your generalization that the dump is dangerous. You can then use that generalization as backing for your claim that it ought to be closed.

HAZARDS OF INDUCTIVE REASONING.   Looks simple, doesn't it? As the foundation of the so-called scientific method, the inductive method is familiar to most of us, and we feel that it is a natural kind of thought process. Undoubtedly it is, yet certain hazards are inherent in the process. The chief one is that we may generalize too hastily from an insufficient sample or from a warped sample.

People who are going to use inductive reasoning effectively in writing must be sure they have enough evidence to convince their readers. In the case of the petition to close down the garbage dump, citing only two or three fires breaking out in a year would probably not be convincing, nor would one incident of a child's being bitten by a rat. And if you were using the inductive method to write an article about trends you see in the new season's television programs, you would not be justified in drawing conclusions if you had analyzed only two or three programs. Moreover, you mark yourself as a careless or naive person if you make what we call the "inductive leap" to a conclusion on the basis of inadequate evidence.

But how big a sample is sufficient? The answer to that question, like the answer to most questions about writing, is "That depends." It depends on the size or extent of the total population or situation about which you are generalizing, it depends on the degree of certainty you want your answer to carry, it depends on how difficult your audience is going to be to convince, and it depends on how important the issue is about which you are writing. If you are writing a paper to convince a skeptical audience—for example, the Federal Drug Administration—that aspirin be made a prescription drug because of its harmful side effects, you would have to document hundreds, probably thousands, of cases in which people had suffered serious consequences from taking aspirin. FDA officials would not be likely to make such a drastic change in the law without a great deal of evidence. If, however, you are writing an article for the college paper on what kind of boots students are buying this year, you could get sufficient evidence by calling half a dozen shoe stores near campus. The topic, though perhaps interesting, is minor, and your audience would probably not be critical; under the circumstances you'd be wasting your time to go to the trouble to conduct an extensive survey.

Probably even more important than the amount of evidence in your sample is the way in which you select that evidence. If you are going to draw honest and useful conclusions from a survey, the evidence in that survey must be chosen randomly; that is your examples must represent a cross section of the population about which you are generalizing. Thus the financial analyst who is writing a report about the kinds of purchases consumers intend to make in the next two years must not only get information from a fairly large number of potential buyers, but those buyers must represent several geographical areas and be taken from a cross section of economic, vocational, and age groups. If, for example, a New York-based analyst chose to gather information only about New York City residents or only from people who read the *New York Times,* he would warp his sample so badly that it would be useless to a national company.

Again, the amount of effort required to make sure that a sample is random and representative depends on how serious and extensive the writing task is and on how many people are apt to read the writing. If you are writing a newspaper feature story on the average price of haircuts in your city, checking a dozen shops selected according to location and sex of the clientele should yield information that is sufficiently assorted for you to draw a valid conclusion. If, however, you were to write a report for the local newspaper about the reading level of the average 12-year-old school child in your city, you would need to get information on several boys and girls from each middle school in the city and be sure that their families represented a cross section of economic, professional, ethnic, and social categories.

GUIDELINES FOR SOUND INDUCTIVE REASONING.　　And finally, when you use inductive evidence as the main focus of your writing, you should be meticulous about three matters. First, be sure your evidence is accurate and is presented clearly. This pattern for writing gives you a chance to show that you have done your research and that you understand the importance of having reliable data from which to draw conclusions. So get the facts straight.

Second, reinforce your credibility and strengthen your case by citing your sources. You can give your references in the actual prose of your report, in parentheses within the text, or in footnotes; any method is satisfactory as long as it allows the readers to check your information if they wish. For informal writing such as opinion pieces or feature articles, you don't need extensive documentation, but you certainly need to let your reader know where you found your material. If you are writing a report or study that has significant and widespread implications, you need to document your sources and carefully describe the method you used in gathering your information. Critical readers will not take you seriously unless you do.

Third, be sure that you do not let the working hypothesis that you started out with dominate your thinking when you choose your evidence. If you come across significant data that does not support your hypothesis, you have an obligation to include it. Not to do so is dishonest and, in the long run, foolish. You can't assume that the people you are trying to convince do not know the contradictory evidence, and if they do, you will have damaged your case irreparably.

Toulmin Logic.

Because the inductive method comes from science, it works especially well for writing in which one is investigating possibilities or citing evidence and drawing conclusions from it. If, however, you want to write a paper in which your primary purpose is to assert an idea and support it, you may want to use a model drawn from the law: a claim/warrant pattern of argument devised by logician Stephen Toulmin. Toulmin believes that most people do not try to use formal logic when they argue; instead, like judges or lawyers, they look for ways to justify claims that they want to make.[3] Their method is to find *data* to support their claims and *warrants* to explain them.

Toulmin and his followers use five primary terms in their analysis of arguments. They are:

CLAIM: The conclusion to an argument. The statement that is advanced for the approval of others. It may be stated or implied.

DATA: The data or evidence available to support a claim.

WARRANT: A statement of general principle that establishes the validity of the claim on the basis of its relationship to the data.

SUPPORT: Any material provided . . . to make the data or warrant more credible to the audience.

QUALIFIER: A qualification placed . . . on some claims (frequently in the form of such words as *possibly, probably,* or *most likely*).[4]

In their basic form, arguments constructed on the Toulmin model use only the first three terms, and they follow this pattern:

DATA ————————————————————→ CLAIM

WARRANT

For example:

DATA: Wholesale beef prices have risen 50 percent in the past six months. ————→ CLAIM: Consumers will have to pay more for steaks in the future.
WARRANT: An increase in wholesale prices causes an increase in costs to consumers.

3. Stephen Toulmin, *The Uses of Argument* (London: Cambridge University Press, 1958), p. 6.
4. Richard D. Reike and Malcolm O. Sillars, *Argumentation and the Decision Making Process* (New York: John Wiley and Sons, Inc., 1975), pp. 77–8.

One might also expand one part of the argument. For example:

DATA: Exhaust fumes cause serious pollution problems in cities.
DATA: Traffic congestion causes serious problems. ⟶ CLAIM: All major cities should ban private autos.

WARRANT: Banning private autos from cities would reduce traffic and pollution problems.

Sometimes, however, the arguments a writer wants to make are more complex, and one or more statements needs to be qualified. When that happens, the writer can add a qualification to any section. For example:

DATA: According to recent government statistics, ⟶ CLAIM: black women do not have an advantage in the job market

WARRANT (implied): Government statistics are reliable.

QUALIFICATION: unless they are college graduates.

Here is another example:

DATA: the declining population in the northeastern states ⟶ CLAIM: will force many New England colleges to close.

QUALIFICATION: Unless demographic patterns change,

WARRANT: (implied) Population shifts affect college enrollment.

Sometimes writers also realize that they must support one or more parts of their arguments. In such cases, another element appears in the Toulmin model for argument. For example:

DATA: on the average, preschool children spend 60 percent of their waking time watching television. ⟶ CLAIM: Modern children are conditioned to be consumers at an early age.

SUPPORT: According to the book *The Plug-in Drug*,

WARRANT: (implied) Watching television conditions people to be consumers.

Here is an example of an argument that is both qualified and supported:

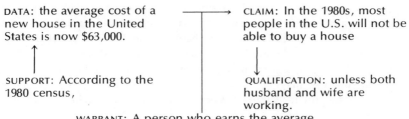

DATA: the average cost of a new house in the United States is now $63,000.

CLAIM: In the 1980s, most people in the U.S. will not be able to buy a house

SUPPORT: According to the 1980 census,

QUALIFICATION: unless both husband and wife are working.

WARRANT: A person who earns the average income of less than $20,000 cannot afford a $63,000 house.

Organizing your arguments in this way has several advantages. The first is that readers who prefer rational arguments are apt to respond positively to the data/warrant/claim pattern because they recognize its resemblance to courtroom procedures. They expect someone who makes a *claim* to *support* it with *data* (or evidence), and they expect him or her to give a *warrant* (or explanation) that shows the reasoning behind the claim. Thus carefully phrased arguments on this pattern have a legitimate ring about them.

A second advantage is that writers can employ the Toulmin approach flexibly, making decisions about how to develop it on the basis of the audience, the purpose, and the writing situation. For example, sometimes a writer does not need to make a warrant explicit. If you were writing to a group of coastal property owners claiming that they should oppose the construction of an offshore port for oversized oil tankers, probably all you would need to point out is that having such tankers near shore greatly increases the chance of oil spills in the area. You would not have to add that such oil spills cause major property damage.

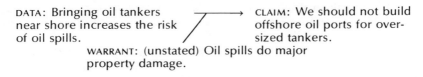

DATA: Bringing oil tankers near shore increases the risk of oil spills.

CLAIM: We should not build offshore oil ports for oversized tankers.

WARRANT: (unstated) Oil spills do major property damage.

If, however, you were writing to the members of the port authority commission who make recommendations about building such ports, you would need to convince them that potential property damage was a serious concern. In that case you would need to state and support your warrant.

DATA: Bringing oil tankers near shore increases the risk of oil spills.

CLAIM: We should not build offshore oil ports for oversized tankers.

WARRANT: Offshore oil spills do major damage to beaches and fishing grounds.

SUPPORT: Facts about 1979 Gulf of Mexico oil spill.

In other situations a writer might recognize that she or he needed to add qualifications to a claim, give expanded support for the data, or provide more than one warrant to clarify the relationship between the data and the claim.

A third advantage of the Toulmin method is that it allows the writer to arrange the parts of an argument in different ways. One might catch the audience's attention by making the claim or major assertion first, then presenting the data to support it. Virginia Woolf uses that approach in the following paragraph:

> [CLAIM] It is unthinkable that any woman in Shakespeare's day should have had Shakespeare's genius. [WARRANT] For genius like Shakespeare's is not born among labouring, uneducated, servile people. [DATA] It was not born in England among the Saxons and the Britons. It is not born today among the working classes. [WARRANT RESTATED AND SUPPORTED] How then, could it have been born among women whose work began . . . almost before they were out of the nursery, who were forced to it by all the power of law and custom?[5]

Woolf could also have begun her argument with the warrant, or, by rearranging her sentences slightly, she could have omitted the warrant and let her readers supply it. And perhaps she would have strengthened her argument by beginning with the qualifier, *"Probably* no woman in Shakespeare's time . . . ''

A writer can decide which parts of an argument might be omitted and which parts need to be stressed only after analyzing audience and purpose. Nevertheless, the following guidelines can help writers make such decisions.

1. In almost every case, make both the claim and the warrant explicit.
2. Include the warrant if the reader is apt to be skeptical or uninformed.
3. Add a qualifier if the truth of the claim is uncertain or relative.
4. Include support for major points that the reader may challenge.[6]

Notice too that Toulmin's approach to constructing arguments allows a writer to combine claim/warrant arguments with inductive arguments just as we do when we argue extemporaneously. We observe individual cases, make a generalization on the basis of those cases (induction), and then we present that generalization as a claim. The paragraph previously cited from Virginia Woolf illustrates the process. She investigated the origins of dozens of people of genius in England and found that none of them were uneducated or had come from the laboring classes. She then generalized that genius is not likely to come from those two groups of people. Using induction again, she exam-

---

5. Virginia Woolf, *A Room of One's Own* (New York: Harcourt, Brace & World, 1929), p. 50.
6. Michael Keene and Kitty Locker, ''Using Toulmin Logic in Business and Technical Writing,'' unpublished paper, 1978, p. 6.

ined the conditions in which women lived before the nineteenth century and realized that almost all of them were uneducated and treated like servants. From that data she generalized that they could not have become great writers.

Finally, the Toulmin model for arguments helps writers to generate material they can use to develop their ideas. Most of us find it easy enough to express our opinions, but sometimes we have trouble when we have to produce evidence (data) to back them or give explanations (warrants) for them. However, writers who habitually ask themselves "What is my warrant for this claim?" or "What supporting data can I find to strengthen my case?" will find that such questions are tools for discovery. They force writers to probe their experience and examine their store of information. Generally that is a thought-provoking process.

Writers who can train themselves to try the Toulmin approach when they undertake a writing task that requires them to make a claim or argue a thesis should find it a time-saving and productive strategy. Going over these four models may help to clarify this strategy.

DATA: The verbal portion of the Scholastic Aptitude Test does not require people to write. ⟶ CLAIM: The verbal portion of the SAT is not a valid test of writing ability.

WARRANT: A test of writing ability must require people to write.

DATA: Because televised football games provide huge audiences for advertisers ⟶ CLAIM: professional football team owners can afford to pay high salaries to their players.

WARRANT: the television advertising makes professional football profitable.

DATA: the value of the dollar in relation to European currencies plummeted this year. ⟶ CLAIM: Fewer Americans will travel in Europe this year.

QUALIFICATION: Although air fares from the U.S. to Europe are the lowest in history,

WARRANT: People prefer not to travel in countries where their money will not buy much.

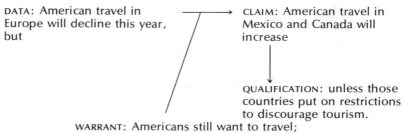

DATA: American travel in
Europe will decline this year,
but

CLAIM: American travel in
Mexico and Canada will
increase

QUALIFICATION: unless those
countries put on restrictions
to discourage tourism.

WARRANT: Americans still want to travel;
therefore . . .

These last two examples demonstrate how the Toulmin approach can be used to construct a chain argument in which the claim from one step of the argument can be used as the data for the next step.

Definition.

Another pattern for organizing writing that seems to reflect a natural thought process is *definition.* When we define, we identify, characterize, and seek to distinguish from other items the person, place, thing, or idea we are focusing on. Moreover, most of us seem to define almost as instinctively as we speak. We define when we say that New York is a dynamic city, the Pittsburgh Steelers are the best team in the National Football League, our penal system is a failure, or solar power is the energy source of the future. We use these definitions as the basis for writing or speech in which we try to persuade, explain, or instruct; in fact, we don't seem to be able to get far in any kind of discourse without using definition. As a method of identifying, classifying, and evaluating our experience, it is basic.

In earlier writing courses you have probably already studied and written definitions, so I will touch only briefly on some methods of definition and suggest ways in which you can use one or more of those methods as a technique for getting started on a writing task.

Method 1: Attributing characteristics.
The ideal motor fuel would be cheap, efficient, and nonpolluting.
A liberated person is one who does not take his or her identity from another.
Comparison/contrast is a subcategory of this method of defining.
Method 2: Analyzing parts. (This can overlap with Method 1.)
The audience for television soap operas consists chiefly of women who stay at home, retired people, and a surprising number of college students.
The stages of the creative process seem to be conception, incubation, execution, and verification.

Method 3: Giving examples.

In the 1970s college administrators found that they had to pay attention to new kinds of students who expected more from their educations: retired military personnel, wives or divorcees returning to school, and already-employed workers returning to school part-time.

The publishing surprise of the decade has been the success of the new magazine with a specialized audience: *Texas Monthly, Working Woman, Rolling Stone,* and *The Runner,* for instance.

Method 4: Stating function.

A psychotherapist is a person trained to treat emotional illness.

A health spa is a facility designed to help people become physically fit.

In practice, as you will recognize, these methods frequently merge or overlap, but you needn't worry about that. No rule says that definitions have to be pure.

USES OF DEFINITION.   One writing situation in which you may find definition useful is that in which you are arguing for change. You can base your entire essay on definitions of what is desirable and undesirable. For example, if you are running for the job of president of the shuttle-bus drivers' union, in your campaign you could define the qualities that an effective union president has to have, then show that you have those qualities. Or if you are writing a paper for a government course on the abuses of the grand jury system in this country, you could define the traditional functions of grand juries and point out that today they often do not serve those functions at all.

Definition is also an effective device for making judgments or evaluations. If, for example, your writing task requires you to argue that some thing, person, or institution is good or bad, effective or ineffective, and to support that judgment, the most logical way to tackle the problem is probably to use definition. You can do it by establishing a standard and applying that standard: this approach also suggests a natural pattern for your writing.

Suppose, for instance, a vice-president in your company has asked you to write a report on and rank the performances of salespeople under your supervision. You could begin your report by defining what you consider a good sales performance: calling on businesses regularly, keeping old accounts, establishing new accounts, getting orders for new products the company has introduced, and so on. Then you could measure the performance of each person against this yardstick, and on that basis judge that person's effectiveness. You would use the same procedure if you were asked to judge an art show, or to file a report on whether a new industry in your area is meeting the state standards for controlling industrial pollution. In each case, you define the standard and apply it.

Finally, defining plays a crucial part when one is debating about principles or ethical issues, so if the paper you must write deals with a moral problem, try definition as your first line of approach. Begin by spelling out the issue for yourself so that you can pin down the basic principle involved. For instance, if you are going to write an editorial protesting the police's dispersal of a Chicano student rally, you would be working from a definition of the students' constitutional rights. If you are charging a person in your organization with sex discrimination, the principle underlying your case is that the law defines everyone as equal regardless of sex.

Such an approach is particularly effective when the basic definition from which you are writing is one that your reader must accept almost without question. For example, one of Abraham Lincoln's most effective arguments against slavery was based on the definition, "A slave is a man." He went on to contend that as a man, a slave was entitled to the human rights guaranteed by the Constitution. This kind of definition is an *a priori* premise, that is, a belief or conviction that the writer simply states and assumes is self-evident. Typical *a priori* premises in our culture are "Free education is a basic right," "All people are entitled to due process of law," "People should have freedom of speech," and "Children's welfare is a proper concern of the government." You can easily think of many more such self-evident statements or definitions. If you have a good sense of your audience, you should be able to decide quickly whether they share your definition of what is right or wrong.

Although structuring your writing around definition often works well, particularly when you need to establish criteria or want to appeal to your audience's sense of what is moral or desirable, the argument from definition has at least two drawbacks. First, you may not be able to find basic premises or definitions that you and your audience will agree on. Second, although your audience may passively accept your definition of what is right, your telling them what they *should* do or about the way things *ought* to be will not move them to action. When you analyze the audience for whom you are writing, you should be able to tell if you face either of these problems. If you do, consider approaching your writing task by using cause and effect.

Cause and Effect.

Speculating about cause and effect is another of those thought processes that we use almost intuitively; it can serve you particularly well when you know that your audience disagrees with you on underlying principles. At such times, you would only alienate your readers by insisting that they accept your definitions of right and wrong. For example, if you are proposing that your state adopt a guaranteed minimum income to replace the present welfare system, and you know that your audience generally opposes welfare, you'd be wasting your time to talk about the government's obligation to the poor. Your audience disagrees, and you are unlikely to change their opinion. If you suggest that their attitude is callous or immoral, they will quit reading or close their minds from the start.

You may, however, win your audience's interest and possible assent by describing the benefits of the guaranteed income and the disadvantages of the present welfare system. You could point out that the proposal you support would eliminate 50 percent of the huge bureaucracy needed to administer the present system, that it does away with most of the opportunities for fraud, that it puts cash directly into the marketplace, and so on. Underlying your argument is the tacit assumption that the government should not let people starve, but you don't mention that. Rather than philosophizing about who owes what to whom, you concentrate instead on a pragmatic solution to a serious problem.

In some communication situations, you have a chance of communicating with your opponent only if you talk or write in terms of cause and effect. When you and your audience are sharply divided and your basic premises are radically different, you will be able to reach them only if you can demonstrate that you and they have shared interests. Then you may appeal to them if you talk in terms of costs, benefits, and tangible solutions. And you have to realize that you may not reach them at all if the benefits from the course of action that you recommend will violate their strongly held principles.

For example, if you were the accountant for a chain of hotels and were to suggest that your clients open casinos in their hotels located in states where there is legalized gambling, and gave as your argument that statistics show that revenues could be increased by 12 percent, you would probably fail if the president of that chain has strong moral objections to gambling. But where lesser issues are involved, you can skirt areas on which you and your audience are apt to disagree and emphasize the results of certain courses of action.

The same kind of pragmatic appeal may work when your audience shares your convictions about what is good or desirable, but will make no effort to put those beliefs into practice. Thus, people may agree that voting is important, that they have a civic obligation to go to the polls, and still not vote. Only if a writer can convince them that their failure to vote will cause them problems are they apt to change their ways. Citing a case in which 23 percent of the eligible voters of a city committed *all* the taxpayers to pay for a six-million-dollar coliseum used primarily for boat and auto dealer shows would probably be more effective than preaching about citizenship. And demonstrating that a smoothly integrated school system is one of management's major concerns when a company chooses a location for building a new plant may be a better argument than an appeal to conscience and goodwill.

Building your writing on a pattern of cause and effect also works well in other kinds of situations. If you must write an environmental impact study or a grant proposal, for instance, your chief task is to describe the effects of proposed actions. If you are promoting a product, a project, or a politician, you are trying to establish a cause and effect relationship in the minds of your audience. And any time that you must justify spending money, you do so by pointing to results, real or anticipated. In fact, so fundamental is the cause and effect process in our thinking that any time you are stuck for a way to get started on a piece of writing, you might save time by trying the causation pattern first.

CIRCUMSTANTIAL ARGUMENT.   Sometimes you may want to present a cause and effect argument in terms so strong that your audience will almost have to agree with you. In that situation you might construct a circumstantial argument, one in which you show that the chain of cause and effect is so strong that if A occurs, B is inevitable.

First, of course, be sure that you have a strong case; your audience will probably not react well to a manufactured crisis. But if you do have a strong case, state it in terms that convey urgency. You can signal a crisis by phrases like "Under the circumstances, we have no other choice but . . . ," "We are forced to . . . ," and "Given this situation, we must . . ." Then go on to give a specific explanation of the circumstances.

For example, in writing an environmental impact statement, you might point out that if a manufacturer continues to use a local lake for cooling the machinery for a proposed new plant, the water temperature will rise enough to create a serious algae problem; you stress that the result is inevitable. Or in presenting the case for an increase in the dues of an association you belong to, you might show that costs for rent, electricity, printing, and secretarial help will otherwise force the association to close. Well-done arguments from circumstances are hard to refute, so if you think you have an unusually strong case to present, reach for those phrases that signal a crisis situation.

You need, however, to observe a few basic cautions when you choose either a plain cause and effect approach or the stronger argument from circumstance as the starting point for your writing. First, don't overstate your case. In most cases, you should be satisfied with pointing out that if A happens, B will *probably* happen too. With a rational audience, you'll enhance your credibility by not getting too far out on a limb. Second, don't oversimplify your case. Complex problems nearly always have complex causes and complex solutions. Suggesting that you have an easy answer for a difficult problem can only make you appear naive or uninformed. Third, explain your reasoning. Don't assume that your audience will accept your analysis of the situation on faith. They want to know how you arrived at your conclusion.

Comparison.

Another of the thought patterns that we often employ when we write or speak is comparison. We explain a process or a situation or justify a proposal by making comparisons, by showing similarities and differences. Using this approach has the special advantage of allowing a writer to tap knowledge that a reader already has to enlighten that reader further.

If, as you search for an approach that will get you started on your writing, you begin to think of cases that are like the one you have to write about, jot down some ideas and see if you can fit them into one of these three methods of drawing comparisons: straight comparison, analogy, or comparison of probabilities (this last is called *a fortiori* argument, which I will explain shortly). In using straight comparison, you would simply want to show likenesses or differences that would clarify the point you are making. For example, if you are asked to write an analysis of the advantages and disadvantages of a proposal that your company adopt a ten-hour day and a four-day workweek, you would show what has happened when similar companies adopted such a schedule. If you are asked to make a recommendation about continuing the use of computer-scored aptitude tests by the personnel department of your company, you would compare absenteeism and worker turnover rate before and after the company began to use the tests. Or if you are writing a paper about the decline of the family farm in the Midwest, you could compare the number of individual-owned farms in 1950 with the number in 1980. You might also use comparison on another level by showing what happened to food prices and property values when the number of family farms declined in the South, and suggest that similar developments can be expected in the Midwest.

ANALOGY.   Hard-fact comparisons like these are often effective and convincing; unfortunately, sometimes they are also dull. For a more dramatic and often more enlightening kind of comparison, you can turn to the analogy, another of our common thought patterns. When we use analogies in writing, we usually do so to draw the attention of our readers to illuminating similarities between something they already know and understand and something we are trying to explain to them. We try to set up a kind of equation in their minds that will help them to comprehend something new by equating it with something familiar. From taking aptitude or intelligence tests, most of you know the form of that equation; it goes A is to B as C is to D, or pump is to water as heart is to blood. At the end of chapter 2, I used the analogy of a person's making unexpected discoveries when hiking toward a destination to illustrate the discovery process that a writer goes through in working out a writing task. And in a recent court case in which a mother whose son graduated from a California high school without being able to read sued that school for failure to do its job, she was drawing an analogy between consumer products and education. That is, *high school* is to *student* as *manufacturer* is to *product*. She was arguing that just as a manufacturer is responsible for the quality of its products, so a school is responsible for the quality of its graduates. (She lost, by the way.)

The ability to draw striking analogies that bring a flash of recognition to the reader is one mark of a good writer; witness, for example, Alfred Kazin's comparison of his boyhood school to a "factory over which has been imposed the facade of a castle,"[7] and James Baldwin's comparison of blacks' resentment of racism to a "rage in the blood."[8] Although such writers may have more talent and stronger imaginative powers than most of us, much of their success comes from their having cultivated their abilities to see likenesses. They are constantly looking for the revealing detail, for the apt comparison, and they keep journals so that they don't lose these insights.

The inexperienced writer can adopt the same methods. If, during a period in which you have a lot of writing to do, you get in the habit of looking around you for incidents from which you could draw analogies, and writing down those observations as soon as you can, you'll take two steps toward improving your writing. First, you'll sharpen your powers of observation and make it likely that you will continue to be a good observer. Second, you'll accumulate a store of illustrative material to draw on when you need it.

Try also to develop the habit of looking for a good analogy when you need to explain a concept or process to your audience. You could make notes on the important features of the thing you are trying to explain and keep reading over them to see what similarities you might find with another concept or process. For example, trying to fill out an income tax form is confusing, frustrating, sometimes even frightening if one thinks of the consequences of not doing it correctly. Looking at those characteristics, you might decide to compare your trying to work your way through it to a rat trying to find his way out of a maze. And I, for example, in trying to explain that the writing process is neither a mystery nor an exact procedure that one can precisely analyze and prescribe, decided that a good analogy for it might be cooking something by an old-fashioned recipe that gives the key ingredients, then says, "Add a pinch of salt, enough milk to moisten, and stir until the batter looks grainy." Both procedures are inexact and messy, but nevertheless, if followed, will help the creator turn out a fairly predictable product. A perceptive writer is certainly capable of drawing similar analogies; to do so, you need to get in the habit of thinking in comparisons.

A FORTIORI COMPARISONS OR COMPARISONS OF PROBABILITIES.   Another pattern into which our thinking seems to fall naturally is that of speculating about logical possibilities; that is, engaging in *a fortiori* reasoning (pronounced ah-for'-shee-or'-ee). The term means "all the stronger"; when we use this kind of reasoning we argue that if a person or group can do or has done a difficult thing, then it is logical to expect that the same person or group

7. Alfred Kazin, *A Walker in the City* (New York: Harcourt, Brace & World, 1951), p. 17.
8. James Baldwin, *Notes of a Native Son* (Boston: Beacon Press, 1955), p. 4.

can do a similar but easier thing—that is, there is "all the stronger" reason to think they can. This kind of comparison lies behind comments such as, "If our university can build a new thirty-million-dollar auditorium, why can't it afford $500,000 for minority scholarships?" or "If Joe has the self-discipline to quit smoking, he should surely have the self-discipline to exercise every day."

As you can see, the "all the stronger" approach to expanding a topic is the kind of commonsense approach that all of us make when we appeal to readers' sense of what is logical and consistent. It is easy to use, particularly when we are trying to make a case for something we think is important. For example, "If this country is willing to spend billions on its space program, it ought to allocate 50 million to cancer research." You should be careful, however, not to let an *a fortiori* argument deteriorate into a simplistic and unsophisticated approach to a topic. Although it is a useful device for pointing up incongruities in behavior and priorities, and sometimes for enlightening your audience, basing your entire piece of writing on the "all the stronger" approach could make you look naive or uninformed. There may be complex reasons why it is easier for a country to spend money on space exploration than cancer research, or why a university does not divert money from building into scholarships. Prudent writers consider those complications, and though they may use this kind of comparison to get into a topic or as a supporting device, they do not totally depend on it.

Narration.

Probably the most natural and perhaps the oldest form of discourse is narration, writing or speaking that recounts a series of events in a straightforward, generally sequential order. We usually think of narration as storytelling, but nonfiction writers can also use it in a number of ways. A company executive writing a report of his visit to a branch office might write a narrative account of his experiences there; an agency staff member writing an environmental impact statement might need to narrate the series of changes that have taken place on a site over a period of years; a magazine writer doing a piece on a famous person would probably use a substantial amount of narration because the audience would want to read biographical anecdotes about the subject; an emergency medical technician would use narrative in writing up the report on an accident victim; and an archaeologist could use narrative to describe the sequence of findings at an excavation. Although none of these writers would use narration exclusively, all would recognize the value of being able to write an accurate and specific account of an event.

If you write chiefly nonfiction, you are not likely to be called on to do much writing that requires only narration, but you should be alert to possibilities for strengthening or enlivening your everyday, working writing by bringing in narrative, especially those short units of narrative called *anecdote* and *incident*. The anecdote is a miniature, self-contained story that usually focuses on a person, but illustrates some point that an author wants to emphasize. For instance, to illustrate how students with poor writing skills must feel when they face a writing assignment that will expose their ineptitude, I frequently tell about my bad experiences in the first few weeks of an intensive course in spoken French.

Incidents are also short and complete accounts that serve a similar purpose, but usually they focus on actions rather than personalities. For example, in her ironic essay about the wedding industry in Las Vegas, "Marrying Absurd," Joan Didion underscores her judgment by briefly describing two weddings she observed: in one incident she tells about a drunk bride in an orange minidress stumbling out of the chapel and falling onto the car; in the other she tells about the father of an obviously pregnant bride making ritual wedding-night jokes to the bridegroom.[9]

Whether you are using the narrative method to write case studies and archaeological reports, or to illustrate your point with anecdotes, keep in mind that good narrators use concrete and specific language. They try to help their readers visualize the events they are describing. In a later chapter I will suggest some guidelines for choosing words that will do that.

Process.

The last of the common prose patterns that many writers use frequently is that of *process*. A process paper is a "how-to" paper; it could range from a sheet of directions on assembling a modular bookcase to a book titled "365 Days to a More Beautiful You." Typically, the person who is doing process writing describes a sequence of steps that lead to a desired result. The writer leads the reader through the stages chronologically, explaining, illustrating, and sometimes mentioning the problems that one might encounter at certain stages. Notice that I followed this approach when I talked about the writing process in chapter 2.

Much of the day-to-day writing that keeps our world running is process writing, and if you are going to function well in business science or technology, you will have to master the art of writing clear process papers. It is not easy, and the demands of some professions require that you take special courses in technical or scientific writing. For the most part, though, people who train and discipline themselves to be good expository prose writers can also become competent process writers. As you learn techniques for writing clear, precise, and economical general-purpose prose, you are also learning to

9. Joan Didion, "Marrying Absurd," in *Slouching Toward Bethlehem* (New York: Dell, 1968), pp. 79–83.

write process papers. We will focus on a particular kind of process writing, the grant proposal, later in the book.

Combining the Methods

Experienced writers probably don't stop to think about what methods or modes of discourse they are using when they start to write; they begin with whatever tricks or rituals they need to get them started, and follow the thought patterns that come into their heads. They could analyze what they are doing— one might say, "I work by getting down specific details first," and another might say, "I try to identify the problem and then show what caused it"—but they don't classify and label their methods. Neither do they try to write primarily in any one pattern; usually they move from one to the other as their topic seems to demand.

But the inexperienced writer sometimes needs to proceed more consciously and deliberately in order to get moving on a piece of writing. Given a writing task, he or she may be able to force the mind out of incubation and into illumination and execution by working through the catalog of natural patterns of writing to see which might prove useful for the job at hand. Here is how it might work.

Assigned writing task: to write a new energy policy for your company.
Possible writing patterns:

INDUCTIVE: Gather data on energy policies of other companies of comparable size.

CLAIM: Using data from inductive study, make a generalization about what a good energy policy would be. Classify present energy policy by applying that generalization.

DEFINITION: List the qualities of a good energy policy. Give examples of good policies from other companies. List functions of good energy policy: to provide adequate energy, provide low-cost energy, provide safe, clean energy.

CAUSE AND EFFECT: Centralizing facilities would reduce costs. Changing to new energy sources would increase costs. Educational campaign would reduce energy consumption.

COMPARISON: Straight: Compare policy to that of other companies.
Analogy: Compare redesigning energy plan for company to redesigning cars to meet new circumstances of high-priced gasoline and problems of air pollution.
A fortiori: If a town succeeded in reducing the crime

rate by education and citizen participation, then a company should be able to reduce energy consumption the same way.

NARRATION: Account of a visit to another company to learn about its energy plan.

Account of what happened at Central Industries when it adopted a new plan.

PROCESS: Explanation of the stages of the new plan, how it will be put into effect, and what the projected results will be.

Some of these patterns overlap or duplicate one another, and a writer would not want to use all of them; that would be overkill. But picking out two or three and developing them would be a practical way to get started writing a paper.

E X E R C I S E S / *Prewriting Activities*

1 Here is an example of a generative sentence that could help you to get started writing a paper on the machine-scored examinations used to screen applicants for most professional schools.

The admissions officers of professional schools have come to rely too heavily on machine-scored tests that are culturally biased and cannot measure motivation, perseverance, or creativity.

Write a similar generative sentence that could help you get started on writing on one of these topics.

A. A comparison of foreign-made and American-made bicycles.

B. A review of a movie or play you have seen recently.

C. An analysis of attendance at athletic events on your campus.

D. An explanation of jet lag.

2 Here is a sample list of details that a writer planning a paper on local art fairs might write down.

booths in tents	handmade jewelry	watercolors
oil painting	weaving	on the spot portraits
stained glass	leather goods	macrame
$10 pictures	pottery	credit-card users

Make a similar list of details for a paper on one of these topics.

A. Cheerleaders for professional football games.

B. Coping with on-the-job stress.

C.   A boat and camper show.

D.   Rodeo clowns.

3   Suppose that your professor of urban planning asks you to write a paper about how airline passengers in your city feel about airport facilities and what improvements they would like to see. What criteria would you establish for taking the survey on which your report would be based? Then answer these questions and explain the basis of each of your answers.

How many people to be interviewed?
What distribution of sexes? Ages? Business travelers? Pleasure travelers?
When would you conduct the interviews? More than one session?
Where would you conduct the interviews?

4   Review the section on Toulmin logic: then write out your claim, warrant, and data for arguing each of these propositions. Add a qualifier if necessary.

A.   Basketball is a better spectator sport than football.

B.   The top stars in the music business make too much money.

C.   Your state should authorize no-fault automobile insurance policies.

D.   People under twenty-one should not be issued credit cards.

5   Define the following activities, objects, groups, conditions, or categories by 1) giving characteristics, 2) analyzing parts, 3) stating function, or 4) giving an example. Use more than one method if you need to.

provincialism	Weight Watchers	hedonism
social worker	low blood sugar	quarter horse
white-water canoeing	a freeway	a fanatic

6   Set up a cause and effect relationship that you could use to argue these propositions.

A.   The state should double the cost of hunting licenses for out-of-state hunters.

B.   The Federal Communications Commission should ban the advertising of junk food on television.

C.   Divorced women as well as men should be liable for child-support payments.

D.   State legislatures should appropriate more money for research in universities.

7 How could you use the following comparisons in developing a writing assignment?

A.   If we can develop the technology to put the astronauts into space, we ought to be able to design a method of transportation that doesn't depend on oil.

B.   The apartment buildings in that part of town are like islands of affluence in a sea of poverty.

C.   Trying to enforce the 55-mile-an-hour speed limit is like trying to enforce the Prohibition amendment.

D.   The average cost of writing a business letter is now $5.41; the average cost of a three-minute out-of-state long-distance phone call between 8:00 A.M. and 5:00 P.M. is $3.32

8 Write a short narrative about a person or incident that you could use to start a paper on one of these topics.

A.   Strengthening enforcement of penalties against drunk drivers.

B.   The growing popularity of fast-food restaurants.

C.   Sexual harassment of women in the armed services.

D.   Backpacking on the Appalachian Trail.

Suggested Writing Assignments

As a part of each writing assignment, write a detailed analysis of your audience. Specify characteristics they have which you need to keep in mind, problems they might present, and what they would expect to get from reading your paper. Also analyze your purpose in writing, specifying what you hope to accomplish in the paper. If appropriate, include an accurate and descriptive title for your paper.

TOPIC 1:
Write a professional brochure for an agency or business, giving as much information as you can squeeze into no more than 600 words. Your writing should be clear, simple, and lively so that the audience can read the brochure quickly and enjoy it. Here are possible topics for such a brochure. You might think of a similar one suited to your own job or interests.

What is a no-fault divorce?
How to establish your credit rating.

Planning your Caribbean vacation.
How to buy a used car.
What is depression?
Getting the most from your micro-
wave oven.

TOPIC 2:
Write an article for your college paper on some campus organization. Define the organization using the methods of definition discussed in this chapter. You could write a strictly informative article or one that is primarily persuasive, that is an argument for or against the organization. You could also
combine the two purposes and write an article that defines the organization
and also tries to persuade people to join it. Here are some typical organizations you could write about:

Student Council
The Hike and Bike Club
Phi Beta Kappa Chapter
The French Club
The Sailing Club
The Pre-Law Association

TOPIC 3:
Write an argument for or against one of the propositions below. Before you
decide on your topic, think carefully about where your paper would be published, who would read it, and what your specific purpose in writing the
paper would be.

A.   The cost of doing business in many parts of the world includes brib-
ing officials. This is a local custom that companies must observe if they are
to do business in that country. Companies who insist this is illegal activity
are being unrealistic.

B.   Movies featuring torture scenes are more obscene and harmful than
movies featuring explicit sexual scenes; therefore they should be x-rated
and people under eighteen not admitted.

C.   The state board of corrections has just recommended building a new
minimum-security prison designed for prisoners who are not habitual crimi-
nals and have not been convicted of a violent crime. The state legislature
will probably approve the recommendation. Your hometown is one of three
sites that the board has mentioned as a good location for such a prison. The
governor will choose among the towns recommended by the board.

Holding Your Reader

IF THERE IS ANY WAY FOR YOUR READERS TO GET LOST, THEY WILL.

That is a warning that all writers should keep in mind constantly as they write. In the world of functional, nonschool writing of the kind that is done at enterprises such as Sears, *Newsweek,* Exxon Corporation, *Cosmopolitan,* the U.S. Department of Commerce, and others, a person reads a piece of writing for two reasons: to be entertained, or to be informed. If the writing does neither, if it confuses or bores or threatens the reader, or if it wastes the reader's time, the writer has lost that reader, usually for good. And whatever response the writer wanted from the reader, he or she will probably not get it.

Unfortunately, most people who are writing in a classroom situation simply do not seem to grasp this problem of holding their audience. They are not able to project themselves beyond the immediate situation to imagine any audience other than their professor. And they assume that, like it or not, professors will read student writing to the end if it seems to make any sense at all. Teachers do not often say, ''I quit reading because I got bored,'' or ''I quit reading because I got lost on the second page.'' But real audiences quit for exactly those reasons, and when writers move out of the school situation and lose their captive audiences, they need to start thinking consciously about specific strategies they can use to hold the capricious and impatient audience they are now writing for. Those strategies include using accurate titles, dividing your writing with internal headings and subheadings, articulating your promise to the reader, and tying the parts of your writing together with hooks or patterns.

Titles

In most cases, you will make the first impression of your audience with your title; therefore it is important that you choose it carefully. As pointed out in chapter 2, you may want to choose a tentative working title to help you start thinking about your topic; after you have completed the writing, you can revise the title to reflect accurately the content of your paper. The working title is for you; the final title is for your reader.

The final title should do several things. First, it should *predict* the content of the paper accurately enough for the reader to decide if he or she wants to read it. For instance, titles like "Energy-Efficient Homes" or "Low-Cost Vacations in Mexico" are precise and direct and will attract readers who are interested in the subjects. Also, such titles are apt to make a good impression on readers because they are honest; they haven't lured them on false pretenses.

Second, a good title *sets limits* for readers, points them in the right direction, and because it prepares them to receive the writer's message, makes it less likely that they will get lost. Both of the above titles meet this standard. For broader, more complex topics a writer can do even more to help the reader stay on the track by adding a colon and subtitle to the main title. For instance, "Trouble in Saudi Arabia: The Conflict between Technology and Tradition" or "The New French Cuisine: Less Trouble and Fewer Calories." Such titles are especially good for papers written primarily to inform because they *signal* to the readers in advance what they should learn from the article, and thus increase their chances of learning it.

Finally, when you write a title you should be thinking of future as well as present readers; you do not want to lose them either. But you probably will if the title you choose for a report or paper is so vague and ambiguous that it may get misfiled or left out of an important bibliography. So when you choose a title, put yourself in the place of a cataloger or researcher. Do the principal words accurately reflect your topic? Have you been specific enough so that the person classifying articles for a computerized bibliography will understand immediately where your paper should go? Under the circumstances, ambiguous or vague titles just won't do. For example, if you chose the title "Star Wars" for an article on rivalry among the hosts of television talkshows it may disappear forever in a bibliography of science-fiction movies.

In general, avoid cute, pretentious, or deliberately ambiguous titles for your writing. They're tempting, particularly if you enjoy puns and have a flair for witty remarks, but they are also a trap. For one thing, it is too easy to mislead your readers. For another, writers who use cute titles, as Aaron Lathan did when he named an *Esquire* article about Elizabeth Taylor "National Velveeta," box themselves into a tone and point of view that may be hard to sustain throughout an article. And of course cute titles are more apt to be misclassified than straight ones. Finally, you need to remember that jokes and puns and pretentious allusions wear thin. The title that today seems witty and urbane may embarrass you when you see it on your résumé five years from now.

Those Critical First Pages

If you ask any editor, executive, or administrator how far he or she reads before making a preliminary decision on most of the manuscripts, proposals, requests, or reports that come across the desk, that person will quickly tell you, ''Two or three paragraphs. A couple of pages at the most.'' It takes only that long for busy and experienced readers to decide whether or not to continue reading; thus what you do in the first page or two is crucial. The surface features are important, of course; you cannot afford misspelled words, glaring grammatical errors, or careless typing. But content is even more important if you want to hold your reader.

Although skilled writers know a multitude of ways to begin their writing—and we will be exploring some of those ways in a later section on paragraphs—most good openings have one thing in common: they let the reader know what to expect. The writer makes a promise to the reader, either directly or by implication, and raises that reader's expectations; the reader assumes that what follows will fulfill those expectations. This kind of opening establishes a pattern, which, if followed, will help to hold the reader. You have learned about ways to develop those patterns in the previous chapters.

Opening promises of writers generally split into two categories: those that intrigue and those that inform. The writer who starts out by trying to intrigue the reader usually does so with an anecdote or an analogy or by citing examples. For example, James Reston began a column about John Connally's aspirations to be president this way:

> Old men running for the presidency of the United States are like old men who take young brides. It's an exciting idea for a while, but it seldom works.[1]

Reston's implicit promise is to tell the reader why Connally will not succeed in his bid for the presidency, and he fulfills it.

The other kind of opening is illustrated by this opening paragraph from the annual report of a major company:

> During 1977, Tenneco once again demonstrated its ability to achieve and maintain a sound and strong financial position—to the benefit of its stockholders, employees, customers, and suppliers alike. Briefly, these are some of the financial highlights of another good year.[2]

And here is the confident opening of a best-selling ''how-to'' book:

> This is the most important book ever written about women's clothes because it is based on scientific research, not opinion.

1. James Reston, ''Connally's Bad Timing,'' *Austin American-Statesman*, 28 January 1979.
2. 1977 Annual Report, Tenneco, Inc., Houston, Texas.

The advice in this book will help women make substantial gains in business and in their social lives. It should also revolutionize their clothes-buying habits.[3]

Both these openers are good because they tell their readers, as briefly as possible, what to expect in the coming pages.

Whether you choose an intriguing opener that hooks the reader with a tantalizing analogy or anecdote, or an informative one that goes directly to the point will depend on your audience and your purpose in writing. The intriguing opener often delays the reader's getting into the real topic, and that is a risk you should weigh in the context of your writing situation. The straight informative opener is safer, particularly for working documents; readers who want to learn from you usually do not want to be put off with diversions. But whichever kind of opening you use, you should try not to digress, confuse, or waste the reader's time with unnecessary introductions or explanations. If you do not get your reader's interest and confidence at the beginning, you will have wasted the time you spent writing the rest of your document.

Hooks and Directional Signals

After you have successfully guided your readers through those first few hazardous pages, you need to think about how to keep them reading to the end. If possible, you want to prevent their having to stop and double back to find your meaning, and you want to prevent their getting sidetracked by a word or phrase that sends them in the wrong direction. If either mishap occurs, you are likely to lose your reader permanently.

Readers lose their way or get bogged down in prose for a variety of reasons, not all of them the writer's responsibility. But it is the writer's responsibility to provide the hooks or links to hold paragraphs together, and to give "directional signals" that keep the reader from straying off the point. Moreover, the expert writer can insert these links and directional signals so deftly that the reader is unaware of being nudged in the right direction. In fact, one of the surest marks of strong and effective prose is its seamless quality. The reader does not notice either the junctures in the writing nor the devices that have been used to disguise them.

All writers need a stock of linking words and phrases at their fingertips to draw from. The traditional ones are *moreover, nevertheless, also, in addition, so, however,* and so on; you are familiar with most of them. It is important to realize, however, that the underlying unity of good writing comes from structure, not from transition devices. Such devices should be used carefully to

3. John T. Malloy, *The Woman's Dress for Success Book* (New York: Warner Books, 1977), p. 15.

reflect the underlying unity of the writing rather than applied from the outside to compensate for poor structure. A reader is most likely to be able to follow a piece of writing when that writing reflects one of the typical thought processes discussed in the last chapter. If those patterns help to hold your writing together, you will need only a few directional signals to supplement them.

Choosing the Right Signals.

You do, however need to be sure that you are choosing the right signals, those that accurately indicate the thought process you are using. Suppose, for example, that you are writing a pamphlet to educate young consumers about credit. Probably at least two methods of development would occur to you: the first would be Definition, because you would want to identify and explain different kinds of credit. The second would be Cause and Effect, because you would want to discuss why people need to establish credit and what can happen if they do not use it prudently. Typical connecting words that would get you from one part of your definition to another are pointers such as *for example, another, first, this kind,* and so on.

Typical words that would help you show cause and effect are *as a result, consequently, thus, so,* and so on. Notice that all these words move the reader forward. If, however, you want to slow your readers for a moment so that they may understand some exception or qualification to the chief idea, you include a slow or caution signal by inserting *however, nevertheless, in spite of,* or a similar phrase. These signals condition readers to expect an interruption or contrasting point so they do not get confused or lost when it appears.

Signals of this kind are important cues for conveying your message to the reader because they reveal the relationships between the parts of your writing. Just as a person looking at a photograph of a large family could not infer the relationships among the people in the photograph unless they were arranged in a way that suggested these relationships, or unless he or she had either written or oral cues, so your reader cannot grasp the connections in your writing unless they are pointed out or are evident from arrangement. And often you need to use both cues and arrangement.

Repetition.

Two more linking devices deserve special attention because inexperienced writers seem particularly afraid of them. The first is repetition; the second is using the conjunctions *and* and *but* at the beginning of sentences.

Repeating key words, phrases, or patterns in a piece of writing can help your readers' attention focused on your central point. And a repeated word or phrase can also serve as an effective hook between paragraphs or between sections, furnishing the cue that keeps readers from straying as they move from one idea to another. This student paragraph furnishes a good example of links within a paragraph. (I have added italics in all following selections.)

After a few months in the Ranger *oil* field, Hamon had saved enough money to buy his first *oil* lease. Soon he was spending every available moment of his time studying *oil* leases and potential land deals. By 1921 Hamon felt he knew enough about the *oil* business to try the drilling end. The first well came in but it was only a "stinker"— producing just a trickle of *oil* by Texas standards. Yet, the well was significant because it signaled the arrival of Jake Hamon into the *oil* business.

The writer uses the word *oil* six times in five comparatively short sentences, yet doesn't tax the reader's patience. Rather the word focuses and unifies the account.

Repeated pronouns can give the same effect. Here an amateur writer repeats the word *his* as one way of holding a book review together.

Stein was disillusioned not only with *his* brief stay in politics, but with the whole lifestyle and stifling educational-bureaucratic structure of the East Coast. *His* years at Yale were nothing but drudgery. *His* bosses at the FTC didn't want him to work on any more cases than any of the other lawyers. He realized that he had lived *his* life to please others. So Stein moved to Los Angeles and began living by *his* own standards and for *his* own approval and happiness.

This and *that* can also work well as recurring pointers that link sentences or paragraphs together.

To link paragraphs together, writers frequently pick up a key word from the last sentence of one paragraph and feature it in the first sentence of the next one. For instance:

That [the Vietnam War] sparked the "youth revolt" that characterized the *generational conflict* of the 1960's; finding their loyalty unrewarded, many withdrew it.

In that period, however, the ground was already being laid for the type of *generational conflict* we are seeing today.[4]

And here is a passage in which one word, purposefully repeated in parallel sentences, reveals the writer's central thesis.

We believe public radio and public television *can* lead the way. Intelligently organized, and adequately funded public broadcasting *can* help the creative spirit to flourish. It *can* reveal how we are different and what we share in common. It *can* illuminate the dark corners of the world and the dark corners of the mind. It *can* offer forums to a multitude of voices. It *can* reveal wisdom and understanding—and foolishness too. It *can* delight us. It *can* entertain us. It *can* inform us. Above all, it *can* add to our understanding of our own inner workings and of one another.

In the conviction that it *can* be so, we make these recommendations.[5]

4. David Elkind, "Growing Up Faster," *Psychology Today,* February 1979, p. 42.
5. From the report of the Carnegie Commission on the Future of Public Broadcasting; in The *Chronicle of Higher Education,* 5 February 1979, p. 9.

All of these writers value repetition as a simple and useful means of unifying their writing and holding their readers' attention. They are not afraid of it. Inexperienced writers, however, often are. Apparently many students who are learning to write become convinced that they should not use the same word twice in a paragraph or even a page if they can possibly help it. They worry so much about repeating a word that they search for awkward alternatives to simple words—"parking structure" for "garage" or "member of the legal profession" for "lawyer"—and when they revise their writing, their first concern is to find substitutes for repeated words.[6] They fail to see that those repeated words can be an asset, particularly if they are strategically placed and used as links.

Using And *or* But.

Apprentice writers often have similar prejudices against beginning a sentence with *and* or *but*. This taboo seems to grow out of the notion that since these two words are officially classified as conjunctions, or joiners, they must always be between two other words. However, they are also strong signal words that cannot be misinterpreted. Readers know exactly what to expect when they encounter either word, and for that reason they work particularly well as the opener for a sentence when you want to stress the relationship of that sentence to the previous one. Notice how the following writers have used *and* and *but* for this purpose. Again, italics have been added.

Harvard Business Review subscribers . . . recently rated "the ability to communicate" as the prime requisite of a promotable executive. *And,* of all the aspects of communication, the written form is the most troublesome.[7]

If we hear a well-constructed, grammatical sentence, the ideas fall easily and quickly into the slots of our consciousness. *But,* if we hear a conglomerate, ungrammatical hodge-podge, we have to sort it out at an expenditure of time and effort.[8]

But works especially well as the opening word of a paragraph that you want to highlight because it states an important qualification or contrast to the content of the previous paragraph. Notice the effect in the examples:

. . . For the most part, readers are assumed to be ideal readers, fully prepared to relate to the fiction or poetry on the author's terms. This expectation is as it should be; it is appropriate for what we regard as creative writing.

6. Nancy Sommers, "Revision Strategies of Student Writers" (Ph.D. diss., Boston University, 1978).
7. John S. Fielden, "What Do You Mean I Can't Write?" in *The Practical Craft,* ed. Keith Sparrow and Donald Cunningham (Boston: Houghton Mifflin, 1978), p. 47. This article originally appeared in the *Harvard Business Review,* May–June 1964.
8. Everett C. Smith, "Industry Views the Teaching of English," in *English Journal,* March 1956. Reprinted in *The Practical Craft,* ed. Sparrow and Cunningham.

But a different expectation exists in business and technical writing where readers are busy executives who want the important findings up front, or are privates last-class who need information at a level they can understand, or somewhere in the bewildering range between.[9]

. . . As my students argue when I correct them . . . : "You got the meaning, didn't you?" Yes, I did, and so do we all get the meaning when a newspaper, a magazine, a set of directions stammers out its message. And I suppose, too, we could travel by ox-cart, or dress in burlap, or drive around with rattling fenders, and still get through a day.

But technical writing in this age can no more afford widespread sloppiness of expression, confusion of meaning, rattle-trap construction than a supersonic missile can afford to be made of the wrong materials, or be put together haphazardly with screws jutting out here and there, or have wiring circuits that may go off any way at all. . . .[10]

These examples, deliberately selected from a collection of articles on business and technical writing, should convince you that it is not a sin, or even a grammatical lapse, to start a sentence with *and* or *but*. If you need additional proof, check the articles in any widely read magazine. You will find an abundance of corroborating evidence.

The Relationship of the Parts of Writing

Fortunately, the number of possible relationships between the clauses, sentences and groups of sentences in a piece of discourse is limited, and easy to describe. There are seven possible relationships:

1. Coordination or similarity; signaled by *likewise, just as, in the same way, similarly,* and so on.

   EXAMPLE: Southerners are greatly concerned about ancestry. *In the same way,* they stress childhood friendships and one's hometown ties.

2. Contrast or qualification; signaled by *however, yet, but, nevertheless, although, in spite of,* and so on.

   EXAMPLE: The Common Market countries quibble constantly about minor issues such as the price of butter. *Nevertheless,* they present a united front on major issues such as immigration.

---

9. Keith Sparrow and Donald Cunningham, "What Are Some Important Writing Strategies?" *The Practical Craft*, p. 114.
10. Morris Freedman, "The Seven Sins of Technical Writing," in *The Practical Craft*, ed. Sparrow and Cunningham, p. 82. This article originally appeared in *College Composition and Communication*, February 1958.

3. Alternation; signaled by *or, either,* or *on the other hand.*

   EXAMPLE: Football is a sport that requires brute strength and endurance. Basketball, *on the other hand,* requires agility and skill.

4. Inclusiveness or accumulation; signaled by *moreover, for example, in addition,* and so on. It can also be signaled by a colon.

   EXAMPLE: In today's market, corporate farms virtually control the supply of grain. *For example,* 13 large producers raise three-fourths of the corn in Nebraska.

5. Consequence; signaled by *consequently, therefore, thus, hence,* and several other words.

   EXAMPLE: Reliable workers seldom prefer to work at seasonal jobs; *consequently,* workers in canneries and cotton gins usually come from the ranks of itinerant, unskilled labor.

6. Causation; signaled by *for* or *because* and sometimes *since.*

   EXAMPLE: Jones Steel Company withdrew from the competition *because* the specifications for the contract were too stringent.

7. Sequence or ranking; signaled by numbers—*first, second,* and so on—or words such as *primary, next, finally, later,* and the like.

   EXAMPLE: For the present, we should concentrate on winning the district contest. *Later* we can think about training for the national meet.[11]

As you compose you should be aware of the relationships you want to establish between your clauses, sentences, and paragraphs, and of the importance of choosing the right directional signals in order to clarify those relationships. If you write *although* when you mean *moreover,* you will mislead your reader.

Here is a student's paragraph that confuses the reader because the writer does not make the relationship between her points clear.

> I am against the proposal to move the American Bar Association convention from New Orleans to protest Louisiana's refusal to ratify the Equal Rights Amendment. This boycott is legally questionable, politically unwise, and socially irresponsible. As a woman and a lawyer, I am committed to advancing the women's movement and maintaining the integrity of the Bar. The ERA and the ABA stand to lose much and gain little by accepting this proposal.

This writer starts out effectively by stating her position clearly in the first sentence and stating some reasons for that position in the next sentence. She

---

11. W. Ross Winterowd, "The Grammar of Coherence," in *Contemporary Rhetoric: A Conceptual Background with Readings,* ed. W. Ross Winterowd (New York: Harcourt Brace Jovanovich, 1975), pp. 229–31.

makes a contract with the reader in those sentences. The reader moves along expecting more expansion and support, but suddenly confronts the sentence, "As a woman and a lawyer, I am committed to advancing the women's movement. . . ." He gets confused because the statement seems to contradict the writer's earlier anti-boycott position, but he has gotten no signal words that would have warned him to expect such a change. Thus he feels the writer has broken her contract with him. And when he reads the last sentence in the paragraph which seems once more to oppose a boycott of non-ERA states, he gets even more confused. Again the writer has not given him a clue that would help him to anticipate the change.

The author of this paragraph could have prevented this confusion and kept her writer directly on the track by adding signals to the beginning of each of the confusing sentences and joining them. If she had said, "Although as a woman and a lawyer, I am committed to advancing the women's movement and maintaining the integrity of the Bar, *I believe* that the ERA and ABA stand to lose much . . . ," the reader would have expected the contradictory clause and mentally processed it without any trouble. The "I believe" would pull him back on the track after the qualification, and he would not have the feeling that the writer had violated the contract of the first two sentences.

Other Aids to the Reader

Frequent Closure.

By providing your readers with links and signals to keep them moving in the right direction, you fulfill an expository writer's chief task: helping the audience to process information as quickly and efficiently as possible. That is, you try to make your writing as *readable* as possible and thus hold your audience's attention. You are trying to keep them from having to reread all or part of what you have written in order to grasp your meaning.

One way to help your readers is not to strain their attention by making them wait too long to discover your meaning. If you can construct your sentences out of phrases or clauses that make sense by themselves, your readers can process those as they read rather than having to hold all the data in their minds until they get to the end of the sentence.[12] For instance, here is a confusing sentence from a student paper:

> Furthermore, *that the United States has the best medical technology in the world, yet ranks sixteenth among countries in successful births per pregnancy* results because impossible medical costs force many people to go through childbirth at home.

12. I owe many of my insights on this matter to Professor E. D. Hirsch, Jr., of the University of Virginia, author of *The Philosophy of Composition* (Chicago: University of Chicago Press, 1977).

The strung-out 22-word subject in this sentence keeps the reader in suspense for so long that he misses the verb, "results," on the first reading. If the writer had rearranged his ideas into manageable units, the reader would not get lost. Here is a rewritten version with the units of thought marked off.

Even though the United States has the best medical technology in the world,/ it ranks below fifteen other countries in successful births per pregnancy/ because impossible· medical costs force many people to have their children at home.

This revised sentence is easier to read than the original because the words are arranged in such a way that the reader can come to *closure* frequently while reading the sentence. When we read, we make *closure* when we come to a point in the sentence where our minds make sense of a string of words; at that point we can let our minds rest for a split second before going to the next part of our reading task. In the revised version the reader can pause twice; in the original version, he cannot pause at all because the mind cannot make sense of the words until the end of the sentence. Thus *closure* is delayed, and the sentence made correspondingly more difficult.

Writers need to keep in mind that, broadly speaking, readers process information more efficiently if it is presented to them in several small, self-contained units rather than in one large, comprehensive one. This principle suggests that writers should not try to squeeze more than four or five units of information into one sentences. If they do, they risk overloading the mental circuits by which we process language. Apparently, if those circuits get overloaded with more information than they can handle, they sputter and malfunction. When that happens, the reader either gives up or has to go back and reread the passage two or three times to absorb its meaning. Such malfunctions are most apt to happen when readers are in a hurry or unfamiliar with your subject matter or vocabulary. For that kind of reader, it is particularly important for you to try to organize your sentences into digestible phrases and clauses.

Because readers can assimilate information more efficiently when it is divided into small units, in most situations a writer should avoid writing a majority of long, complicated sentences. Frequently, just their appearance on the page frightens off readers. But long sentences in themselves do not necessarily cause reading problems; if *closure* occurs frequently, a sentence of fifty or sixty words or more can be read easily. Marking off the units of closure in this 108-word sentence from Tom Wolfe's *The Right Stuff* shows this.

A career in flying was like climbing one of those ancient Babylonian pyramids/ made up of a dizzy progression of steps and ledges,/ a ziggurat,/ a pyramid extraordinarily high and steep,/ and the idea was to prove at every foot of the way up that pyramid/ that you were one of the elected and anointed ones who had *the right stuff*/ and could move higher and higher and even/—ultimately, God willing, one day—/ that you might be able to join that special few at the very top,/ that elite who had the capacity to bring tears to men's eyes,/ the very Brotherhood of the Right Stuff itself.[13]

We know, then, that grouping words into clusters that have meaning in themselves facilitates reading. And when those clusters, whether they are clauses or sentences, are hooked together by linking terms or significant punctuation marks, reading becomes even easier. Using this kind of grouping and linking works especially well if you are guiding the reader through a complex, information-packed piece of prose.

In the final analysis, the central problem that a writer has in putting together a piece of prose that will hold the reader comes down to figuring out how to do two things at once: make the reader comfortable by referring to the known and the familiar, while at the same time catching the reader's interest with new material. Writers improve their chances of doing this successfully if they realize that when people read, they are simultaneously going through three steps of language processing. They are holding in their minds what they have just read, assimilating what they are reading at the moment, and anticipating what they are going to read in the next sentence and the next paragraph.

Effective writers help their readers master this triple task in two ways. First, they group their words together in manageable units so the reader can absorb and store them. Second, they link those units together with signs or tags that enable the readers to connect the words they are reading at the moment with those they have already read and those they are going to read. By doing so they create a thread of continuity through what otherwise might be a confusing maze or words.

Probably most authors are not consciously aware how they use tags, at least not in the first draft, and certainly very few of them think about linguistic theory as they write. The good ones just know from experience that a reader cannot handle too much information at one time, and that they need to help readers make connections. But there is no reason why the apprentice writer cannot benefit from trying to do consciously what the professional author does unconsciously. So as you write, keep checking to see that you are providing your readers with tags and cues that remind them where they have been and where they are going. And be especially alert when you read over your first draft because that is the time when gaps or glaring *non sequiturs* should be most obvious; on a second or third reading you may have become used to them.

Divisions, Headings, and Subheadings.

The principal way that writers reveal the design behind a piece of writing is by breaking it into parts: chapters or sections, divisions and subdivisions,

13. Tom Wolfe, *The Right Stuff* (New York: Farrar, Strauss, Giroux, 1979), p. 24.

and paragraphs. Similar parts are grouped together so that the reader gets a sense of continuity, and transition devices link the parts so that the reader can move smoothly from one to another. The way that you decide to divide your writing, and your method of indicating those divisions, will have much to do with how well you are able to hold your readers.

To some extent, your decisions on these matters will be governed by the kind of writing you are doing. Different professions call for different conventions about writing formats, and if you are writing a proposal or a report, it would be a good idea to look over typical work from the agency or company you are writing for. There may be a standard format. However if there is not, or if you are writing a piece for which you have no model, here are some guidelines.

1. When a piece of writing is long—ten pages or more—it is particularly important to break it frequently, and label the divisions.
2. When writing deals with complex matters and uses difficult or specialized vocabulary, it is important to break it frequently and label the divisions.
3. When your audience is unfamiliar with your subject matter, they particularly need clearly labeled divisions.
4. When your audience is diverse and of various educational levels—for example, the audience for *TV Guide* or for a brochure on social security benefits—clearly labeled divisions are important.

In general, if you are in doubt about whether to divide and label, you should probably do so. And keep in mind that the more important a piece of writing is, the more you need to help your readers find their way with divisions and headings. As one expert puts it, "One might say that [by headings] the reader of a report is provided with road signs; in the headings he has a means of making his way through the report without getting lost and with the assurance that he will reach his destination safely."[14]

In doing general expository writing you can usually get by with three kinds of headings. The first, used to designate a major division, is the heading in capitals that is centered on the page. In a paper about TV it might be:

THE NEW TELEVISION SHOWS

The second, used for the first division within this major category, is the left-margin heading, also in capitals, and on a separate line.

---

14. J. Raleigh Nelson, "Sectional Headings as Evidence of Design," in *The Practical Craft*, ed. Sparrow and Cunningham, p. 270.

DRAMAS

The third kind of heading, which would indicate a subdivision within the second category, is also at the left margin and on a separate line, but with capitals only at the beginning of each word. For instance,

Situation Comedies.

In writing a fairly long report, you would probably want to use all three kinds of headings, arranging them carefully in order to guide your readers through your presentation and to draw their attention to your most important points. And even in shorter pieces, if the content is rather technical or difficult for the reader to grasp, you should give them all the help you can with good headings and subheadings. But if you are doing straightforward writing on an issue that is not particularly serious and complex, and the chief purpose of divisions is the psychological one of breaking your prose into chunks so that it will look less formidable to the reader, you can probably get by with just one kind of heading: the left-margin caption on a separate line with only the first letters of words capitalized. For example, an article entitled "Notes of a West Point Woman" in the December 1978 *Cosmopolitan* was divided into about four equal parts; the sections were headed

The Lady's a Cadet
Boys and Girls Together
A Plebe's Life
The West Point Way

The headings were not really necessary to indicate the content of the article, but they eased the eye. They may well have been added by an editor.

And that is the final reason to split your writing up into sections and put in your own headings and subheadings. If you don't, an editor may do it for you. Editors are so conscious of their readers' need to be guided through a piece of writing that frequently they will add whatever cues they think would be helpful. And as any professional writer can tell you, you will be happier if you anticipate and respond to the readers' needs yourself rather than letting an editor perform corrective surgery on your work.

Some Psychological Hazards

Finally, writers who want to hold their audiences should keep in mind the psychological as well as the intellectual impact of their words. You will lose your readers not only if you bore them, you waste their time, or confuse them, but also if you intimidate or threaten them.

To avoid doing so, *focus on showing respect for your audience*. Demonstrate that you understand their attitudes and are sympathetic with their problems. If there is common ground between you and your audience—and there usually is if you look for it—stress the ways in which you agree rather than the ways in which you differ. Write as if you are addressing people of intelligence and goodwill, and honestly assume that you are.

Remember also to *use objective language and stress facts rather than opinions*. If you use *strong* biased and emotional words, especially at the beginning of a piece of writing, you may set off defensive feelings in your reader and close his or her mind to the rest of the article or letter. As behavioral therapists point out, when one makes a strong statement, either positive or negative, the audience does not receive that statement neutrally; rather they usually react emotionally. Thus, in some kinds of communication situations, people take sides very quickly, and once they do, the chances for real communication drop sharply. So begin neutrally, and your audience is more apt to keep reading.

Third, *write provisionally, not dogmatically*. When you are stating your views or proposing an action, use terms like, "We might consider . . . ," or "It is possible . . . ," or "One possible solution might be . . . ," instead of coming on strong with phrases such as "Obviously the best plan is . . . ," or "Any fool can see that . . ." A strong, positive tone suits certain kinds of writing and certain audiences—fund-raising pamphlets or political rallies, for instance—but when you sense that your audience may be cool to your proposals or contradict your assertions, you have a far better chance of holding that audience if your tone suggests that your proposal is tentative, and that you welcome advice about it. What you are trying to do is create an atmosphere of cooperation in which your audience can pay attention to you because it is not forced to protect itself.

EXERCISES / *Prewriting Activities*

1 Here are some titles chosen from the table of contents of an essay anthology. How useful do you find them as forecasters of what the reader would find in the essay? Which titles do you think are the most informative? Which are the least informative?

> The Fear of Being Alone
> Business As Usual
> Bag Man
> The Full Circle: In Praise of the Bicycle
> The Truth about Cinderella
> The New Illiteracy
> Work in an Alienated Society

Lessons of the Street
The Lesson of the Mask
Techno-Politics

2 Try to think of titles that would accurately reflect the content of a
paper you might write on these topics:

A. Exercise as one of the major components of a good health program.

B. Credit cards as a contributing cause to the inflationary spiral.

C. An argument for or against instituting a payroll tax in your city. Such a tax
would be levied on everyone who worked in but did not live in the city.

D. A review of a major art show in which all the artists were American
women.

3 Evaluate these opening paragraphs taken from papers by advanced
student writers. Do they pull you on to want to read the paper? Do you
get lost in any of them?

If you're feeling confused, depressed, and totally void of self-confidence, you could be experiencing the common state of "college stress
syndrome." At one time or another students go through this unpleasant
phase. Stress refers to the way in which your body reacts to a mentally or
emotionally disturbing influence. This anxiety enters our lives in many different forms. According to Dr. Richard Nemic, director of the psychiatric
section of the Student Health Services Center, there are three basic sources
of student stress: procrastination, career choice, and exams.

Every year, our highways needlessly slaughter many thousands of people. And every year, people are reminded that wearing their protective
safety belts would dramatically increase their chances for survival. And yet
people continue to ignore such advice and suffer the consequences. In an
attempt to solve this problem, this country has gone as far as to install systems that virtually force occupants of automobiles to wear protective safety
belts. What happened? People resisted to such a degree that the legislation
was finally repealed. So, obviously, another solution is needed if the population is to reap the benefits of being protected from their cars. Air bags are
such a solution

Humans often complicate simple situations by not using the basic abilities that are unique to our species. Sounds like another way of saying
humans don't think. But not really. I think it is more accurate to say that
humans are so busy thinking about big problems that we neglect small
problems. Confusing? Let me try again. Remember the straw that broke the
camel's back? It was the straw that did it. No one ever mentions the tree that

fell on the poor animal, only the straw. To me, airports are good examples of how a straw can have the impact of a tree. If you allow yourself plenty of time, read the direction signs, and carry an assortment of change, you will probably have no problem getting where you are going.

4 Write an opening paragraph for one of the topics given in the second exercise above. Before you begin to write, think about what information you should include in order to get your readers started off in the direction you want them to go.

5 Rewrite these paragraphs with transition devices that will help to keep the reader on the right track.

You will develop a sales approach as you become more acquainted with your job. Every individual prefers to handle customers in his own way. Keep in mind, however, three basic rules: be assertive, be helpful, and be pleasant at all costs. Remember serving the customer is the number one priority. You must keep busy. There is always something to be done: cleaning, dusting, displays, shifting stock, and setting up windows. You will be expected to perform these duties and others on a daily basis. Working in the stockroom and performance on the floor are equally important.

Mandatory installation of air bags is definitely a good idea. It will save many lives and prevent many people from being crippled or maimed. It will also save many thousands of dollars in hospital and treatment costs. The big question is whether or not it will get the support it needs to stay mandatory. Let us hope the citizens of the United States have more control over the government than do the automobile manufacturers.

6 Here are two long but fairly readable sentences from professional writers. Mark each of them off into units of closure that reveal how the content is organized.

Once that fact is recognized, it may be possible to think again about the proper building blocks of a meritocracy—measures that do not seal fate at an early age, that emphasize performance in specific areas, that expand the pool of talent in more than a hit-or-miss way, and whose limits are always visible to us, so that we are not again deluded into thinking we have found a scientific basis for the order of lords, vassals, and serfs.[15]

I yield to no one in deploring prejudice against the young, but I found it unsettling to learn that Mr. Schroeder, five years out of the University of Michigan, and four other young men of approximately the same experience constitute the entire legal staff of the FTC's Bureau of Consumer Protection,

15. James Fellows, "The Tests and the Brightest," *The Atlantic*, February 1980, p. 48.

the body that now proposes to reform one of the nation's venerable technical institutions.[16]

7 Here are two sentences from student papers. Rearrange them so that they are easier to read.

Although there are many quality foreign-made cars, trouble finding labor and expensive parts, on the average 35 percent higher than parts for American cars, takes away whatever edge their dealers have.

I want to point out the effects of raising young girls within the confines of a chauvinistic sex role on later confrontations with success.

Suggested Writing Assignments

As a part of each writing assignment, write a detailed analysis of your audience that specifies characteristics they have which you need to keep in mind as you write, problems that such an audience might present, and what the audience would expect to get from your paper. Also analyze your purpose in writing, specifying what you hope to accomplish in the paper. If appropriate, include an accurate and descriptive title for your paper.

TOPIC 1:
Imagine that you write for the entertainment section of a local newspaper or magazine. One of your weekly jobs is to eat at one of the major restaurants in the city and write a 300 to 500 word review of your experience there for the Saturday paper. Although all the better restaurants advertise in the paper or magazine, your editor wants an honest review that will let potential customers know what they can expect if they eat there. You are gradually building a reputation as a fair and reliable judge of restaurants and so you should keep that in mind as you write. Don't forget to mention prices.

TOPIC 2:
The regents of your college or university are having hearings to determine whether they should tear down the low-rent student housing that was built 35 years ago from second-hand army surplus buildings. The housing is unsightly and needs repairs; some of the regents have said that they think it is unsafe. If it is torn down, however, the apartments that would replace it would rent for almost twice as much as the present units, and the campus would be without any low-rent housing for at least two years.

Prepare a 10-minute talk (no more than 1000 words) against tearing down the buildings to be delivered at the meeting that the regents are going

16. Samuel C. Florman, "Standards of Value," *Harpers*, February 1980, p. 67.

to hold. You will be the spokesperson for the married students who now live in the university housing.

TOPIC 3:

Write a letter to the vice-president for marketing of a major firm such as General Foods or Johnson Products trying to persuade him or her that the network should no longer run a particular television commercial that you find offensive. Specify what you find offensive and why, and try to give the vice-president a good reason for dropping the commercial.

CHAPTER 6

Choosing Your Words

Students who sometimes have trouble finding the right words to express their ideas often think that writing teachers and professional writers have special talents or ways to tap a storehouse of words that are not available to ordinary people. We don't, of course, but because most of us read widely and have fairly large vocabularies, when we need a word, we are more conscious than the average person of the options open to us. And if you aspire to be a facile and effective writer, you also need to read and develop your vocabulary. There is simply no substitute; you can't choose good words if you don't know very many.

But having a stock of big or unusual words will not in itself help you to become a better writer; in fact, in some writing situations you should avoid using big words even if they are a part of your working vocabulary. You do need, however, to keep noticing words and learning new ones so that you develop a sensitivity to the way words sound and look, and to their connotations. You have to get a feel for the way they affect the reader. That is why inexperienced writers should not rely on a thesaurus, or dictionary of synonyms, for finding new words to enhance their writing. Unless writers already understand the fine shades of meaning that distinguish synonyms from each other, they cannot use a thesaurus as it should be used; that is, to refresh one's memory about a familiar, but temporarily forgotten word.

But let's assume that you have a fairly good vocabulary. What you would need now are some techniques for tapping that vocabulary and some guidelines for choosing one word instead of another in a particular writing situation. And such guidelines do exist, although they are necessarily broad and necessarily flexible. Different kinds of writing require that you make different kinds of word choices, and since you might be doing writing tasks that vary from drafting the inaugural address for a new governor to writing up the case history of a person being admitted to a mental hospital, you must be able to adjust your word choice to the occasion. But in general, one can say that the kind of words that communicate most effectively are those that are concrete and specific. The kinds of words that communicate least well, and must often be explained or illustrated, are those that are abstract and general.

Abstract/Concrete and General/Specific

Abstract words designate intangible qualities, concepts, ideas, or attitudes; they refer to matters that we know only through our mental processes, not through our senses. Words like "loyalty," "existentialism," "evil," "criticism," and "agreement" are abstract. Concrete words refer to tangible, verifiable qualities or characteristics that we know through our senses. Words like "green," "dog," "bench," "hot," and "sugar" are concrete words. One can say we *conceive* the abstract through our intellect; we *perceive* the concrete through our senses.

The distinction between general and specific is similar. We use *general* terms to refer to large classes or broad areas, and we use *specific* terms to refer to particular items or individual cases. Words like "colleges," "the French," "housing," and "doctors" are general; words like "Austin College," "Simone de Beauvoir," the "Wayside Apartments," and "Dr. Zhivago" are specific. Often, but not consistently, the general and the abstract overlap, as do the concrete and specific.

But most words do not fall so neatly into these either/or categories. Instead we have to classify them according to a scale, place them somewhere on what semanticists call the *ladder of abstraction*. It is from that metaphorical ladder that we derive the term *level of abstractions;* we are also referring to that ladder when we talk about *high level* or *low level* abstractions. Here is how the ladder works.

8. ideologies
7. religions
6. western religions
5. Christianity
4. Protestantism
3. Baptists
2. Southern Baptist Convention
1. First Baptist Church of Memphis, Tennessee

None of these terms refers to anything tangible—"Church" on level 1 refers to a community of worshipers, not a building—but "First Baptist Church of Memphis" is much narrower and thus much less abstract than "ideologies."

We also can have levels of generality. For example,

7. communication media
6. printed material
5. books
4. nonfiction books
3. textbooks
2. composition texts
1. *Successful Writing*

While all these terms refer to something tangible, at the lowest level we have a single identifiable item, and at the highest level we have a classification so broad that we have trouble thinking of all the things it includes. One could also arrange a series of sentences or phrases on this scale.

We need to use language at all levels in both ladders if we want to communicate well, if we want to philosophize, hypothesize, draw conclusions, tell stories, give advice, or inform people. Thus, we cannot say that specific or concrete language is always preferable to the general and the abstract; an effective writer uses all of them, mixing and changing levels as the topic and the audience demand. But we can say that in most cases, a writer needs to help the reader by reinforcing the general and abstract with the specific and concrete.

Reasons for Using Concrete Language.

There are good reasons for this. Although a major function of our intelligence is to abstract general principles from particular cases, and to think about concepts that we can't see or touch, if we go too long without using specific terms that give readers a visual anchor, we lose them. Sophisticated and experienced readers can probably stay with very abstract writing longer than inexperienced ones, but even they will wear out rather quickly and either quit reading or have to stop at intervals to go back and reread. Both groups of readers have problems for the same reason: highly abstract or general prose engages only a part of their learning faculties. It does not engage their senses or produce images.

As Arthur Koestler points out in *The Act of Creation,* "Thinking in pictures dominates the manifestations of the unconscious—the dream, the hypogogic half-dream [fantasy], the psychotic's hallucination. . . . Pictorial thinking is more *primitive* . . . than mental thinking.''[1] And it is through encouraging this kind of pictorial thinking or concrete thinking that a writer can make the reader *see* things; literally through description and images, or figuratively through metaphor and analogy. Perhaps it is because pictorial thinking is more primitive that some people writing on highly intellectual topics neglect to use it. Rather they write stupefying prose like this.

It is evident to the point of platitude that the normal formation of a multitude implies the coincidence of desires, ideas, ways of life in the individuals who constitute it. It will be objected that this is just what happens with every social group, however select it may strive to be. This is true; but there is an essential difference. In those groups which are not characterised by not being multitude and mass, the effective coincidence of its members is based on some desire, idea, or ideal, which of itself excludes the great number. To form a minority, of whatever kind, it is necessary

1. Arthur Koestler, *The Act of Creation* (New York: Macmillan, 1964), p. 168.

beforehand that each member separate himself from the multitude for *special*, relatively personal reasons. Their coincidence with the others who form the minority is, then, secondary, posterior to their having each adopted an attitude of singularity, and is consequently, to a large extent, a coincidence in not coinciding.[2]

Notice that there is not a single concrete or visual word to help the poor reader decipher this passage.

In contrast, the Greek philosopher and teacher Plato seemed to know that his students needed visual illustrations if they were to grasp the highly abstract and elusive theories he wanted to teach them. For instance in the *Phaedrus*, he describes the soul by comparing it to a team of horses driven by a charioteer; the white horse represents the pure instincts, the black horse the sensual drives.

> The horse that holds the nobler position is upright and clean-limbed; it carries its head high, its nose is aquiline, its color white, its eyes dark; it is a lover of honor . . . temperance, and decency. . . . It needs no whip, but is driven by word of command alone. The other horse, however, huge, but crooked, a great jumble of a creature with a short, thick neck, a flat nose, dark color, grey bloodshot eyes, the mate of insolence and knavery, shaggy-eared and deaf, hardly needing whip or spur.[3]

Perhaps Plato realized that because his students only *listened* to him, and did not have a printed text to refer to if he lost them, they badly needed for abstract theory to be reinforced with the specific and concrete.

But even with printed material an audience can grasp abstract concepts more easily if the author reinforces them with concrete examples and specific references. Unfortunately, many of the people who write books about philosophy, economics, or other topics seem to have forgotten this. It may be that by the time experts write books, they know their topic so well that they forget that they are supposed to be explaining it to the uninformed, and as a result, they forget to move down from high-level abstractions to illustrate their points. This is an example of the kind of writing that they sometimes produce.

> Physical things from far ends of the earth are physically transported and physically caused to act and react upon one another in the construction of a new object. The miracle of the mind is that something similar takes place in experience without physical transport and assembling. Emotion is the moving and cementing force. It selects what is congruous and dyes what is selected with its color, thereby giving qualitative unity to materials externally disparate and dissimilar. It thus provides unity in and through the varied parts of an experience. When the unity is of the sort already described, the experience has esthetic character even though it is not, dominantly, an esthetic experience.[4]

2. Jose Ortega y Gasset, *The Revolt of the Masses* (New York: W. W. Norton, 1932), p. 14.
3. Plato, *Phaedrus*, trans. W. C. Helmbold and W. B. Rabinowitz (Indianapolis: Bobbs-Merrill, 1956), p. 38.
4. John Dewey, "Having an Experience," in *On Experience, Nature and Freedom* (Indianapolis: Bobbs-Merrill, 1960), p. 165.

Unfortunately many students who encounter this kind of dull and obscure writing assume that it is "good academic prose," and represents the kind of writing they should do in college. So they adopt a model for college writing that makes them produce papers that start like this: "Current television programs air a disproportionate number of nonnutritive food product commercials designed specifically to induce consumption of these products."

A person who writes "nonnutritive food product commercials" instead of "ads for junk foods" is probably trying to sound dignified and informed, but succeeds mainly in sounding pretentious and in slowing down readers, who have to stop and translate "non-nutritive food products." The sentence is also wordy; "commercials" doesn't need to be modified with "designed specifically to induce consumption of these products." That's what ads are for. So all the writer really needs to say is: "Currently there are too many junk-food ads on television." Not a scintillating sentence, but it is clear and specific.

Downshifting[5]

Frequently, however, one must use abstract or general terms because there are no concrete or specific equivalents. When you face that situation you can help your reader by *downshifting,* that is, by adding explanations or illustrations that are on lower levels of generality. For instance:

(4) Existentialism is a philosophy of personal responsibility. (3) It holds, as Sartre puts it, that "man is condemned to be free." That statement means that (2) no one can claim that he is a victim; (2) he alone is responsible for his behavior. (1) If other people exploit him, it is because he allows himself to be exploited.

There are four levels of generality here. The paragraph moves from level 4, abstract statement, to level 3, illustration of statement, to level 2, two specific interpretations of level 3 statement, and finally to level 1, a specific example to illustrate the level 2 interpretation. You will learn more about this useful technique of *downshifting* in the chapter about paragraphs.

Concrete Sentence Subjects

For several reasons, writers who can train themselves to use concrete and specific subjects for their sentences as often as possible will almost certainly

5. This term was coined by the grammarian Francis Christensen, in his book *Notes toward a New Rhetoric* (New York: Harper and Row, 1967).

improve their writing. First, they will avoid strung-out, drab constructions like these:

> There is an existing possibility that we will lose the appeal.
> The affordability of the hotel's rates was the deciding factor.

Second, the writer who starts out with an abstract subject is more apt to write the kind of wordy, flat sentences that delay closure and keep the reader from getting to the point. For example,

> The offering of low-interest loans to students on scholarship is a primary objective of his program.
> An undesirable situation from society's point of view is brought about by free access to heroin.

Sentences like these are dull and plodding because they drag on through too many abstract words tacked together with prepositions. Yet many writers work at these kinds of sentences, hoping to sound elegant and solemn, properly "academic." Formal writing at its worst is full of such pale, inflated sentences, but writers who want to interest and please their audiences should systematically weed them out whenever possible.

Third, writers should get rid of abstract sentence subjects when they can because they narrow their choice of verbs and often eliminate the most interesting ones. They limit their verb options because abstractions cannot act. A "consideration" cannot *do* anything; it just is. An "aspect" cannot move or change; it just exists. Occasionally one can smuggle in a metaphor by creating such combinations as "equity calls for" or "morality overrides," but the best way to keep open options for good verbs is to use concrete subjects—personal subjects, if possible.

Finally, writers should avoid abstract subjects because once they have chosen one, they are apt to choose a passive verb to go with it. Then they have increased the probability of writing out a colorless and vague sentence. For example,

> Several aspects of the problem will be explored.

or

> This inactivity was caused by lack of funds.

If you want to get your prose up off the ground, streamline it, and make it vigorous and readable, you need to keep your abstraction detector in operation constantly as you write and as you revise. And it needs to be in good working order because the abstract subject seems to be the first kind to come to mind when one starts a sentence. It's so easy to start a sentence with "Integrity is a quality . . . ," rather than think of a concrete example or a specific statement that really says something about integrity. It is also easy to settle for words like *aspect, facet, consideration,* and *approach* instead of finding the specific word that fits the context. Train yourself to examine the words that you are using, and think about how they affect the reader. For instance, if you begin to write, "the recognition of this problem is crucial to success, "stop to think whether it wouldn't be better to write, "We must recognize this problem in order to succeed."

You can do this in your mind as you formulate the words you are going to write down, you can do it as you look at your words just after they have come from the typewriter or pen, or you can do it as you rework your first draft. Don't wait too long to weed out abstractions, but don't let worrying about them interfere with your creative momentum either. Gradually you will let fewer abstractions get through your filter, and gradually you will tighten and strengthen your writing.

Of course, you must use abstractions often; they furnish the skeleton of almost any intellectual inquiry. But when you do, clarify and reinforce them with concrete examples and specific language. Often too, you must use abstract sentence subjects; you can't and shouldn't manipulate all your sentences to avoid them. If you look through this book, you will see hundreds of sentences with abstract subjects. What you will not see is how many hundreds more I crossed out, revised, rearranged, or never put down at all after I thought about them.

Verbs

Verbs are the lifeblood of writing. They keep it moving, set its tone, hold it together, and control its rhythm and tone. They can serve as one of a writer's most important tools; thus here I offer some guidelines for choosing verbs that will strengthen your writing. I also offer a warning about the hazards connected with using certain verb forms.

Varieties of Verbs.

When talking about verbs, I like to use words that one ordinarily applies to people, not to parts of speech; words like *strong, plain, vigorous, energetic, lively, pretentious, straightforward, pedantic, imaginative, dull, routine, flashy, colorless, flabby, lifeless,* and so on. Like people, certain verbs work better than others in particular situations, and one cannot generalize that vigorous verbs are always best or that there is no place for colorless and routine writing. But weak verbs, like weak people, are seldom an asset in any situation, and an efficient writer, like an efficient manager, should learn to identify them and replace them.

So your first job is to learn to recognize verbs that do their job well. For example:

No one really *likes* the work. No one really *likes getting out* in the Texas sun and *skinning* his knuckles on heavy sections of steel pipe or *wrestling* with a spinning chain or *climbing* to the top of a rig where a single slip *can lead* to a ninety-foot fall or *mixing* drilling mud that gets in work clothes and *combines* with the grease, sweat, and oil *to make* a smell that no amount of washing can remove. No one *likes to put up* a rig in one isolated spot then *take it down* later only *to put it up* again in another isolated spot miles away. And no one *likes* the long hours and graveyard shifts and the endless driving back and forth to the job and coming home, as one roughneck put it, to "warmed over coffee and an asleep old lady."[6] [Italics added.]

These are straightforward, unpretentious verbs, but most of them are also energetic and visual; they create movement and images that make you see what is happening. Rewriting the paragraph with weak verbs and nonvisual adjectives would change the effect.

Working on oil rigs *is* not pleasant. It *is* hot and exhausting and often hazardous. It *is* also dirty and sometimes even boring. Probably no one really *likes* this kind of work.

The rewrite keeps the idea, but all the life has gone out of it because a succession of sentences built on the subject+is+complement pattern generally produces flat, routine prose.

Although the verb *to be* in all its forms (*is, am, are, was, were, will be, have been,* and so on) remains the central verb in our language, careful writers use it sparingly. Granted, constructing sentences with *is* plus an adjective or noun takes less time and trouble than digging out more precise and stronger verbs, but when you make such constructions a habit, you sacrifice quality. For example:

Even though good meal planning *is* the most important job of every homemaker, many families don't eat well. The problem *is* most acute among poor families. Usually, they *are* ignorant of nutrition. Just as often, they *are* unable to pay for foods rich in vitamins.

The student paragraph is respectable, but dull, and wordier than it needs to be. Notice the improvement when we replace "is" with more precise verbs and close up some of the sentences.

Although all homemakers *should make* meal planning their most important job, many families don't *eat* well. Poor families *suffer* most from the problem because not only do they *know* little about nutrition, but they cannot *afford* vitamin-rich foods.

6. "Working the Rigs," *Texas Monthly,* October 1978, p. 124.

And notice what the varied verbs do for this student paragraph.

So Stein *rented* furniture, *ran* into an old girlfriend, *started doing* lots of grass, *flirted* with cocaine, and *began buying* his groceries at a store which sold every soft drink known to man. He *extended* his personality with a Mercedes 450SL and *immersed* himself in a lifestyle known as California-weird. Incredibly, he *found* a kind of happiness.

Describing Stein's personality with verbs works much better than saying "Stein was this" and "Stein was that."

Still, not all writing needs to be vigorous and colorful, and there will be times when your writing task calls for you to use plain, utilitarian verbs. For instance:

In an era of educational accounting and educational accountability, it *would be* helpful to have a way of determining what the essential and most valuable "core" of a university education *is* and what *is* peripheral and mere tradition. What *are* the actual effects of a liberal education, this most persistent of Western ideals? It *is* sobering to realize that we have little firm evidence.[7] [Italics added.]

Perhaps the paragraph could be improved if the authors worked on getting rid of the *is* verbs, but in this context where they are speculating on matters that are necessarily abstract and intangible, this style works.

So I do not recommend, as some writing teachers do, that you try to eliminate forms of *to be* from your writing entirely. Use it when you need to, but do it consciously and cautiously.

Certain other drab, flat verbs contribute to making writing grey and listless. One is *exists,* a noncommittal word often used as a substitute for *to be*. For example, "There exists a need for action in this area," or "Conditions exist that are hazardous to workers' health." The sentences come alive if we throw out *exist* and say, "We need to act," and "These conditions endanger workers' health."

Other lifeless verbs that crop up frequently are *experience,* and *evidence*. Notice that these words are also abstract nouns, and when one turns them into verbs they become even more vague. If a student writes about "experiencing a French course" or a columnist writes that a company is "experiencing new activity in oil exploration," the reader gets only a fuzzy notion of what is going on. "The falling Dow Jones average evidences lack of confidence in the government" is a drab and potentially confusing sentence. There are other bland verbs that, when used vaguely rather than in their exact and limited sense, make writing flabby. Some of those are *seem, appear, constitute, lack,* and *relates to*.

7. David Winter, Abigail Stewart, and David C. McClelland, "Grading the Effects of a Liberal Arts Education," *Psychology Today,* September 1978, p. 69.

Finding Good Verbs.

When you are trying to find good verbs for your sentence, keep at least two things in mind. First, choose the one-word, direct form of a verb when possible rather than strung-out verb phrases that include a noun or an adjective. For instance, write "I recognize" rather than "I am cognizant of"; write "emphasize" instead of "put the emphasis on"; write "try" rather than "make an attempt to"; write "reflect" rather than "is reflective of." These stretched-out verb forms, while not wrong, are ponderous. One such phrase here and there does little damage, but when you accumulate them, your writing sags badly and loses vitality.

Second, choose an active, preferably specific or concrete verb when you can find one that fits the particular writing situation. In your mind run over such possibilities as *trigger, suffer, reflect, slump, grow, fight, fear, consume, collapse,* and so on. Such words are not fancy or impressive in themselves, but they are specific and vivid. And don't scorn those plain, useful verbs like *make, cause, know, believe, show,* and so on; you need them too, particularly when you are writing primarily to inform.

The change to specific and vivid verbs tightens your prose, makes it move faster, and saves the reader effort.

Avoiding Passive Verbs.

Finally, use passive verbs sparingly. Passive verb constructions (those in which the subject doesn't do anything, but instead has something done to it) have several effects on writing. First, they slow it down and flatten it out. Generally you need more words to write a passive construction than you would an active one, and some of those words are colorless auxiliary terms. For example, not only does "Action on the issue has been taken by the board" take longer to read than "The board acted on the issue," but it also takes longer to process and comprehend because it has an abstract subject and the reader has to wait until the end to find out who acted. If you have just one or two passive sentences on a page, that delay probably doesn't matter, but if you pile up several passive constructions, the effect is deadening.

Second, too many passive verbs drain the color from your writing because as the number of passive verbs increases, the number of people decreases. For example, notice this passage in which I have bracketed the passive verbs.

In this situation, it is surprising that in recent years so little work [has been done] on the theory of philosophical argumentation. Indeed, the only sustained inquiry into it [has been undertaken] by the logical positivists. But this inquiry [is circumscribed] by that very assumption whose doubtfulness [has just been indicated]; the assumption, namely, that the principles which govern philosophical disputes [can be strictly identified] with those of hitherto established methodologies.[8]

A reader has a hard time getting a hold on this paragraph because there is neither a person nor a thing to focus the senses on, and one cannot tell who is doing the "undertaking" and "circumscribing" and "indicating" and "identifying." The passive voice obscures identities.

Since the passive voice often conceals identities, it contributes to a third problem: *vagueness*. Consider the dilemma of the reader who encounters a piece of writing with a number of sentences like these.

Giving bribes is considered a legitimate business expense.
The government was overthrown three days ago.
Outside agitators are being blamed for the looting.

The reader who wants to find out the facts—*Who* thinks bribes are legitimate? *Who* overthrew the government?—becomes frustrated when he or she encounters this kind of evasive statement. That reader might conclude that the writer is too lazy to find out important details or so evasive that he does not want to take the responsibility for his statements. Thus if you want to maintain your credibility with your readers when you are writing about important actions, avoid the faceless passive voice if possible.

Sometimes you can't avoid using the passive, and you shouldn't always try. It has its place because there are times when a writer wants to focus the reader's attention on the action rather than the agent doing it, or when the acting agent is unknown or unimportant. For example:

Pompeii *was buried* by a volcano 2,000 years ago.
Hundreds of spectators *were injured* in the riot that followed.
The operation *has been duplicated* in dozens of hospitals.

People doing technical writing or some kinds of report writing may also need to use the passive voice frequently in order to center their readers' attention on a process or mechanism or case history. Such writers do not want to distract their readers by introducing names or personalities so they use phrases like "The mechanism was mounted . . ." or "The patient was examined . . ." If that kind of writing reflects the approved style for assignments that you must do, you should probably not try to defy the conventions of your profession. You can try to keep your passives to a minimum, however, and make your writing as direct and simple as is acceptable. There are even signs that

8. Henry W. Johnstone, Jr., "A New Theory of Philosophical Argumentation," in *Philosophy, Rhetoric, and Argumentation,* ed. Maurice Natanson and Henry Johnstone (Philadelphia: University of Pennsylvania Press, 1965), p. 126.

some professions are trying to improve the writing in their journals and texts by encouraging people to break out of the drab bureaucratic writing style.

If you have developed a fondness for passive verbs, take a look at your writing. Would *you* want to read it? Do *you* think it is interesting and easy to understand? If not, try going through it and cleaning out most of the passives, and see if that helps. Almost certainly it will. Then try to become conscious of passive constructions as you revise, and each time you use one, ask yourself, "Do I have a good reason for putting a passive verb here?" If you do, keep it; if you don't, rewrite the sentence with an active verb.

Choosing Nouns, Verbs, and Modifiers

When you write, try to find good combinations of subjects and verbs, combinations that are clear and forceful enough to carry most of your meaning by themselves without being shored up by adjectives, adverbs, or modifying phrases. Searching for subject-verb combinations that work well by themselves will force you to pick out words that are precise and strong in their own right, and thus help you to compress more meaning into your words. For instance, to write "Many powerful and important people were present at the impressive and colorful inauguration ceremonies" gives your readers a general opinion, but few specific details. They would get more information and a visual image from this sentence: "Senators, judges, corporate presidents, and flag officers watched the inauguration ceremonies, which took place before a display of flags and marine battalions in full-dress uniform."

A good example of writing that shows what a writer can do with only nouns and verbs is this opening sentence from George Orwell's essay, "Marrakech":[9] "As the corpse went past the flies left the restaurant table in a cloud and rushed after it, but they came back a few minutes later." By creating *images*, Orwell works directly on the reader's senses and makes a far stronger impression that he could with any number of adjectives that *told* the reader about the smells and gruesome sights in the streets of Marrakech. He shows; he doesn't tell. Try to do the same thing when you can. Substitute the visual noun and strong verbs for what Orwell calls "decorative adjectives," words like *spectacular, splendid,* or *tremendous.*

Choosing Modifiers.

You must use adjectives and adverbs, of course; they are indispensable for indicating quality, size, comparison, classification, and differences. Well

9. George Orwell, "Marrakech," *A Collection of Essays* (New York: Doubleday & Company, 1954), p. 186.

used, they add strength and color and particularity to your writing. Certain kinds of modifiers, however, do not describe things and events in themselves, but rather your personal reaction to them: words like *wonderful, fantastic, marvelous, devastating, gorgeous*, or *catastrophic*. Such words work well enough in casual conversation, where one may not want to stop to search for the most precise term, but they seldom contribute anything to writing.

Try also to avoid adjectives or adverbs that show strong bias. For instance, the writer who asserts "The *ridiculous* practice of hiring women and minorities to fill quotas is *dictatorial* and *absurd*" is using a circular statement that would probably not impress an audience who does not already agree. The words don't *show* the drawbacks of the practice; they are only table-thumping adjectives that bully rather than persuade.

Intensifying adjectives used to express horror or distress often fail for similar reasons. To write "The *unbelievable* anguish and *excruciating* agony that a rapist inflicts upon his *helpless* victims justifies the death penalty" may not be as strong as the more restrained "The trauma and pain endured by rape victims may justify demanding the death penalty for the crime." The second sentence invites readers to come to their own conclusions. You can also usually improve your writing by cleaning out those routine intensifying words *very, extremely, really*, and *definitely*. Most of us use such words more from habit than the desire to express strong feelings.

Careful writers also try to avoid adjectives and adverbs that seem to attach themselves to other words as if drawn by magnets. When you find yourself writing phrases like *common courtesy, fundamental difference, underlying cause, paramount importance*, and *final destination*, ask yourself if you need the modifier. Does putting *final* before *destination* or *common* before *courtesy* sharpen your meaning? Probably not.

Special Problems with Qualifying Modifiers.

One kind of modifier, the qualifying word or phrase, raises particular problems. Terms that belong in this category are *rather, somewhat, often, probably, partly, in some cases, generally, for the most part*, and so on. There are dozens of such words that signal exceptions, limitations, or caution, and prudent writers use them frequently to temper their writing and avoid sounding dogmatic or simplistic. The writer who asserts, "In the 1980s only people who do well on machine-scored tests are going to get into medical and law schools" makes an extravagant claim that immediately exposes him or her to challenge. If that same writer says, "By the 1980s *it may be* that only people who do well on machine-scored tests can get into medical or law school," the qualification changes the statement from a dogmatic pronouncement to an arguable hypothesis.

Such qualifiers are necessary. If you skim over this book, you will find that most of my assertions are qualified by *probably, often, in general, most people,* and other phrases. I have my favorites, as do most writers, which I use to keep from overstating my case. I am protecting myself and building my credibility with my audience by not making extreme claims and by avoiding terms like *always* and *never.*

A writer can, however, easily carry this kind of caution too far and end up sounding timid and insecure rather than prudent. That can happen when a hesitant writer who is afraid to express strong opinions begins sentences with phrases like, ''It is somewhat the case that . . . ,'' ''It rather seems as if . . . ,'' ''It is possible that one could say . . . ,'' or some equally timid statement. Weak openers like this give the impression of a person raising an arm over the head to fend off a blow. They are not likely to command the attention or respect of the reader.

So you need to strike a balance between brashness and timidity, between sounding dogmatic and sounding insecure. It's a matter of controlling your tone. In most writing situations you can create a confident but courteous tone by making positive statements that you tone down with an occasional mild qualifier. Examples of such statements might be, ''1980 should prove a profitable year for cattle raisers,'' or ''Most depressed people can benefit from psychotherapy.''

Metaphorical Language

Another way in which writers can make their writing stronger and more concrete is by using metaphors, preferably fresh ones. Although most of us sprinkle our everyday speech with metaphors such as ''that job is a pressure cooker,'' or ''that guy is an accident looking for a place to happen,'' we forget that we could also be using colorful figures of speech to clarify and enliven our working writing.

Metaphors to Add Vigor.

Now you may think that plain writing, free from imaginative language, works best for the kind of writing tasks you usually have to do, and you may be right. If you are a nursing student writing a clinical history, your supervising professor may not want that history enlivened by striking metaphors. Or if you are a business major doing a report on shifting trends in consumer buying, you may think that you need to keep that report strictly analytical and report only the straight facts. In either instance, you should try to anticipate what kind of language your audience expects. But don't always assume that metaphors or images have no place in serious writing. No audience really wants to be bored, and you may be able both to interest your audience and make your point more clearly by bringing in an occasional metaphor.

For example, a business writer used the following metaphor: ". . . New York designer Martin Stachely unveiled a chiffon dress beaded with so many sequins that his model blazed like a one-woman laser light show."[10] And a writer describing the responses of a mental patient to an experimental therapy program used this metaphor:

> For Richard Lee, a tall Chinese kid, the salvo of words was something to dodge. With each surge of verbiage, Richard would wince and back up, then spin and sit down, only to stand and turn again. Richard was a matador turning away from the words and motion cast in his direction.[11]

In both cases the metaphors add a visual dimension to the writing and make it more likely that the reader will get a fuller impression of what the writer is trying to convey.

Metaphors That Persuade.

Writers also use metaphors to persuade. They do this by creating in the readers' minds an association between the two things that are being compared, thus encouraging readers to transfer their attitudes about one item in the metaphorical equation to the other item. For example, in his essay "Notes of a Native Son," when James Baldwin compares his reaction to racial prejudice to the behavior of a puppet controlled by external forces, he wants his readers to believe that in certain situations he was no more responsible for his actions than the puppet would be. He also plays on his readers' emotions by calling hatred a disease that destroys people.

When writers and speakers use metaphor, they count on their audiences having predictable responses to the creatures, objects, institutions, and events that all of us are familiar with. For instance, most people seem to react negatively to machines, positively to living things; most people react negatively to cages and traps and prisons, but positively to open spaces and creatures who are free. Writers tap these emotional responses through metaphor. Notice how John Stuart Mill builds one into his argument in this passage:

> Human nature is not a machine to be built after a model, and set to do exactly the work prescribed for it, but a tree which requires to grow and develop on all sides, according to the tendency of the inward forces which make it a living thing.[12]

By equating human nature with a growing plant, as he does in several passages throughout the book, Mill enlists his readers' support for his view that there is an inherent human potential that can be developed only if society does not impose limitations on free thought.

A feminist writer, Brigid Brophy, uses a vivid extended metaphor to per-

---

10. John Bloom, "Vanity Fair," *Texas Monthly,* October 1978, p. 118.
11. O. N. Jones, "Confrontation Summer," *Psychology Today,* March 1979, p. 83.
12. John Stuart Mill, *On Liberty* (Indianapolis: Bobbs-Merrill, 1956), p. 72.

suade her readers that although today's woman may have few legal barriers to her freedom, strong social forces prevent her full development.

Cage bars are clumsy methods of control, which excite the more rebellious personalities inside to rattle them. Modern society, like the modern zoo, has contrived to get rid of the bars without altering the fact of imprisonment. All the zoo architect needs to do is run a zone of hot or cold air, whichever the animal cannot tolerate, round the cage where the bars used to be. Human animals are not less sensitive to social climate. . . . The zones of hot and cold air which society uses to perpetuate its uneconomic and unreasonable state of affairs are the simplest and most effective conceivable. . . . Tell a man that he is not a real man, or a woman that she is not 100% woman, and you are threatening both with not being attractive to the opposite sex. No one can bear to be unattractive to the opposite sex. That is the climate which the human animal cannot tolerate.[13]

Metaphors to Clarify.

Finally, metaphor, along with analogy, is an invaluable device for clarifying and illustrating abstract concepts because it allows writers to explain the unfamiliar by putting it in terms of the familiar. Probably one reason that Plato has remained a well-known and influential philosopher for 2,500 years is that he had a gift for finding an illuminating metaphor that would help his listeners translate a theory into visual terms. The passage on page 106 is an example. And here is an example in which a physiologist uses metaphor to explain a modern abstract concept, jet lag.

Like a clock on a home thermostat, brain clockwork turns down the body temperature at night and turns it up at dawn. Adrenalcortical and other hormones, sodium and potassium salts, and many other substances are similarly regulated through a daily cycle. The clock appears to run a little slow, normally—about an hour later every day. This tendency for the clock to run a little slow is corrected daily at sunrise, when the brain resets it for the correct time.

To the traveler flying westward from New York to California, the sun appears to rise at a later hour, and the brain merely receives the reset-signal a little late, affording another hour or two of sleep. Since we naturally function on a 25-hour free-running cycle, it is not surprising that most people adjust to westward travel and a longer day easily.

Flying eastward—to Europe, for example—is more stressful. The sun appears to rise earlier: six, seven, or more hours before the brain is ready to begin a new day. At that point, the sunrise may not be very effective in setting the hands of the brain's clock ahead.[14]

When you have to explain something that you sense your audience is going to have trouble understanding, see if you can coax a metaphor out of

13. Brigid Brophy, "Women Are Prisoners of Their Sex," *Saturday Evening Post*, 21 November 1963.

14. Monte S. Buchsbaum, "The Chemistry of Brain Clocks," *Psychology Today*, March 1979, p. 124.

your subconscious to do the job for you. Look first to that ready source of familiar examples, your own experience. For instance, I might draw on my experience in making clothes to draw an analogy between writing a first draft of a paper and basting a garment together to get an idea of how it is going to look when it is finished.

Other rich sources of metaphor are experiences, activities, or events that would be familiar to your average reader. For example, I can illustrate the concept of ethical appeal (see p. 52) by saying that a person builds his or her ethical appeal just as a person establishes a credit rating in a community: by consistently carrying out promises, meeting obligations, and acting reliably. A radio commentator one morning evaluated the results of President Carter's attempts to salvage Israeli-Egyptian treaty negotiations by saying, "He hasn't cured the patient, but it's still alive." You can make good metaphorical use of your knowledge about games, travel, business, education, fixing a car, or running a household. Isaac Asimov, explaining Princeton scientist Gerald O'Neill's theories about space colonies wrote: "Ultimately, a new row of space colonies should be built as easily as a new row of houses in the suburbs."[15]

One of the bonuses of using metaphor is that by doing so you can simultaneously enrich and condense your writing. The right metaphor invigorates your writing by dramatizing your idea. For instance, the sociologist David Riesman illustrated his theories of inner-directed and outer-directed personalities by saying that the inner-directed people make decisions by consulting internal gyroscopes that have been set by parents and society, and the outer-directed people make their decisions by putting out radarlike signals to the society around them.[16] He thereby enriched his writing by giving it a visual dimension. He also conveyed an idea much more economically than he would have if he had tried to spell it out in literal terms. In prose as in poetry, good metaphor acts as a kind of shorthand that squeezes an abundance of meaning into a few words.

Allusion

The most economical kind of metaphor is an allusion, a reference to an event or story or cultural institution that evokes a whole body of knowledge or associations with a single phrase or word. The names Judas or Midas are such allusions; so are Romeo, Don Juan, Falstaff, or King Lear. Each brings to mind a particular kind of personality. Historical reference to the Gold Rush or the Spanish Inquisition reminds a reader of the attitudes and kinds of behavior

15. Isaac Asimov, "Gardens of Space," *Saturday Review,* July 1975, p. 8.
16. David Riesman, *The Lonely Crowd* (New Haven: Yale University Press, 1950), pp. 31, 37.

that characterized those two events. Biblical allusions can compress a moral statement into a few words, and a reference to the labors of Hercules or to a Procrustean bed triggers rich associations for readers who know Greek myths.

You can also find an abundance of useful allusions on the contemporary scene. Popular songs, movies, television, advertising, sports—any experiences that you and your readers share—provide resources for conveying a lot of information in a few words. For instance, the expression "life in the fast lane" describes a whole lifestyle to most modern American readers. Comparing someone to Pete Rose compresses a description of an attitude and a pattern of achievement into two words. Calling a political convention the Republican Super Bowl would communicate the atmosphere of prefabricated merriment and extravagant publicity that characterizes both.

However, writers who strengthen their writing with allusions, either traditional or modern, must have an acute sense of audience, or they risk mystifying or alienating their readers rather than enlightening them. The person who drops references to a "Trojan horse" or an "Achilles' heel" when writing for an audience not familiar with *The Iliad* is being short-sighted and inconsiderate. So is the writer who uses a rock group or a progressive country band as a central reference in a piece written for people past 50. So think carefully about your audience and the assumptions you can make about them before you choose your allusions. Well used, they are fine writing tools; poorly chosen, they can do more harm than good. But once in a while gamble by bringing in an allusion even if you are not sure of the effect it might have; better that you should miss occasionally than write consistently flat, colorless prose.

Jargon, Gobbledygook, or Doublespeak

When you encounter writing that is not only flat and colorless, but hard to read because it is wordy, heavy with abstractions and passive verbs, and padded with qualifiers and evasive language, you should suspect that you are encountering jargon. In its original sense, the word *jargon* means the specialized language of a profession or trade; lawyers, for instance, have to talk about *habeas corpus* and *writs of mandamus,* and editors have to talk about *layouts* and *corrigenda.* In such contexts specialists are justified in using specialized terms. But writers who use intimidating and confusing language when they are writing for an average audience, or use highly specialized and unfamiliar terminology when it is not necessary, are writing another kind of jargon, that confusing and pretentious kind of language that is sometimes also called gobbledygook, doublespeak, or bureaucratese. This kind of jargon is another form of the emperor's new clothes language discussed in chapter 1.

Certain kinds of evasive or puzzling words and phrases tend to crop up in this kind of writing. The most common are euphemisms, such as *career apparel* for *uniforms,* or *quality control person* for *inspector;* vague words such as *viable, interface,* or *meaningful;* foreign words or phrases such as *modus vivendi* or *comme il faut;* or gimmicky words like *actualize* and *prioritize.* All of these terms can cause problems for readers; they may have to stop and ask themselves, "Now what is a *quality control person?*" or "What does *interface* mean?" and if they don't know what *modus vivendi* means, they either have to stop to look it up or go on without understanding. And a reader who bumps into a term like *prioritize* will usually do a double take. In fact, perhaps the earliest signal a reader gets that he or she may be getting bogged down in jargon is that feeling of the mind glazing over and the words not penetrating. When that happens a reader has to backtrack and start over again.

Almost certainly people *learn* to write jargon; it does not grow out of a genuine need to communicate. Students seldom write it until the last years of high school or until they get to college. People who do write it do so, I think, for several reasons. At one extreme they use euphemisms to disguise unpleasantness—*sanitary land fill* for *garbage dump*—or to gloss over realities—*happiness passport* for *charge account.* At the other extreme writers may use doublespeak to conceal the truth or whitewash harsh facts. No one has described that kind of jargon better than George Orwell in his essay, "Politics and the English Language":

Defenseless villages are bombarded from the air, the inhabitants driven out into the countryside, the huts set on fire with incendiary bullets, and this is called *pacification.* Millions of peasants are robbed of their farms and sent trudging along the roads with no more than they can carry; this is called *rectification of frontiers.* People are imprisoned for years without trial, or shot in the back of the neck or sent to die of scurvy in Arctic prison camps; this is called *elimination of unreliable elements.* Such phraseology is needed if one wants to name things without calling up mental pictures.[17]

Students most often use jargon for reasons that fall somewhere between these extremes. They use it because they think it sounds impressive—the emperor's new clothes again—they use it to protect themselves—if the reader is not sure what they mean, he or she can't get too angry about it—or they use it because they're lazy. It really is much easier to string together abstract words and fuzzy phrases than it is to write precise, clear prose. Here is an example from an advanced writer.

He [the protagonist in *Goodbye, Columbus*] is confused about the coexistence of happiness and money. . . . His immaturity in this manner is common to the American people. Many are as incapable of relating sex with love as they are relating material

17. George Orwell, "Politics and the English Language," in *Shooting an Elephant and Other Essays* (New York: Harcourt, Brace & World, 1945), p. 88.

goods with the immaterial. Americans have grown so accustomed to separating the material from the immaterial, and to the overabundance of tangible luxuries that emotions, passions, and intellect are consistently overlooked.

The example illustrates fuzzy, abstract writing that at first seems to be saying something, but which upon examination proves to be an undecipherable accumulation of smooth-sounding words. It represents the kind of writing that uses language as a protective barrier rather than as a tool of communication.

Finally, here is an example of authentic military jargon used as a classroom exercise by a colleague who teaches future officers to write at the U.S. Air Force Academy.

Subject: Pilferage of Dining Hall Common-Use Items
To: Wing Group, Staff, Squadrons and Tenant Units
1. Every attempt is made to provide quality service to all patrons of the Dining Hall; however, the excessive pilferage of silverware, cups, glasses, plates and dispensers (salt, pepper, and sugar) has degraded service. Due to supply delays these items cannot always be replaced in a timely manner; additionally replacement of these items consumes funds that could be better utilized for improvement. The cost of these items has steadily increased, thereby requiring a greater expenditure of funds for replacements. Reduced fund allocations dictate maximum utilization of all commonuse items and the cooperation of all personnel.
2. It is requested that all barracks, offices, work shops, etc. be cleaned out and these items returned to the Dining Hall.
3. All personnel should be apprised of this subject and the detrimental effect it has on service and morale.

Notice how stiff and flat this writing is, and how wordy. By writing *in a timely manner* instead of *quickly, fund allocations* instead of *funds,* and *utilization* instead of *use,* and by relying heavily on passive verbs, the faceless author projects a pompous, fussy image that will probably make no impression on the people he is trying to reach.

Once you have formed the habit of hiding behind jargon, it takes constant work to break that habit because all of us are tempted to settle for the ready-made phrases and the catchall words that crowd into our minds when we begin to write. But as you can do exercises to keep your body lean, you can develop certain habits that will keep your prose lean. Here are some of them.

1. Keep your language as specific and concrete as possible; when you use abstractions, ask yourself if you need to illustrate or reinforce them with examples.
2. Watch your verbs; keep them active if possible, and avoid inert, colorless verbs that get lost in your sentences.

3. Use direct and straightforward language, not ambiguous euphemisms, for example, write *students,* not *those engaged in higher education.*
4. Get rid of foreign words and phrases whenever possible, and avoid trendy words like *interface* and *viable.* Use the simpler term when you have a choice—*use* instead of *utilize, visit* instead of *visitation.*
5. Don't be afraid to show your face occasionally; even technical and objective writing does not have to be bland and faceless.

Following the suggestions in chapter 9 on revision will also help you to weed the jargon out of your writing.

Sexist Language

In recent years, editors, administrators, and officials have imposed a new requirement on writers: they must avoid using sexist language; that is, they should not use words or examples that suggest sex discrimination or stereotyping. For instance, they should not consistently use the words *man* or *men* when they mean *person* or *people,* they should not consistently use the pronouns *he* or *his* when the referent for those pronouns is not specifically male, and they should not habitually use the pronouns *he* and *his* to refer to people in professions such as medicine or engineering, and *she* and *hers* to refer to people in professions such as nursing and teaching. Neither should they use anecdotes or phrases that suggest sex-role stereotyping; for example, most editors will no longer permit nonfiction writers to use phrases like *dizzy blonde* or the *weaker sex.*

Many people, particularly authors who have been writing for years without worrying about whether they were using sexist language, protest that the fuss about masculine pronouns or the generic term *man* is ridiculous; that when they use those words they refer to everyone. They also frequently claim that having to consider such matters when they write inhibits them and forces them to write awkward sentences. They consider themselves fair and open-minded people, and they do not think they should continually have to prove their virtue by writing "his/her" or "he and she."

One can sympathize with this point of view. Certainly writing is demanding enough without adding one more guideline for authors to worry about. Nevertheless, I think that the prohibition against sexist language is here to stay, and that for several reasons responsible authors are going to have to work at keeping it out of their writing.

The first reason is economic. Editors, public relations people, people in charge of fund drives or promotions, and ad writers realize that women make up a large segment of almost any writer's audience, and they are not going to risk offending those women with sexist references or word choices.

The second reason is legal. In most cases, an administrator or executive cannot restrict persons of either sex from applying for a job or a scholarship or from enrolling in a school or program. Therefore it is important that any announcement or literature that promotes or describes academic programs, job opportunities, or tax-supported services or facilities should not suggest, either directly or by implication, that an agency or institution discriminates against either sex.

A third reason is practical. The writer who consistently uses *he* as a referent for every personal noun is often inaccurate. One can no longer assume that 95 percent of doctors, lawyers, scientists, mail carriers, or taxi drivers are male, nor that those who like to read about food are women and those who like to read about investments are men.

A fourth reason is psychological and ethical. Language really does shape thought, and the writer who persists in using masculine pronouns probably has images of males in mind as he or she writes, and projects those images into the mind of the reader. Take this passage, for example:

> I recently asked a roomful of eighteen-year olds to tell me what an adult is. Their deliberate answer, after hours of discussion, was that an adult is someone who no longer plays, who is no longer playful. . . . Of course they did not want to remain children, or teens, or adolescents; but they did want to remain youthful, playful, free of squares, and free of responsibility. The teen-ager wants to be old enough to drive, drink, screw, and travel. *He* does not want to get pushed into square maturity. *He* wants to drag the main, be a surf bum, a ski bum, or dream of being a bum. *He* doesn't want to go to Vietnam, or to IBM, or to buy a split-level house in Knotty Pine Estates.[18] [Italics added.]

So the words *man* and *he* are really not neutral, and the writer who wants to be nonsexist has to find substitutes for them.

Guidelines for Nonsexist Writing.

Cleaning sexist connotations out of one's writing takes ingenuity and effort, but the person who works at it can finally make writing nonsexist prose as much of a habit as spelling and punctuating acceptably. Here are some guidelines:

1. When feasible, use plural nouns and eliminate the need to choose a pronoun of specific gender; often this is the simplest remedy. For example: "Painters who want to exhibit their work, not "A painter who wants to exhibit his work."

18. Mervyn Cadwallader, "Marriage as a Wretched Institution," *The Atlantic Monthly*, November 1966, p. 64.

2. Reword the sentence to eliminate the gender pronoun. For example: "The average American drives a car three years," instead of "The average American drives his car three years."

3. When feasible, substitute the words *person* or *people* for *man* or *woman*, or *men* or *women*. For example: "A person who wants to get ahead in business," instead of "A man who wants to get ahead in business." "People who want to become nurses," instead of "Women who want to become nurses."

4. When feasible, substitute *one* for *he* or *she* or *man* or *woman*. If appropriate, you can also substitute *you* for a gender word. For example: "If one plans ahead, one can retire at 60." instead of "If a man plans ahead, he can retire at 60."

5. When it seems indicated, write *he or she* or *his* or *her;* as long as you do not use the phrases too often, they will not be conspicuous.

6. If you wish, consistently write *he/she* and *him/her*.

7. Sometimes use *she* and *her* instead *he* and *him* as general pronouns. For example: "The driver who is renewing her license must now pass an eye test," and "An officer who makes an arrest should show her badge."

8. Instead of identifying people by their sexes, identify them in other ways; for example, student, applicant, customer, voter, patient, parent, official, and so on. For example: "Customers are protesting rising food costs," instead of "Housewives are protesting rising food costs." "City officials will call for bids tomorrow," instead of "City fathers will call for bids tomorrow."

9. Refer to women by their own names, such as Julia Walsh or Francis Fitzgerald rather than by their husband's names, Mrs. John Walsh or Mrs. Frank Fitzgerald. Avoid references to their marital status unless it is important that your reader know that status. If you are including men's professional titles, include women's professional titles too. For instance, "Professor Joseph Keith and Professor Jane Kennedy," not "Professor Keith and Mrs. Kennedy."

10. Be consistent when you are referring to people by their last names. For instance, if you write "Hawthorne" or "Melville," then also write "Dickinson," not "Emily Dickinson." If you write "Carter" and "Ford," then write "Thatcher," not "Margaret Thatcher."

11. Avoid special female designations when it is feasible to do so. For instance, you don't need to call a woman poet a "poetess" or a woman author an "authoress."

12. When possible, replace occupational terms ending in-*man* or -*woman* with another term. For example, "firefighter" instead of "fireman," "mail carrier" instead of "mailman," "salesperson" instead of "salesman," and "janitor" instead of "cleaning woman." Probably you do not need to go to the extreme of writing "waitperson," instead of "waiter" or "waitress."

13. Be careful not to stereotype people by profession or by supposedly sex-linked traits. For example: "Young people who want to become doctors should realize that they will be in college at least ten years," not "The young man who wants to be a doctor should realize he will be in college at least ten years"; "Emotional people should not go into high-stress jobs," not "Emotional women should not go into high-stress jobs."

14. Avoid referring to a woman's physical appearance unless it is relevant to the purpose of your writing, or unless you would mention a man's physical appearance in the same context. For instance, if you were writing a credit history on a client, you would not write, "Mary Jones is an attractive redhead," unless you are also prepared to write "Fred Jones is a handsome blond" in the same kind of report.

Writers who want to develop a style that is free from sexist overtones have to do three things. First, they have to become conscious of those overtones; that may be their greatest hurdle since many people seem genuinely to believe that consistently using *man* and masculine pronouns does not indicate any bias. Second, they have to develop the habit of continually editing their writing for lapses into the traditional male-centered style. Probably the apprentice writer should not worry too much about such lapses on the first draft, but plan on making necessary changes the second time through. Third, they have to believe that developing a nondiscriminatory style matters. I hope I have convinced you that it does.

But single words, however carefully chosen, must be combined into sentences and paragraphs in order to convey messages. Some of the techniques a writer can use for making those combinations effective is the subject of the next chapter.

EXERCISES / *Prewriting Activities*

1   Rewrite the following sentences using concrete and specific language whenever possible.

A.   The article is intended for people who are unaware of the status of housing growth in this country.

B. The program means elimination of access to artificially produced foodstuffs.

C. The mere indication of legislative intent would serve as an incentive to constituents.

D. A knowledge and understanding of the law is a necessity for those who want an alteration of it.

2 Rewrite these sentences using people or a person as the subject of the sentence.

A. The load of responsibility on the lender is great.

B. A stringent self-evaluation is needed to remedy your problem.

C. The anxiety that accompanies choosing a profession is a major cause of stress.

D. Careful selection of foods containing all the various nutrients is important for maintaining health and adequate energy.

3 Rewrite these sentences with more vigorous verbs.

A. Abortion as a method of population control is ineffective in lessening the birthrate.

B. There are several advantages that will be achieved by this ruling.

C. Vitamins are substances the body requires in small amounts.

D. There are many things to examine when looking for a used car.

4 Rewrite these sentences to replace the passive verbs with active verbs.

A. Women are faced with similar anxieties every day.

B. Such information should be made available to the consumers in case they ask.

C. What should be considered is the capability and suitability of an individual for the job.

D. It is recommended by state officials that action be taken immediately.

5 Photocopy a magazine article in which the author uses metaphor or allusion and bring it to class. Analyze what the writer's reason for using allusion and metaphor seems to be. Do you think the technique is effective?

6 Interpret these jargon-laden sentences and then rewrite each of them to make it clearer.

A. The configuration of human and technical talents to be mobilized often transcends the jurisdiction of formal educational institutions.

B. "Once upon a time, a small person named Little Red Riding Hood initiated plans for the preparation, delivery, and transportation of foodstuffs to her grandmother, a senior citizen residing at a place of residence in a forest of indeterminate dimensions."—Russell Baker

C. Our investments are generating a negative capability.

D. Nelson prioritized the company's objectives in terms of viability and expense factors.

7 Rewrite the following passages to eliminate sex-biased language.

A. A student will be judged not on how effective he will be as a practicing lawyer, but on the number of correct answers he gives on a multiple-choice test.

B. The businessman who is trying to achieve racial and sexual balance among his employees will have to advertise in a variety of places.

C. The nurse who wants to work in a small town often finds that she has been replaced by unlicensed nurses' aides.

D. Hemingway, Fitzgerald, Katherine Anne Porter, Steinbeck, and Joan Didion are among the authors who have kept notebooks on their writing habits.

Suggested Writing Assignments

As a part of each writing assignment write a detailed analysis of your audience and specify the characteristics they would have that you need to keep in mind as you write, the problems such an audience might present, and what the audience would expect to get from reading your paper. Also analyze your purpose in writing, specifying what you hope to accomplish with the paper. If appropriate, include an accurate and descriptive title for your paper.

TOPIC 1:
Go and observe carefully a street, neighborhood, building, or small area in your city and write an objective report on it that might be used for a paper in an urban sociology class or course on city government. Use concrete and specific but neutral language; appeal to the senses as much as possible and avoid using vague adjectives. Think about what kind of information your reader would want to get from the report and what use that information

might be put to outside of class. Some possible topics for description might be the following:

> A deteriorating Victorian house that would be worth renovating and preserving.
> A vacant lot that could be converted into a playground.
> A block close to campus that is being invaded by x-rated bookstores and porno movie houses.
> The county courthouse that was built in the last century.

TOPIC 2:

The generous retirement pay of people who have served 20 years or more in the armed services costs U. S. taxpayers a substantial amount of money. For example, a colonel may retire at 42 and receive over $1,000 a month retirement pay while holding down another job; a four-star admiral may retire at the age of 60 with a pension of more than $40,000 a year. These benefits also have the advantage of being tied to the cost of living so that they increase as the price index rises.

Assume the persona of someone who defends or opposes these benefits and write an article expressing your views. Think carefully about the consequences of your argument and support your points. Direct your paper to a specific audience.

TOPIC 3:

Write a short article for elementary school children from ten to twelve years old explaining a few main points about some concept, theory, or activity in your special field in words simple enough for them to understand. Use concrete illustrations or analogies with processes or events that they would be familiar with to help you make your point. Some topics that children this age might enjoy learning about are these:

Behavior modification	Theatre in Shakespeare's time
Biological adaptation	Off-shore oil drilling
Orbiting space stations	The electric car
School desegregation	Weather forecasting

7 Sentences

Why Sentences?

At some point in the development of written language, writers—or more probably editors or scribes—invented the marks that we use to indicate sentences in a piece of writing. They did not invent the sentence itself; that already existed. Students of language think that sentences must be natural language units because even people who are totally illiterate seem to be able to form effective sentences intuitively without consciously thinking about what they are doing. When we write, however, and cannot depend on the pauses, gestures, and changes in tone that speakers use to signal divisions or to indicate shifts in direction or emphasis, we have to start thinking about constructing and punctuating our sentences in ways that will help readers to follow and understand them.

Writers need to remember that the whole purpose in dividing writing into sentences—or paragraphs or sections or chapters—is to make life easier for the reader. A few years ago when I was recording for Recordings for the Blind, I had to read out loud a long, completely undivided and unpunctuated section from a book by an author who liked to use unconventional prose forms to create certain effects. It was the most difficult piece of reading I have ever had to do. Not only did I have to figure out which groups of words made sense when they were put together, but I had to spot transition terms and decide which sentences they went with in order to show how units related to each other. Usually I had to try two or three times before I could put together a group of words that seemed to make sense. That experience taught me a lot about why we divide and punctuate our writing.

Yet professional writers probably don't consciously plan ahead about how they are going to write a sentence or what kind of patterns they will use. They don't say to themselves, "I think I will write this article mostly in complex sentences," or "I think I will use a lot of parallelism and subordinate structure for this paper." Rather they focus on what they want to say, keep in mind their audience, and begin to write, using any of the dozens of different sentence patterns available. Sometimes they are satisfied with their first choice; sometimes they cross it out and try two or three others before getting a sentence the way they want it. Sometimes they leave all the sentences in their original form on the first draft and change many of them later, splitting them up, deleting, combining, adding material, rearranging words, and so on. They tinker with them until they look right.

This tinkering with words and adapting sentence structure to fit content, purpose, and audience might be called *sentence packaging*. Sentences are containers in which we arrange our ideas, and different kinds of sentence packages work well in different kinds of communication situations. This term suggests how many different kinds of sentence packages writers have available, a variety ranging from two-word fragments to long, complex/compound sentences punctuated with semicolons. A writer can choose packages that are plain or fancy, large or small, bulky or streamlined, and so on. They can stuff a lot of information into comparatively few large packages, or they can divide it and package it in smaller, more manageable containers.

But before we can consider some guidelines and techniques for packaging sentences, we probably need to review the minimum terminology a person needs to know, not to write sentences, but to talk about them.

Terminology

PHRASE: A word cluster that acts as a part of speech; it does not have a subject or verb.

CLAUSE: A group of words with a subject and verb. A subordinate or dependent clause is incomplete by itself; an independent clause is complete and could act as a sentence.

SIMPLE SENTENCE: A sentence with one independent clause and no other clauses; it may, however, contain modifying words or phrases.

COMPLEX SENTENCE: A sentence with an independent clause and at least one subordinate clause.

COMPOUND SENTENCE: A sentence made up of two independent clauses joined by a conjunction or semicolon.

COMPOUND/COMPLEX SENTENCE: A sentence with two independent clauses and one or more subordinate clauses.

MODIFIER: A word, phrase, or clause that gives information about another part of the sentence.

APPOSITIVE: A special kind of modifier inserted directly after a noun or pronoun to give more information.

COMPLEMENT: In sentences, the word or phrase that completes the verb. Subject-verb-complement is the most common sentence pattern.

PARALLELISM: A pattern of the same kind of structure in the separate clauses or phrases of the sentence.

SUBORDINATION: Having one clause in a sentence dependent on an independent clause for its meaning.

CLOSURE: The point in a sentence at which a group of words assumes meaning for the reader (see page 93).

Options for Sentences

Simple Sentence.

The simple sentence usually works well for direct assertions, definitions, straightforward reports, and statements of fact. Three examples of this sort of sentence follow.

The high cost of energy is the chief cause of inflation.

The patient was wheeled into surgery at 7:30 A.M.

The average single-family dwelling in the United States now costs $62,000.

Sentences like these are particularly good for calling attention to a key point or introducing your reader to your topic.

Simple sentences don't have to be short. You can keep the plain package but get more information into it by adding appositives or other kinds of modifiers. For instance:

Children need security, *physical and emotional,* in order to flourish.

Her grandmother, *a staunch Catholic,* enrolled her in a convent school in Philadelphia.

Today, *perhaps for the first time in history,* hundreds of thousands of middle-aged people are going to school.

So simple sentences don't have to be simplistic. You can qualify them, enrich them, or make them more colorful, concrete, or informative and still keep them easy for the reader to follow. But a writer should be careful not to pad simple sentences or embellish them needlessly. The bare, short, direct sentence serves special needs.

First, writers use the stripped-down simple sentence for emphasis. It's an attention-getter, a good opener. For example:

Fame is an aphrodisiac.

or

Success is a frame of mind.

Sentences like these catch the reader's eye and spark interest in what will follow. Modifiers would weaken them.

Second, writers can put variety into their writing and break up a monotonous rhythm by consciously mixing crisp, simple sentences with longer, complex ones. For instance:

> Make a friend of a plant. . . . Plants never complain. They don't criticize, demand, pontificate, eye you lasciviously, nag, tell you you're putting on weight, you're late, you're lazy, you're dull. They are gratifyingly receptive to tender loving care, good music, and gentle conversation. There's much joy to be derived from discovering that your spider plant is about to bear lots of little spider plants, that the wandering Jew you stuck in water a week ago is starting to send out roots.[1]

If, on reading over your first draft, you find that it is overloaded with long sentences of 25 to 30 words or more, try breaking some of them into shorter sentences and creating a more varied pattern for the reader.

Third, writers who want their writing to move quickly, either because they know their audiences are impatient or because a brisk tone suits their topic, will increase the tempo of their prose by frequently inserting short, simple sentences into their writing. For instance:

> Fiesta is the axis around which San Antonio turns. Poor people save up for Fiesta. Rich people rest up for Fiesta. Hotel people build up for Fiesta. Shopkeepers stock up for Fiesta. Garbage collectors pick up and jetsetters pack *after* Fiesta. And during Fiesta every April, San Antonio is possibly the world's most enchanting party, a gentle, unfrenzied Mardi Gras.[2]

By putting together a series of short simple sentences that repeat words and patterns, the author has created a tight, swiftly moving piece of prose.

Compound and Complex Sentences.

Although one can pack a lot of information into a technically simple sentence by adding modifiers and introductory qualifying phrases, the writer who wants to express qualifications, exceptions, consequences, or reservations probably needs to write complex or compound sentences. Their flexible structure allows a writer to show relationships between ideas, bring subtleties into writing, and pack more information into a sentence by packaging two or more ideas in one container. That first trait of complex/compound sentences, their capacity for connecting ideas, may be the most important. In fact a reliable mark of skilled writers is their ability to package information efficiently by using the right connecting words and phrases in a complex sentence. Compare these two student examples.

> But in 1913, he got a big break when, after a lengthy court battle, he secured a court order granting the Oil Belt permission to cross the tracks of the rival Texas and

1. Sue Wendt, "Living Alone—But Do You Like It?" *Working Woman,* April 1979, p. 38.
2. Mike Greenberg, "Fiesta!" *Texas Monthly,* March 1979, p. 100.

Pacific Railroad outside Ranger. On the same night that the order was granted, Hamon's crews labored by torchlight to complete the crossing, while armed guards kept watch.

Education is the most important function of Recordings for the Blind. Literature is the fundamental tool of learning. In the past, books printed in braille have been the most widely used material for educating the blind. A better method has been developed to replace these books. We have learned that the use of tapes is much more effective.

The first passage is smooth and tight because the writer has tied his clauses together with words like *when, while, but,* and *on the same night.* The second passage is hard to follow because the student has written a series of independent sentences, and given no hints about the connection between them. The same amount of information could have been packaged more efficiently in two complex sentences. Notice the difference:

Because literature is the fundamental tool of learning, education is the most important function of Recordings for the Blind. Today tapes have replaced the books printed in braille, which used to be the most widely used material for educating the blind.

To construct good complex sentences that express contrasts, qualifications, or nuances, a writer needs to develop a stock of single terms which let the reader know what to expect. The old standbys are *moreover, however, in spite of, nevertheless, also, if, since,* and so on (see page 87). The difficult task for inexperienced writers may be to make discriminating choices among those words and choose the one that indicates precisely the relationship between two clauses or sentences. For instance, *despite* and *moreover* are not interchangeable; neither are *since* and *although.*

The signal words that a writer chooses trigger specific expectations in the reader's mind, and skillful writers make sure that the sentence or phrase that follows those signal words meets those expectations. For example, notice how different signal words before or after the same sentence change the reader's expectations.

Hanson has never earned more than $10,000 a year; *nevertheless*
a. he considers himself a successful man.
b. he pays more income tax than some millionaires.
Hanson has never earned more than $10,000 a year; *moreover,*
a. he probably never will.
b. his wife does not work.

Although gasoline costs more than $2.00 a gallon in Europe,
a. people there buy more passenger cars each year.
b. the consumers do not complain.
Since gasoline costs more than $2.00 a gallon in Europe,
a. most people drive two and four-cylinder cars.

b. millions of people commute to work by bicycle.

In order to develop your skills as a writer, you need to experiment with using various signal words to tie the parts of your sentences together. Would *although* or *nevertheless* best show the relationship you want to express? Should you choose *but* or *and* to join your clauses? If you're uncertain, try two or three ways in your rough draft and see if you can sense the difference. You'll occasionally make poor choices, but gradually you'll improve your writing as you develop a sensitivity to the differences among signal words. Apprentice writers have to risk losing their way in complex and compound sentence structures now and then in order to develop the skills to express what they want to say. If they don't, they cannot grow as writers.

Choosing between Compound and Complex Sentences.

In describing the part of a complex sentence, I have used the term *dependent clause* rather than *subordinate clause* because one cannot always assume that the dependent clause in a sentence is necessarily less important than the so-called main clause. A qualifying or modifying clause may be *structurally* dependent—that is, it could not stand by itself as a sentence—but nevertheless dominate the content of the sentence. For example:

(dependent clause)
Although he was only 34 when he made his historic discovery, Perkins had been a practicing scientist for years.

So you should not assume that you have to decide which of two ideas is the more important before you can write a complex sentence.

Neither should you assume that you can show the subordination of one idea to another only by writing a complex sentence; if you choose the appropriate signal words, you can also use compound sentences. For example:

John has never enjoyed exercise, *but* he conscientiously runs two miles a day.

Gerald did not do well on the Medical College Admissions Test; *nevertheless,* he was a straight A medical student.

The most important considerations to keep in mind when you are joining ideas in any kind of sentence—simple, complex, compound, or complex/compound—are the relationships you want to show and the emphasis you want to achieve. When you make those decisions, you can try out various linking terms (see p. 87) and move your clauses around to get the effect you want. But usually when you want to express interdependence and qualifications, you will find that you need complex or complex/compound sentences.

Many stylists suggest that when you are making more than one point in a sentence, you should put the idea you want to emphasize at the end. For example:

> While it is true that the United States does not import as much as it did five years ago, our balance of payments is still unfavorable.

or,

> No matter what kind of writing you do, you should never ignore your audience.

Don't, however, feel that you have to build to a climax in every complex sentence you write. Your best guideline is to try various patterns for your sentences and see which seems to give you the effect you want.

BALANCED SENTENCES.   You can use compound sentences for at least two purposes that complex sentences cannot fill. One is to compare or contrast points of equal importance; the second is to compress a number of points into one sentence by setting up parallel clauses. Both kinds of sentences are "balanced," but the first is most often used to stress contrasts. For instance:

> The Romanticists believed Man was divine; the Calvinists believed he was depraved.

or

> All of us talk about our freedoms; few of us talk about our obligations.

The second kind of balanced compound sentence more often stresses similarities. For example:

> If you love animals, they will be affectionate; if you nourish them, they will flourish; if you train them, they will be a pleasure.

Learning to construct both these kinds of balanced sentences significantly increases your command of sentence strategies.

Sentence Combining

Embedding.

Writers who are trying to construct smoother and more efficient sentences can often do so by finding ways to combine the contents of two or three sentences into one sentence that is more tightly packed. One technique for this kind of combining is called embedding, putting the information from one sentence into the body of another one by inserting a modifying word, phrase, or clause. Notice how it can be done with these examples from student papers.

a. Jennifer is always fighting off the advances of the station manager.

b. She is his secretary.

a/b. Jennifer, the station manager's secretary, is always fighting off his advances.

a. The psychologist Ollie Pocs told *Psychology Today* that "married couples over 40 have little or no sex life."

b. He made this statement in June 1977.

c. Pocs is on the faculty of Illinois State University.

a/b/c. In June 1977, Illinois State University psychologist Ollie Pocs told *Psychology Today* that "married couples over 40 have little or no sex life."

a. Meetings of the new chapter of the Sierra Club will be held in the South Austin Natural Science Center.

b. The first meeting will be on Thursday, September 22, at 7:30 P.M.

c. The meeting will be presided over by Bill Hollingsworth, state president of the club.

d. Hollingsworth will talk on activities of the Sierra Club.

a/b/c/d. At 7:30 Thursday evening, Bill Hollingsworth, state president of the Sierra Club, will preside over the first meeting of a new chapter of the club at the South Austin Natural Science Center; Hollingsworth will talk about Sierra Club activities.

And here is a student example that shows how much one can pack into two sentences with skillful embedding.

Estimated at more than 2,000, the crowd on the main mall stood in a light drizzle yesterday as ex-President Ford and G.O.P. gubernatorial candidate Clements staged a political pep rally. Addressing the largest crowd assembled on campus since graduation last May, Ford and Clements thundered Republican rhetoric as they stood before a round-up of bright white shirts, leather chaps, and burnt-orange bandannas.

As writers become more practiced, they learn to embed modifiers and qualifiers into their prose as they write a first draft, but inexperienced writers often don't see that they could have compressed the content of several sentences into one more efficient one until they have written those several sentences. And even the best writers frequently cannot decide how they want to arrange a sentence until they have tried it several ways. Consequently, many do much of their changing and embedding on the second or third draft.

What skilled writers know and what aspiring writers need to remember, is that a sentence is not fixed and set once it is written. It can be broken into and pieced out to make it more comprehensive, it can be qualified by inserting a word or phrase, or it can be shortened into a clause or phrase and tucked into another sentence.

Transforming.

One can also produce more effective sentence packages by using a sentence-combining technique called *transforming,* that is, joining, revising, and rearranging two or more sentences into one tighter and smoother sentence. One can transform sentences in a number of ways. The most common are these:

- Make one sentence into an introductory clause or phrase for another sentence.
- Make one sentence into a subordinate clause and embed it into another sentence.
- Condense a sentence into a modifier and insert it in another sentence.
- Join several sentences together as balanced or parallel clauses.

Often a writer can think of several good ways to redo two or three loose sentences into one compact sentence. For example:

ORIGINAL: The causes of inflation are multiple. Easy consumer credit is one cause. Rising cost of energy is another. Still another is the feeling buyers have that they should buy now because next year everything will cost more. This last may be the hardest to cure.

REVISION 1:   Although there are many causes of inflation—for example, easy consumer credit and the rising cost of energy—the most difficult to combat may be the buyers' feeling that they should buy now because next year everything will cost more.

REVISION 2:   Officials trying to control inflation think it may be more difficult to combat people's attitude of "buy now because it will cost more tomorrow," than to control the cost of energy or tighten up consumer credit.

Notice that bringing personal subjects and strong verbs into the second revision makes it an improvement over the first.

Here are some examples from student papers, along with suggested transformation by sentence combining.

ORIGINAL: The President bases his plan on several assumptions. He assumes a large majority of the population heard his requests. He assumes that just as large a majority understood these requests. And he assumes that this same group will obey his requests. These are very large assumptions in my opinion.

REVISION: In my opinion, the President bases his plan on several shaky assumptions: that most people heard his requests, that they understand them, and that they will obey them.

ORIGINAL: First, I need to find out what the most serious problems are. Through a national survey, these problems will become apparent. After I discover the problems, research can be directed specifically toward them.

REVISION: After making a national survey to find out what the most serious problems are, I will be able to direct my research toward solving them.

ORIGINAL: There are three courses of action that the legislature may wish to choose. All involve the appropriation of money designated specifically for this purpose. First, a bill appropriating enough money for a multilevel parking structure could be considered. Second, an appropriation to cover half the costs, with the other half coming from increased parking fees, could be considered. Thirdly, a bill allowing for the Board of Regents to raise building fees charged to the students.

REVISION: The Legislature could choose among three alternatives, all involving appropriating money: first, they could appropriate enough money to build a multilevel garage; second, they could appropriate half the cost of the garage and get the rest from increased parking fees; third, they could pass a bill allowing the Board of Regents to raise building fees paid by the students.

In each case, the revision is easier for the reader to process and understand because it eliminates padding and repetition and because the relationship between ideas is easier to see. Through transforming and tightening, the ideas being expressed have been brought under better control.

Sentence Strategies

In general, writers who consciously begin to combine sentences are going to produce longer and more complex sentences. Usually, those combination sentences are better, more efficient sentences than the originals, but no writer should, for that reason, begin to assume that long sentences are good in themselves, or are necessarily better than short ones. Sometimes short ones do the job well, and sometimes a writer will deliberately use a series of short sentences to speed up the rhythm of writing, to catch the reader's attention, or because the intended audience might be intimidated by a series of long sentences. And sometimes by using short sentences, one can create a tone that would be difficult to duplicate with long sentences. For instance:

In winter the warehouse is cold and damp. There is no heat. The large steel doors that line the warehouse walls stay open most of the day. In the cold months, wind, rain, and snow blow across the floor. In the summer the warehouse becomes an oven.[3]

But people who aspire to be competent writers have to learn to construct a variety of sentences and to make intelligent judgments about sentence length. Unfortunately there are no simple rules to go by; however, here are some guidelines that may be useful.

3. Patrick Fenton, "Confessions of a Working Stiff," *New York* Magazine, April 1973, p. 78.

Vary your sentence length. A paragraph made up entirely of long, or even middle-length sentences tends to get dull and monotonous. The eyes— and the inner ear—welcome an occasional short sentence to break the monotony. For example, here is a paragraph that begins with short sentences, moves through a series of information-packed middle length sentences, and culminates in a long and skillfully constructed complex sentence.

> Then, in the forties, came affluence. Money. It was not the solution to what ailed them, but to men and women who had been poor all their lives it offered a novel escape. Until the forties, a great many Texans *had* been poor all their lives, and when they began to come into money it was natural that they should over-rate it and expect the wrong things of it. They had imagined it would make them happier with one another, and they resented one another all the more when it didn't. Men made money and women spent it. If one spent unstintingly, sexual poverty might be disguised. . . . New houses, new cars, new clothes, wall-to-wall carpets and wall-to-wall bric-a-brac, gadgets and appliances, living room sets so uniformly ghastly one would have liked to burn the factory that made them, these were the order of the day in the forties.[4]

Another reason for varying sentence length is that stringing a series of long complex and compound sentences together makes your writing seem *dense,* particularly if those sentences are loaded with a lot of prepositional phrases. (By dense I mean difficult to process and absorb.)

One has to realize also that many readers are intimidated just by looking at a paragraph made up of 30–40 word sentences, particularly if those sentences have little internal punctuation. They just assume that the passage will be hard to read, just as one assumes that a paragraph that runs for an entire page will be hard to read.

Keep long sentences readable by providing frequent closure. This principle, already mentioned on p. 93, emphasizes once more that readers process language better when it is divided into manageable units for them. Closure comes at the point in a sentence when the reader makes sense of a group of words; that group can be a phrase, a clause, or the entire sentence. If a writer constructs a sentence in which the reader must hold a large number of words and phrases suspended in the mind before he or she can discover the meaning of them, then that sentence is going to be harder to read than one that might be longer but is made up of a series of units that make sense in themselves. In the following sentences, which are about the same length, the first is comparatively easy to read because it divides into self-contained units. The second one is more difficult because the reader must go a long way before being able to discover the point of what he or she is reading.

> If you wanted to find a woman in New York who had made it on her own, someone who had raised her children and paid her bills and made her job work, someone

---

4. Larry McMurtry, *In a Narrow Grave* (New York: Simon and Schuster, 1968), p. 70.

who had done all this and grown stronger and more interesting with the years, you couldn't find a better specimen than Sylvia.[5]

The power of parents to influence their children—the power to mold them, the power to make them do things and prevent them from doing things—according to their wishes is an aspect of a more general capacity which all human beings have, the capacity for witchcraft.[6]

Use a majority of comparatively short sentences when writing for an audience who is unfamiliar with your topic or whose reading skills may be poor, or when you are writing something to be read aloud. By comparatively short, I mean sentences from 10 to 25 words in length. Given the same subject matter, short sentences are usually easier to read and understand. And when writing speeches and oral presentations, an author needs to be acutely conscious that the audience cannot go back and reread what they don't grasp the first time; therefore writing short, carefully constructed and tightly connected sentences with frequent closures may make the difference as to whether one will lose or hold an audience.

Have some plan in mind for key sentences before you begin to write them. Probably a writer should not try to plan each sentence out before starting to write it; that would inhibit discovery and experimentation. Nevertheless, you ought to have some idea what you want to do in key sentences when you begin to write them. Are you going to start out with a qualification and then go to the main clause? Are you going to write a definition or give a straight statement of fact? Are you going to give a series of examples, or contrast two points? Try rehearsing different openings in your mind and thinking about how you might develop them. And although sometimes you will discover exactly what you want to say only at the point of utterance, it's not a good idea to depend totally on inspiration to construct your sentence for you. Too frequently that method will produce a rambling, confusing sentence in which the reader cannot figure out purpose or relationships.

Sentence Punctuation

Just as inexperienced writers sometimes let their anxiety about the rules of sentence structure prevent them from trying to express complex ideas, they also sometimes allow their fear of making punctuation mistakes keep them from attempting the sentences they would like to write. You do need to know a few rules of punctuation in order to mark off your sentences so that your readers can process them efficiently, but they are neither mysterious nor difficult to master. Here are the most important ones.

5. Ellen Goodman, *Turning Points* (Garden City, N.Y.: Doubleday, 1979), p. 277.
6. Claude M. Steiner, *Scripts People Live* (New York: Bantam Books, 1975), p. 76.

Use a comma to mark off an introductory subordinate clause. Although this rule does not always have to be followed, it is a good idea to get in the habit of putting in a comma when you come to the end of a qualifying or modifying clause at the opening of a sentence. For example:

> Although the flood damage was not as bad as expected, the insured losses ran into millions of dollars.

> After all the problems were solved and the satellite was launched, the engineers breathed a sigh of relief.

The longer your introductory subordinate clause, the more important it is that you mark it off so that your reader can see the divisions of your sentence.

Usually use commas to mark off introductory words or phrases that put important qualifications on your sentence. For instance:

> Nevertheless, she will serve out her term of office.
> On the whole, nonsmokers live longer than smokers.
> In spite of this, the scores continue to fall.

Subordinate clauses and qualifying phrases that come *after* the main sentence usually do not have to be marked off with a comma. for instance:

> We will begin our research next summer if we get the grant.
> Martin will not take the job in spite of that.

Use commas to mark off appositives, that is, inserted phrases or words that give additional information. For example,

> Harvard, *the oldest university in the United States,* is also one of the best.

> Faulkner, *an American Nobel prize winner,* has never been a popular novelist with the general public.

> Kissinger, *a Jew,* often supported Arab causes.

> Harrods, *a department store,* is famous all over the world.

Use commas to mark off nonessential relative clauses, that is, clauses that give additional information about a noun, but are not absolutely necessary to the sense of the sentence. For example:

> The Swiss, *who are reputed to be the thriftiest people in Europe,* have a high standard of living.

> Karl Marx, *who was a prophet before his time,* did not live to see his doctrines become widely accepted.

> Iowa, *that bastion of conservatism,* sometimes elects women to office.

But relative clauses that are essential, that is, clauses that must be in the sentence for it to convey the meaning, should *not* be marked off by commas. For instance:

Drivers *who do not renew their insurance* will not be allowed to register their cars.

Drama courses *that do not include movies and television* are obsolete.

In general, mark off parts of a sentence that cause significant interruptions with commas or dashes. Dashes are useful to indicate to the reader that you are taking a momentary detour but are coming back. For instance:

If literary critics wrote novels themselves—and they almost never do —readers might taken them more seriously.

When one takes any hobby seriously—photography, sailing, bird watching, or skiing—it usually becomes expensive.

Set off with a comma a modifying clause that comes at the end of a sentence. For example:

He planned to travel everywhere but West Texas, a place he never wanted to see again.

Emerging nations always want to improve transportation, an industry closely related to defense.

Put a comma before *the conjunction that connects two independent clauses.*

The governor of New York has been sharply criticized by the press, but he intends to run for election again.

Laughlin was a witness for the defense, and some people think he was bribed.

Sometimes sentences don't really require a comma in such constructions, but you probably should form the habit of putting one in to avoid the confusion that might result if the reader were to miss the pause and run on into the next phrase.

Use a semicolon to join closely related independent clauses. For example.

A few years ago a two-income family was unusual; today it is commonplace.

Jones is not politically sophisticated; he understands neither patronage nor party platforms.

The problem is not how we can prosper; it is how we can survive.

One could divide any of these compound sentences into two simple sentences, but the construction would not be as tight.

Use semicolons to join a series of clauses that have internal punctuation that might cause confusion. For example:

The people who signed the contract were George White, the architect and builder; Phyllis Young, the woman who had given the money for the building; John Graves, formerly associated with Buckminster Fuller, the noted inventor; and Tom Eggerton, a developer and banker, formerly of Dallas.

The board must take several problems into account: the price of oil, especially imported oil; the shortage of skilled workers in the area; the unstable political situation in India, where most of the raw material will come from; and a possible increase in taxes on exports from that country.

Use a colon in a sentence to introduce a series or to indicate that an explanation will follow. For Example:

They will have four cities from which to choose for the convention: Denver, San Francisco, Houston, and New York.

Cartright has only one requirement of his employees: loyalty.

The purpose of professional associations is dual: to maintain standards within the profession, and to lobby for special interest bills.

Common Sense about Punctuation.

Writers need to master these conventions primarily because, like any other activity, writing becomes easier when one knows the chief rules well enough to quit worrying about them. Practicing writers should also know, however, that in nonschool writing situations, attitudes about punctuation are relaxing. In magazines, books, and many business documents, one simply sees fewer commas than most usage handbooks would have one think are necessary. For example:

Women strong or otherwise accounted for a good part of the snuff consumed in Texas and elsewhere until not too long ago. But female dippers were dwindling in numbers even when I was a kid, and in the present degenerate day when sexiness up to the age of 75 or so is an apparent common aim, the practice seems to be confined mainly to a few ancient and unreconstructedly country types.[7]

7. John Graves, ''The Snuff of Dreams,'' *Texas Monthly,* October 1978, p. 200.

A strict grammarian would have put commas around the phrase "strong or otherwise," and before "when sexiness . . ." to set off that subordinate clause. Editors, however—and they are the people who gradually modify the rules about grammar—seem to follow a policy of getting rid of commas if the writing is clear without them. If you don't want to take that risk, or if the person evaluating your writing is a strict constructionist, stay with the handbook. That's certainly the safe way.

If, however you want to approach punctuation from a pragmatic point of view, I would suggest two guidelines. First, *put in commas to mark natural pauses and junctures in your writing,* places where the reader needs to stop to absorb the words or become aware of a logical division. So when you are listing items in a series, you need commas between them so they won't seem connected to each other. You also need them after most introductory clauses so that the reader can grasp the qualification or context.

Second, set off with commas elements that interrupt the flow of a sentence. Such elements are usually appositives, nonessential phrases or clauses, explanatory words or phrases, terms of address, and many signal words such as *nevertheless, for example, consequently,* and the like. Remember that the sole purpose of punctuation is to help the reader; therefore you should put in commas at places that, if they were left unmarked, the reader might get confused.

And remember the semicolon. It can rescue you from many punctuation dilemmas.

Fragments and Minor Sentences

Just as today's editors and practicing writers are relaxing their attitudes about punctuation, they are also becoming more tolerant about sentence fragments, that old bugaboo of traditional grammarians. In years past amateur writers have thought—and with good cause—that they must never violate that well-known rule, "Always write in complete sentences." A complete sentence was defined as one that had a subject and verb and expressed a complete thought.

In many writing situations, writers would still do well to abide by the familiar rule. My survey of professional people's response to lapses from standard usage (see page 244) revealed that more than 65 percent of them said that they would object strongly to finding these sentence fragments in writing that came across their desks.

He went through a long battle. A fight against unscrupulous opponents.

The small towns are dying. One of the problems being that young people are leaving.

44 percent said they would object strongly to the following sentence fragment, and 32 percent said they would object a little.

> Cheap labor and low costs. These are two benefits enjoyed by Taiwan firms.

I think one must conclude from this evidence that most people in decision-making positions want the writing they see to conform to the rules for sentences that they learned in school.

But any person who notices sentence structure as he or she reads contemporary writing will recognize dozens of groups of words that are punctuated as sentences but don't fit the definition just given. They occur not only in advertising where they are used for their eye-catching, emphatic effect, but in expository prose at both ends of the literary spectrum. For example:

> It's fashionable to knock TV news. Always has been. Thirty years ago, the news on television was amateurish. Not much different from newsreels. Superficial. Today, it's slick. Too many Adonises and Venuses posing as reporters. It's also too controversial. Or not controversial enough. Too liberal. Too conservative. Too heavy on foreign news. Too heavy on local news. Just headlines.[8]

> This millionaire—in real estate, antiquities, and royalties—who came out of the austere world of the early pioneers, the first child born in the first kibbutz. Sullen, introverted, impatient with his fellow mortals. Too easily bored. "Charismatic" in a country in which that designation, in the eyes of many, is a compliment. Feline, artful, a notorious womanizer, yet probably without a single close friend: incapable of companionship among equals. Emotionally blocked, estranged from his sons as he himself had been from his father. A lover of power, money, good food, fast cars, and all manner of creature comforts. Acquisitive.[9]

Obviously both these passages work, and work well. They communicate their ideas clearly, economically, and forcefully, yet they employ almost no traditional sentences; the second one has none.

The puzzled student writer might well ask why these writers feel free to use sentence fragments when traditionally they are considered unacceptable. The answer, I think, is that the so-called fragments that these writers use are not really incomplete groups of words; rather they are what one team of modern grammarians call "minor sentences" or "formal fragments." This new definition recognizes that when we can read a group of words and make sense out of it, we mentally process it as a sentence whether or not it has all those elements that a sentence is traditionally supposed to have. Or to put it another way, readers can sometimes reach closure at the end of a group of words even if that group does not have a subject or verb; when that happens, that group

8. Edward Bliss, Jr., "There Is Good Journalism on TV," *TV Guide,* 15 July 1978, p. 39.
9. Amos Elon, *New York Times Book Review,* 14 January 1979, p. 3.

can be marked off with a period and called a "minor sentence." [10] It is a legitimate division of writing.

Groups of words that really are sentence fragments, that is, incomplete pieces of a coherent whole, are those that *don't* work by themselves. There may be several reasons why they leave the reader in suspense. They may begin an idea and not carry it through, they may express only part of an idea and thus confuse the reader, or they may form a phrase or clause that does not makes sense by itself and yet is not attached to anything else. Here are some typical examples:

> There are few assertions in the article and little evidence to support them. *An example being, "It is unclear whether these intruders had anything to do with the crime."*

The italicized words here need to be attached to a base; although they are punctuated as a sentence, they make no sense by themselves.

> Unlike doctors, lawyers are ready to practice when they get their degrees. *Although it is often necessary to take an expensive course in order to pass the bar exam.*

The italicized portion should be joined with the sentence; otherwise the "although" raises expectations that the writer does not meet.

> To understand how all knowledge is related. That is the goal of a liberal education.

The writer would get a more economical sentence by starting out, "The goal of a liberal education is. . . ."

> Harrison lived out a legend in his own time. *A man who came from nowhere and created a billion dollar business empire.*

The italicized portion here is really an appositive and doesn't work well standing by itself.

Probably the best guideline to keep in mind about writing sentence fragments is that if you are in doubt, don't use them. And if you do use them, be sure you are constructing minor sentences that convey a finished idea, not broken-off sentences that puzzle or annoy your audience. If you punctuate a group of words as a sentence, but realize it leaves your reader in suspense or seems not to fit with anything, then attach it to a sentence or rewrite it.

Also, when you make decisions about using minor sentences or word groups that are technically sentence fragments, think carefully about your au-

10. Charles R. Kline, Jr., and W. Dean Memering, "Formal Fragments: The English Minor Sentence," *Research in the Teaching of English* (Fall 1977), p. 97.

dience and your purpose. Not only professionals, but also professors, particularly English professors, usually prefer that you write straightforward, traditional sentences that will convey your meaning efficiently and not raise any distracting usage problems. Many other audiences, such as a supervisor reading a report or an evaluation committee reading a proposal, feel the same way because, as with most educated readers, their school background has conditioned them to react against sentence fragments. The thoughtful writer knows and respects those attitudes. So if you want to be sure that a serious piece of explanatory or persuasive writing gets a careful, unprejudiced reading from a serious audience, avoid writing fragments.

If, however, you are writing descriptive prose in which you want to communicate impressions or if you are writing an informal, breezy article for a general audience, you may find that putting in an occasional minor sentence or fragment will help to create the tone and tempo that you want. If so, don't be afraid to try using them. Often they are appropriate and effective. But do know what you are doing, and in a writing class, be prepared to defend your choices.

E X E R C I S E S / *Prewriting Activities*

1 Join these pairs of simple sentences into one complex or compound sentence using linking words that will show the relationship between the contents of the clauses. For example, you could join

Almost every math problem is workable if the student has mastered college-level skills.
The skills themselves are not tested.

    into

Although every math problem is workable if the student has mastered college level skills, those skills are not tested.

    Pair 1
The problems must be worked in an average time of 21 seconds each.
Most students must glance quickly at the problem and then randomly select one of five answers.

    Pair 2
Even if he failed in his effort, he knew that he had made an attempt.
It gave him a sense of control over his life.

    Pair 3
A bill similar to the one passed in New York has been introduced in the Texas legislature.

Both houses are unlikely to act until the consequences of the New York law are evident.

Pair 4
An important part of student life involves meeting new people.
It is equally important that you be wary when dealing with new acquaintances.

2   Combine these groups of sentences into one more tightly packed sentence. First, review the sentence-combining options on page 132.

The brochure will be distributed in the Student Health Center.
It supplies information about nutrients that people should include in their diet.
The brochure is a service of the American Medical Association.

There is an old theory that used car dealers aren't to be trusted.
To a certain extent this is true.

In school, teachers allow little boys to be aggressive and domineering.
Girls are taught to be sweet, quiet, and courteous.

They had no knowledge of cultivation of crops.
They had no word in their vocabulary for sea or boat or war.
They had never tasted salt or smoked tobacco.

Procrastination is an avoidance technique.
It can be cured.
There are psychologists on campus who can help you.
They have devised study programs to help you budget your time and set goals.

3   Punctuate these sentences in a way that will help the reader comprehend their meaning.

A.   At the same time the doctor urges that therapy be used as a form of punishment not imprisonment in "dangerous and miserable" conditions but punishment that will effectively rehabilitate the individual.

B.   Surely we cannot expect the U.S. and the USSR which have known nothing but fear for each other since the first World War to completely let down their defenses and enter into a trusting relationship.

C.   Inflation robs the dollar of its worth naturally causing higher prices of goods and services and affecting all sorts of investments even so-called gilt-edged securities.

D.   Gold has become an anxiety investment and as long as the world is upset by political and economic uncertainty investors will turn to gold for reassurance and tranquility.

4   Decide which of the italicized word groups are effective minor sentences and which are broken sentences that do not function effectively.

A.   *Low wages and cheap energy.* These are the natural resources of Brazil.

B.   You should not depend on living on your pension. *Even though it seems adequate.*

C.   He fought an exhausting battle. *A battle against corruption, indifference, and cynicism.*

D.   The candidate was nervous about voter apathy. *That being the most serious problem in her district.*

E.   Trying to prove his point, he overstated his case. *Which was not very well thought out in the first place.*

Suggested Writing Assignments

As a part of each writing assignment write a detailed analysis of your audience and specify the characteristics they would have that you need to keep in mind as you write, the problems such an audience might present, and what the audience would expect to get from reading your paper. Also analyze your purpose in writing, specifying what you hope to accomplish with the paper. If appropriate, include an accurate and descriptive title for your paper.

Topic 1:
Imagine that you work for a local bank that sponsors one of the two major credit cards—Mastercharge or Visa—and your boss has asked you to write a brochure of not more than 600 words that the bank will give to people who come in to apply for a credit card. The brochure should both educate and promote; that is, the bank wants people to become credit-card customers, but it also wants them to use the cards intelligently and responsibly. Your job is to write a positive but cautionary brochure that explains how credit cards work and what problems people sometimes have in using them. Think carefully about your audience.

Topic 2:
You own 50 acres of land 25 miles from a major city—e.g., Chicago, St. Louis, Dallas, Minneapolis—and other property owners in your area want to have the land zoned to limit development to no more than one dwelling per five acres. They are trying to persuade the county commissioners to call an

election to pass such an ordinance, which would effectively stop owners from selling their property for subdivisions. The county commissioners are under heavy pressure from both sides and have not yet decided whether they want to bring the issue to a head by putting it on the ballet. Write to the commissioners arguing for or against holding such an election.

Topic 3:

You are a state senator's administrative aide, responsible for doing research on problems that may become political issues in the next legislative session. The senator has asked you to research and report on a one-block area of substandard housing close to the capitol. Some civic leaders are saying that it should be razed because it is so unsightly that it gives people a bad impression of the city. The residents of the area, however, contend that with a subsidy from the state they could repair and paint their houses, and that the state would be doing them serious harm to condemn and tear down their homes.

The senator wants not your opinion, but facts on which to base a decision. Make your report as specific, brief, and objective as you can and still give the senator adequate information on which to act.

8 *Paragraphs*

Why Paragraphs?

Skillful writers realize that the length of their paragraphs and the way those paragraphs are arranged affect the readability of their prose. Not only do length and arrangement affect the rate at which a reader can process and comprehend writing, but they may also determine whether a person decides that he or she is going to read a piece of writing at all. For instance, you may have had the experience of thumbing through a book or magazine article and feeling intimidated when you encountered several pages of unbroken print. Most readers react the same way to even one page of unbroken print.

Thus writers paragraph partly for purely visual reasons, to reassure readers that the material is divided into manageable units that they are going to be able to handle without strain. Those divisions may also have other psychological effects because by breaking writing into divisions that readers perceive as separate units, an author signals to those readers that he or she does not intend to overload their information processing circuits; rather the writer is trying to present material in modest portions that can be easily assimilated.

Good writers make decisions about paragraphing partly on what they know about their audiences. When they are writing for general audiences with varied educational backgrounds—say, the readers of *Family Circle* or *TV Guide*—they write shorter paragraphs than they would for more sophisticated audiences—say, the readers of *Scientific American* or the *Atlantic*. Probably their reasoning is that the audience for the two latter publications is made up of practiced readers who can handle larger units of discourse and are less apt to be intimidated by seeing long paragraphs.

These examples illustrate extremes, but a writer trying to meet the needs of an audience can draw helpful conclusions from them. If your audience is made up principally of unsophisticated or inexperienced readers, keep your paragraphs short, that is, from five to seven sentences, perhaps even fewer. If you have a well-educated audience of habitual readers, you can extend your paragraphs to eight to ten sentences or more.

Most people who write proposals, reports, brochures, position papers, environmental statements, or working documents for either general or specialized audiences favor comparatively short paragraphs just as they favor comparatively short sentences. By "comparatively short" I mean paragraphs of seven or eight sentences, paragraphs that do not fill up an entire column or printed page. One can find many exceptions, of course, but in general editors and writers of nonfiction seem to believe that most audiences want their reading divided at frequent intervals, and so they use these divisions.

Avoiding One-Sentence Paragraphs.

Unfortunately, some mass-market writers let their enthusiasm for short paragraphs carry them to the extreme of habitually writing a series of one- or two-sentence paragraphs that are really not paragraphs at all. They are only separated sentences. For example:

> Once upon a time there was a little girl in a small town in South Dakota who dreamed of speaking French.
>
> So when she grew up and went off to college, a prestigious school in the East, she was ready for her dream to come true.
>
> "I had a miserable French teacher—I was disappointed," recalled Ann Clark, the chef behind Austin's La Bonne Cuisine School of French cooking. "So I dropped out of school and a girlfriend and I went to France."
>
> There the two worked as *au pair* girls, live-in housekeepers earning some money and gaining an entry to the ethos of France that had seemed so inviting.[1]

Although writers for newspapers construct such short paragraphs because the narrow columns of a newspaper make long ones look intimidating, this kind of writing is choppy and hard to follow; the reader has to jump from one point to another without any help from an organizing pattern or from connectors. It also violates the fundamental principle that underlies paragraphs in the first place; that is, they are units of discourse that develop ideas.

That principle does not mean that you should never use one-sentence paragraphs. Sometimes they serve the useful function of emphasizing a point, and sometimes they can act as a transition from one paragraph to another. Usually, however, skillful writers avoid writing one-sentence paragraphs because they are distracting and disrupt the reader's train of thought.

Guidelines for Breaking Paragraphs

The traditional rule for paragraphing says that you should start a new paragraph when you begin to discuss a new idea or topic. Although this rule is useful as far it goes, it does not cover all the decisions that a writer must make

1. Carolyn Bobo, "France Makes Rich Life for Cook," *Austin American-Statesman,* 21 December 1978, p. G–1.

about paragraphing. For example, one topic might require several pages of explanation, but commonsense would tell most writers that they should not write three-page paragraphs.

A better guideline, then, is that you *can* start a new paragraph when introducing a new topic, but you can also start a new paragraph when you come to a place in which you want to indicate a time or space separation or when you sense you are making a slight shift in direction. When you sense that you have reached closure with a group of sentences, you can probably also make a paragraph break.

For example, notice that it is possible to break up the following paragraph at the points indicated without seriously affecting the unity of the prose.

Our national veterans policy seems to be misguided. Most people will agree that public expenditures for former soldiers should go primarily to assist those who have been injured in military service and to help bring the men fresh from war back into the fold. But federal policy tends to spread benefits thinly, so that a great many get something to be grateful for (presumably they will reward their legislators at election time). Meanwhile the relative few whose needs are truly related to military service tend to get short shrift. / The situation will probably get worse. Under existing law, the hospital system remains open to all veterans. Those over 65 not only have a statutory entitlement to VA medical care regardless of financial need, but they are also eligible to receive VA pensions. There are 13 million World War II veterans. Their average age is 56. According to very rough estimates, the annual cost of pensions could rise from about $3.5 billion in 1978 to about $7.5 billion in 1995. / Senator Alan Cranston is attempting reform, but the reformed program would also be expensive and would still constitute a large welfare program just for veterans. Aside from the question of whether or not existing policies and such possible reforms are fair to nonveteran Americans is the question of how great a burden the World War II veterans are going to place on the VA's substantial but finite resources. If the VA's energies are increasingly directed toward this group, which has been described as "a wave about to break," what will happen if there is another war anytime soon?[2]

Each created subdivision still makes a separate point, and it groups together sentences that are necessary to the development of that point.

Paragraph Development

The crucial quality of a good paragraph is unity. It has boundaries, and the reader can move smoothly from one sentence to the next, sensing that each flows naturally from the one that precedes it. There are no unpleasant surprises, no disappointments; readers find in the latter part of the paragraph what the earlier part led them to expect.

2. Tracy Kidder, "Soldiers of Misfortune," *The Atlantic,* March 1978, p. 87.

But how do writers go about constructing these ideal paragraphs? Probably they do it partially by using their trained intuition, by following one or more of the typical thought patterns discussed in chapter 4. They write deductive paragraphs that begin with generalizations and draw inferences; they write inductive paragraphs that begin with examples and move to a conclusion. They write cause and effect paragraphs, narrative paragraphs. paragraphs describing process. or paragraphs built around analogies. And they write paragraphs that seem to mix two or three patterns. Here are some examples of a variety of patterns.

DEDUCTIVE PARAGRAPH:

It is virtually impossible for twentieth-century people to imagine the enormous job of food preparation in colonial times. Cooking was done on an open hearth that had to be tended constantly. Kettles, made of iron, often weighed forty pounds. Without refrigeration, meats had to be preserved by salting or pickling. Rich and spicy sauces were the style, since they were needed to preserve food or to cover the taste of food that had been badly preserved. Women kept their own gardens, every fall putting up vast amounts of home-grown vegetables and fruit. They ran home bakeries and dairies, did the milking, made butter, and kept the hen yard.[3]

CAUSE AND EFFECT PARAGRAPH:

According to the linguistic school currently on top, human beings are all born with a genetic endowment for recognizing and formulating language. This must mean that we possess genes for all kinds of information, with strands of special, peculiarly human DNA for the discernment of meaning in syntax. We must imagine the morphogenesis of deep structures, built into our minds, for coding out, like proteins, the parts of speech. Correct grammar (correct in the logical, not fashionable, sense) is as much a biologic characteristic of our species as feathers on birds.[4]

NARRATIVE PARAGRAPH:

During the week, her husband didn't get home in time to help prepare dinner. What's more he hated a mess in the kitchen. It drove him nuts, he said, when she had an evening class and left the dishes soaking in the sink when she went out. He got mad every time he walked into that messy kitchen to take a beer out of the fridge. After all, he sometimes yelled, it was the wife's *duty* to keep the house clean! When he came home from that hectic office where he made the money they lived on, he had a right to expect a clean house, peace and quiet, and some tender loving care.[5]

ANALOGY PARAGRAPH:

The writing teacher must not be a judge, but a physician. His job is not to punish, but to heal. Most students are bad writers, but the more serious the injuries, the more

3. Carol Hymowitz and Michaele Weissman, *A History of Women in America* (New York: Bantam Books, 1978), p. 5.
4. Lewis Thomas, *The Lives of a Cell* (New York: Penguin Books, 1978), p. 91.
5. Betty Friedan, ''Does Equality for Women Have to Threaten Men?'' *Family Circle,* 20 February 1979, p. FC4.

confusing the symptoms, the greater the need for effective diagnostic work. When an accident victim is carried into the hospital emergency ward, the doctor does not start treating the patient at the top and slowly work down without a sense of priority, spending a great deal of time on the black eye before he gets to the punctured lung. Yet that is exactly what the English teacher too often does. The doctor looks for the most vital problem; he wants to keep the patient alive, and he goes to work on the critical injury.[6]

INDUCTIVE PARAGRAPH:

When combat threatens, the caveman reaction occurs. The heart starts beating faster; blood pressure rises; the digestive system slows down; and numerous other changes take place, all automatic and all aimed against the enemy. These changes occur not only to an infantryman in combat, but to a child frightened by strange noises in the night, to boys fighting on the playground, and to men and women caught up in the rarefied game of office politics. The changes are useful to the infantryman and to the boys; but they only make the frightened child more fearful, and in the long run they can have a deadly effect on the ambitious person trying to outmaneuver competitors. These are physical changes designed to facilitate physical action. When we need to fight or run, they help us, but when we don't, they still occur—and if the emergency doesn't pass, if the threat isn't met and solved, these changes persist and become chronic, wearing out the motor of the body without taking us anywhere.[7]

You could also use a comparison/contrast pattern either within a paragraph or to alternate between paragraphs.

Probably the truth is that most of the time writers don't consciously plan what kind of paragraphs they are going to write any more than they plan what kind of sentences they are going to write. Rather they begin with an idea and think in terms of developing that statement. Then they choose their methods of development according to their audience and purpose. They realize that sometimes they need to catch the reader's attention with details and gradually work into the thesis; other times they need to stress the main point by putting it first. And if they cannot seem to find a pattern, they may mentally review their options in the effort to find a way to get started. Less experienced writers can use the same approach: start out by trusting your organizational instincts, but if they seem not to be working well, pick out one of the traditional methods of development and try it. It helps to know that you have a system to fall back on when inspiration fails, as it frequently does with every writer.

Commitment and Coherence

But regardless of how they work out problems of development, all writers need to keep two requirements for paragraphs in mind as they write: first, they

6. Donald Murray, *A Writer Teaches Writing* (Boston: Houghton Mifflin, 1968), p. 91.
7. Walter McQuade and Ann Aikman, *Stress* (New York: Bantam Books, 1975), p. 7.

should make commitments and then meet them, and, second, every sentence in a paragraph should fit into the pattern of that paragraph.

Making a commitment or promise to the reader at the beginning of a paragraph or essay or report is one major way in which writers hold their readers' attention and keep them from getting lost. The commitment sentence or paragraph guides the readers' expectations and they continue reading in order to fulfill these expectations. They are satisfied if they get the information or explanation they expected, and they are frustrated if they don't. So the writer's obligation is always to do what he or she contracted to do: meet the commitment.

Kinds of Commitments.

Commitments in paragraphs take many forms. (I have italicized commitment sentences in the following examples.) They can take the form of a *generative sentence,* one that suggests more details will follow. For example:

Even if Mother had not been such a pretty woman, light-skinned with straight hair, he was lucky to get her and he knew it. She was educated, from a well-known family, and after all, wasn't she born in St. Louis? Then she was gay. She laughed all the time and made jokes. He was grateful. I think he must have been many years older than she, but if not, he had the sluggish inferiority of old men married to younger women. He watched her every move and when she left the room, his eyes allowed her reluctantly to go.[8]

Commitments can also take the form of a *question that the writer undertakes to answer.* For example:

What functions do dreams serve today? One view, published in a reputable scientific paper, holds that the function of dreams is to wake us up a little, every now and then, to see if anyone is about to eat us. But dreams occupy such a relatively small part of normal sleep that this explanation does not seem very compelling. Moreover, as we have seen, the evidence points the other way: today it is the mammalian predators, not the mammalian prey, who characteristically have dream-filled sleep. Much more plausible is the computer-based explanation that dreams are a spillover from the unconscious processing of the day's experience, from the brain's decision on how much of the daily events temporarily stored in a kind of buffer to emplace in long term memory. The events of yesterday frequently run through my dreams; the events of two days ago, much more rarely. However, the buffer-dumping model seems unlikely to be the whole story, because it does not explain the disguises that are so characteristic of the symbolic language of dreams, a point first stressed by Freud. It also does not explain the power affect or emotions of dreams; I believe there are many people who have been far more thoroughly frightened by their dreams than by anything they have ever experienced while awake.[9]

8. Maya Angelou, *I Know Why the Caged Bird Sings* (New York: Bantam Books, 1971), p. 58.
9. Carl Sagan, *The Dragons of Eden* (New York: Ballantine Books, 1977), pp. 151–52.

Notice that the author also makes and fulfills commitments *within* the paragraph; he mentions and responds to three theories about dreams.

Another way a writer can make a commitment is to *start a narrative* in the first sentence, thus conditioning the reader to expect the narrative to continue. For example,

> *But as a boy I idolized him for the connection with America-at-large that he had made as a painter on the Union Pacific Railroad.* He had gone West with the railroad, had been offered a homestead, had seen the great country that my illiterate housebound mother would never know. I lovingly enlarged every morsel of our walks to museums, parks, libraries; our working-class solidarity, father and son, as he described great labor struggles and the struggle for Socialism—in my childhood the only Jewish religion that could take him out of himself. I saw him break down when Eugene V. Debs died, when Robert M. La Follette lost the Presidency, when Sacco and Vanzetti went to the chair.[10]

Here are two inductive paragraphs that make their commitment by *opening with descriptive anecdotes,* which lead the reader to anticipate an explanation.

> A New York cabdriver jams on his brakes as a car bearing Iowa license plates runs a red light on Forty-second Street. The cabbie's eyes bulge, he bites his lower lip, and then he stabs viciously upward with the middle finger of his right hand. He doesn't say a word, but his message could not be clearer if he shouted it.

> A Hollywood starlet appears on a television commercial for mattresses. As she looks meltingly into the eye of the camera, she allows her tongue to protrude slightly between her teeth, and slowly slides it over her lips. Lying down on the mattress, she cants her hips forward and stretches sensuously as a cat. Her message could not be clearer if she whispered it.[11]

So writers can choose a variety of ways to communicate their promises to the reader. The important point is to follow through on the promise, not to leave the reader dangling or puzzled because the sentences that followed the commitment did not do what the reader had been led to expect. For instance, here is an opening paragraph from a student theme that frustrates the reader's expectations:

> Most students at major universities across the country are financially supported by their parents. With the rise in tuition and the cost of living, parents must find different ways of saving money to send their children to college. But more and more students rely on this money with the thought, "Well, there's more where this came from." I feel that this impractical attitude and constant spending spree by college-age adults can be changed.

The opening sentence is a statement of fact that could lead somewhere, but it doesn't. Because the second sentence is not related, the reader is thrown off

10. Alfred Kazin, *New York Jew* (New York: Alfred A. Knopf, 1978), p. 10.
11. Albert C. Wassmer, "Talking to People without Words," *Cosmopolitan*, October 1978, p. 146.

the track and only begins to pick up the thread again at the end of the paragraph.

Downshifting.

Another important way in which writers meet their commitments to their readers is by creating discernible patterns within and among paragraphs. Often they create those patterns simply by following a certain method of development: cause and effect or comparison/contrast, for example. Other times they create them by using a writing technique called *downshifting,* already mentioned on page 107. This technique was given its name by discourse analyst Francis Christensen, who pointed out that "when sentences are added to develop a topic or subtopic, they are usually added at a lower *level of generality.*"[12] Downshifting thus is a metaphor that compares moving down the ladder of abstraction (see page 104) to shifting into a lower gear when driving. And the most effective writers are those who can shift gears easily and operate at several levels of generality. They move up and down the ladder of abstraction, choosing the level of generality they need to make their meaning clear.

A paragraph diagramed to illustrate downshifting looks like this:

Although the court had forced Cullen to cough up nearly $4000 for her current medical expenses, Priscilla was strapped.
> The mansion's monthly electric bill alone was $150.00.
> The country club bills averaged $500.
> Priscilla had been forced to borrow a considerable sum of money from a bank, using her jewelry and a $23,000 Ching dynasty jade carving as collateral.
>> The jade and the jewelry (including a 16.31 carat diamond and platinum bracelet) were still in hock, and the money was almost gone.[13]

Notice that all the sentences on the second level expand on the first sentence, and the final sentence gives more information about the second level sentence just preceding it.

The following diagram shows an author moving between higher and lower levels.

Timing is very important when you buy a car.
> At the end of the month many salesmen and dealers are trying to meet a monthly quota or win some sort of monthly contest.
>> If a salesman is behind in his quota or eager to win the contest, he may give you an especially good deal.
> The best bargains are also made when business is slow.
>> The weekend is the busiest time at a dealership, so plan to make your deal early in the week.

12. Francis Christensen, *Notes toward a New Rhetoric* (New York: Harper and Row, 1967), p. 56.
13. "Solitary Confinement," *Texas Monthly,* May 1979, p. 130.

Midmorning and midafternoon are the slowest times during the day, so arrive then.

Take advantage of any time the auto industry is in a slump; it's a good time to buy.

In July, August, and September, dealers usually discount that year's models to make room for the new ones arriving in September.

However, if you do buy at the beginning of a model year, you'll have longer to use the car before taking the first year's depreciation.[14]

Other Unifying Devices

Those useful transitional terms mentioned in the earlier section on sentences (see chapter 7) also play an important part in unifying paragraphs. By signaling the relationships between the sentences of a paragraph, they help to hold it together and keep the reader moving along. But a particularly useful unifying device *within* paragraphs is the simple pronoun. By repeating a relative pronoun throughout a paragraph, a writer can hold the reader's attention while developing a point. For instance (italics added):

His head is small and compact, nut-like, with a tight rug of greying hair. *His* face is boyish and alert, the eyes blue, with sclera rinsed clear white. A bow-shaped upper lip projects over a row of small neat teeth. *He* smiles and laughs a lot, eyes puckering in crow's feet, and *he* has a habit of slapping a thigh and stamping a foot when he finds something particularly good. Standing, *he* plunges *his* hands deep in *his* pockets, shoulders hunched, head slightly tilted. *He walks like an amiable and angular Chaplin, his* feet flipping out. *His* voice is naturally high, but *he* can deepen it thunderously when mimicking.[15]

Numbers and words indicating quantity are also good unifying devices for a paragraph. If you are going to make three points, mark them with numbers. Words like *both* and *several* in the opening sentence of a paragraph also help readers to anticipate what is coming. And words like *primary, secondary, next,* and *final* also point the reader in the right direction and help to hold the sentences of a paragraph together.

In a tight and coherent paragraph, all the sentences focus on the main idea, and they follow each other in an order that seems logical and natural, each sentence evolving from the previous one. Ideally, an editor could not cut the paragraph up into separate sentences and rearrange them without affecting

14. Stephanie Kegan, "How to Outsmart the Car Salesman Trained to Outsmart You," *Self,* January 1979, p. 98.
15. Brian O'Doherty, "A Visit to Wyeth Country," in *The Art of Andrew Wyeth,* ed. Wanda Corn (San Francisco: The Fine Arts Museum, 1973), p. 14.

the meaning. So if you read over a paragraph you have written and find that the parts of it could be moved around almost randomly, like checkers on a board, you have a problem. Probably you need to start over again and try one of the modes of development discussed in chapter 4.

Opening Paragraphs

Like titles, opening paragraphs should serve three principal functions: 1) they should engage the reader's attention, 2) they should shape expectations, and 3) they should give the reader a reason to continue reading. In most cases, they should also state, or at least suggest, the commitment or promise that the writer is making to the reader. The first paragraph lays down the tracks for both reader and writer, and because it does, deserves special attention.

But it is difficult to generalize about opening paragraphs because there are almost as many different kinds of introductions as there are kinds of writing. Grant proposals require one kind, technical reports another, case studies another, and credit histories still a different kind. Writers of book or movie reviews, feature stories, travel articles, or personality profiles might use a wide variety of opening paragraphs, all of them effective. What it comes down to finally is that practical writers make decisions about their opening paragraphs only after they have identified their purpose and their audience. They know *what* they want to do in that first paragraph or two, but they decide *how* to do it according to the writing situation. And because that decision must be such a flexible one, I will touch on only a few of the many kinds of good opening paragraphs that can be used.

STRAIGHTFORWARD ANNOUNCEMENT. For many kinds of writing tasks, a writer probably does best to make the most direct, economical, and clearest opening statement that he or she can. Certainly this guideline applies to any documents whose main purpose is to convey factual information to a busy person: documents like technical reports, case studies, market analyses, grant proposals, or requests for information. In these cases, the writer shows respect for the reader by coming straight to the point because the audience for this kind of writing wants the key information as quickly as possible—no anecdotes or preliminaries. For example:

This report analyzes the data gathered from a four-year study on the composing processes of blind students at the University of Washington. Working with four students who composed their papers for an advanced writing class by using tape recorders and three students who composed with a braille typewriter, our research team gathered information that has allowed us to compare the composing habits of blind students to

those of sighted students, and to draw some useful inferences from those comparisons.[16]

Only two sentences, but they answer the questions Who, Why, When,
Where, and What, and set up a contract between writer and reader.

Equally direct opening paragraphs also work well for term papers or
other kinds of academic writing. For instance, here is the opening paragraph
from a paper done for a course in international business.

> Lockheed Aircraft and Gulf Oil were recently prosecuted by the federal govern-
> ment for giving bribes to foreign businessmen in order to make their products more at-
> tractive to those potential clients. During indictment proceedings both corporations
> contended that their cash payments were both necessary and common among interna-
> tional businesses. The question then is how common is bribery in foreign nations, and
> should the United States prevent our corporations from offering bribes even when
> doing so is a common and accepted practice?

A third kind of writing task in which a writer should usually begin with a
clear and direct statement is writing that asks for something. Although many
of us are reluctant to get to the point when we have to ask people for time or
money or favors, most of the time people prefer a straightforward request to
an indirect opening that wastes their time. Consider the psychology of the situation. If you were writing the Ford Motor Company to complain about a
faulty transmission in your new Mustang, or to Mastercharge to protest about
an incorrect billing, you would waste no time on unnecessary explanations or
introductions in the opening paragraph. You would get to the point immediately because you would be in a businesslike frame of mind and want action.
The people whom you write to ask for grants or guest lectures consider those
requests in a businesslike way too. If your request is legitimate and reasonable, you should state it quickly and clearly so the reader can deal with it in
the same way. For instance,

> On September 5 and 6 information specialists from all the state branches of the
> Missouri Mental Health and Mental Retardation Agency will meet in St. Louis for a
> two-day workshop on outpatient clinics. Since you have done so much work on this
> kind of clinic, we would like very much for you to address the workshop on the after-
> noon of September 6, speaking on any topic of your choice. We are able to offer you
> an honorarium of $250 plus your expenses.

or

> As a native Texan and a writer about Texas who has published articles in *Texas
> Monthly* and the *Houston Post,* I qualify for the J. Frank Dobie Paisano Fellowship of-
> fered each year by the Texas Institute of Arts and Letters. I am applying for that

16. Anne Gere, "The Composing Processes of Blind Students" (Paper delivered at Conference
for College Composition and Communication, April 6, 1979, Kansas City, Missouri).

fellowship and enclose copies of my articles, a biographical data sheet, and the names and addresses of several references.

OPENING ANECDOTES OR NARRATIVES.   In other writing situations, an author must find a way to entice the audience with the promise of something interesting to come. In nonschool writing situations, often the audience has no particular obligation to read what you write and will do so only if you can catch them in the first paragraph or page. Experienced freelance writers know a multitude of ways to meet this challenge, but one of the most common is the anecdote or description that draws the reader into the world that the author wants to show. For instance:

Walter Cronkite sits at his table in one of his favorite lunch places in Manhattan, the Copenhagen, watching a waiter pour akvavit straight to the rim of a small goblet set in front of him. He ponders the feat of getting the liquid to his lips without spilling it, explaining to his companion how the tension of the bubbles at the top holds the stuff in the glass, and how you know when you've had enough: when you can't drink without spilling. Behind his head is a small gold plaque initialed "C.C." for "Cronkite's Corner." On the table is a bowl of fresh dill, which is supplied only to special friends of the restaurant. Within the crowded room are a few old acquaintances to whom he nods warmly.[17]

or

Kathleen G. has two children, ages two and five. About a year ago she was waiting with them in the checkout line at the supermarket and began to feel dizzy and faint. Her heart was beating rapidly. Unable to leave the store, she asked someone to call her mother, who lived nearby, to take her and the children home. The next time she needed to get groceries, Kathleen was afraid of having another "spell" and insisted that her husband accompany her. Within several weeks she became afraid of leaving the house unless her husband would go with her. Even at home, however, she found herself feeling increasingly anxious and unable to cope with the routine tasks of running the house.[18]

These are honest, nongimmicky openings, but nevertheless they are vivid and give readers a good idea of what to expect if they continue to read.

Solving the Opening Paragraph Dilemma.

Even experienced writers often find themselves caught in a dilemma about opening paragraphs. On one hand, a good opening paragraph is critically important if you are to catch your readers and get them moving in

17. Lyn Tornabene, "Walter Cronkite Cannot Tell a Lie," *Cosmopolitan,* Oct. 1978, p. 97.
18. Carolyn Kott Washburne and Dianne L. Chambless, "Afraid to Leave the House? You May Have Agoraphobia," *Ms.,* Sept. 1978, p. 46.

the right direction; thus a careful writer puts a lot of time and thought into the introductory paragraph. On the other hand, just knowing how important that opener is can cause a writing block. Nothing you put down seems right, yet you know you have to get those tracks down and get going.

Probably the best solution to this dilemma is to remember the advice on getting started from chapter 4. Start free-writing, circling, or nutshelling to get your generative juices going. Get down something, anything that bears on your topic: a question that you intend to answer in the paper, a statement of the problem you want to solve, a sketch of a person who will figure in the paper. Even if what you write is obvious and dull, getting that first paragraph on paper where you can read it over will help. So put something down, knowing that you can certainly discard it later. When you finish, go back and take a critical look at it. If it doesn't meet those three criteria for an opening paragraph—if it does not engage, entice, or inform the reader—get rid of it and write another one. Now that you have finished with your first draft, you can almost certainly do a better job of writing the opening paragraph than you did when you started. And as a bonus, you may find that you don't need a separate introduction. The paragraph that you intended to make the second one may do very well as the first.

The Concluding Paragraph

Concluding paragraphs pose another kind of dilemma. Although one finds tremendous variety among opening paragraphs—questions, anecdotes, definitions, assertions, and so on—some patterns do emerge. Such patterns are not, however, obvious among concluding paragraphs, except for technical and business reports or proposals and case studies for which the form is traditional. In that kind of writing, the author summarizes findings and, if required, makes recommendations. Such endings are clearcut and predictable, not hard for the learning writer to conform to when necessary.

In other kinds of writing, such as persuasion or an expository academic paper, the writer often needs to restate main ideas or arguments at the end of the paper, particularly when that paper runs to 15 or 20 pages, and the reader may need to be reminded of statements made earlier. In such cases, it is a good idea to indicate to the reader that you are drawing together the threads of the argument or restating your conclusions. You can give such reminders with words or phrases such as, *finally, in conclusion, in the end, then,* or *in the final analysis*. The structure for this kind of presentation is comparable to that which a trial lawyer uses to persuade a jury: make the claim, give the evidence, sum up the findings.

For other kinds of writing—book or movie reviews, biographical essays, promotion brochures, to name just a few—writers often struggle with composing a good ending. Giving the reader a sense of closure, of completion, is important, yet often there is no point in a recapitulation or a summary that would just bore the reader. The best advice I can give is to put in some signal terms such as *finally, to conclude, last,* or *it seems then* and don't belabor points that have already been made. If you have led your reader to the conclusion of your ideas, probably it is best just to stop. The best conclusions, like the best transitions, grow out of the structure of your writing. They are not something you tack on at the end to achieve an effect.

E X E R C I S E S / *Prewriting Activities*

1 Read over these two paragraphs to see where you think you could break them without seriously interrupting the train of thought.

Bradley is one of the few basketball players who have ever been appreciatively cheered by a disinterested away-from-home crowd while warming up. This curious event occurred last March, just before Princeton eliminated the Virginia Military Institute, the year's Southern Conference champion, from the NCAA championships. The game was played in Philadelphia and was the last of a tripleheader. The people there were worn out because most of them were emotionally committed to either Villanova or Temple— two local teams that had just been involved in enervating battles with Providence and Connecticut, respectively, scrambling for a chance at the rest of the country. A group of Princeton boys shooting basketballs miscellaneously in preparation for still another game hardly promised to be a high point of the evening, but Bradley, whose routine in the warmup time is a gradual crescendo of activity, is more interesting to watch before a game than most players are in play. In Philadelphia that night, what he did was, for him, anything but unusual. As he does before all games he began by shooting set shots close to the basket, gradually moving back until he was shooting long sets from twenty feet out, and nearly all of them dropped into the net with an almost mechanical rhythm of accuracy. Then he began a series of expandingly difficult jump shots, and one jumper after another went cleanly through the basket with so few exceptions that the crowd began to murmur. Then he started to perform whirling reverse moves before another cadence of almost steadily accurate jump shots, and the murmur increased. Then he began to sweep hook shots into the air. He moved in a semicircle around the court. First with his right hand, then with his left, he tried seven of these long, graceful shots—the most difficult ones in the orthodoxy of basketball—and ambidextrously made them all. The game had not even begun, but the presumably unimpressible Philadelphians were applauding like an audience at an opera.[19]

19. John McPhee, "A Sense of Where You Are," *The John McPhee Reader*, ed. William Howarth, 2d ed. (New York: Vintage Books, 1978), pp. 2–3.

In outline it was a good plan, but it quite failed to take into account the mentality of buzzards. As soon as they were wired to the tree they all began to try and fly away. The wires prevented that, of course, but did not prevent them from falling off the limbs, where they dangled upside down, wings flopping, nether parts exposed. It is hard to imagine anything less likely to beguile a moviegoing audience than a tree full of dangling buzzards. Everyone agreed it was unaesthetic. The buzzards were righted, but they tried again, and with each try their humiliation deepened. Finally they abandoned their efforts to fly away and resigned themselves to life on their tree. Their resignation was so complete that when the scene was readied and the time came for them to fly, they refused. They had had enough of ignominy; better to remain on the limb indefinitely. Buzzards are not without patience. Profanity, firecrackers, and even a shotgun full of rock salt failed to move them. I'm told that, in desperation, a bird man was flown in from L.A. to teach the sulky bastards how to fly. The whole experience left everyone touchy. A day or so later, looking at the pictures again, I noticed a further provocative detail. The dead heifer that figured so prominently in the scene was quite clearly a steer. When I pointed this out to the still photographers they just shrugged. A steer was close enough; after all they were both essentially cows, "In essence, it's a cow," one said moodily. No one wanted those buzzards back again.[20]

2 Develop a deductive paragraph from the following opening sentence:

The student who enrolls in a pre-medical program can look forward to a grueling four years.

3 Develop a cause and effect paragraph from the following opening sentence:

After the baby boom of the sixties, the birth rate in the United States began to fall steadily.

4 Develop a narrative paragraph from the following opening sentence:

When the rock star stepped on stage, he flashed a sexy smile at all the girls in the front row.

5 Develop an inductive paragraph from the following opening sentence:

In Israel the cost of gasoline has gone to more than $3.00 a liter.

20. Larry McMurtry, "Here's HUD in Your Eye," in *In a Narrow Grave* (New York: Simon and Schuster, 1968), pp. 10–11.

6 What commitment has the writer made to the reader in these opening sentences from the paragraphs of professional writers?

"Some of us who live in arid parts of the world think about water with a reverence others might find excessive."—Joan Didion

"The weeks after graduation were filled with heady activities."—Maya Angelou

"There are, it seems, three principal states of mind in human beings: waking, sleeping, and dreaming."—Carl Sagan

7 How well does the student writer meet the opening commitment in each of these paragraphs?

Utilitarians argue that punishment is justified because it promotes utility, or the best ends for society. Punishment, they say, deters crime, incapacitates the criminal, and reforms him. It should be severe enough to provide the greatest benefit to society. If Jones is caught shoplifting, for example, he should be punished *just enough* to deter further shoplifting and to reform him. This might mean five days in jail, but certainly nothing too severe (like capital punishment) because that hurts society more than it helps.

Much of the economic strength of this country is based on mobility, and I rely on mobility through my car to make my living. The lowered speed limit has tended to endanger this economic strength, while failing to achieve the goals which it was meant to. The National Drivers Association report of Fall, 1977, stated that 14 percent of all fuel is consumed by motor vehicles, and the General Accounting Office of the United States has reported that the 55-mile-per-hour speed limit has lowered consumption by 1.8 percent, which translates to a total fuel saving of only two-tenths of one percent. The National Science Foundation and the Illinois Department of Transportation have reported that only five percent of the reduction in highway deaths are attributable to lower speeds.

8 Write a paragraph starting with one of these opening sentences and downshifting to two or three levels.

The average county jail houses an astonishing variety of lawbreakers.

Divorced fathers are getting increasingly aggressive in demanding custody of their children.

A casual observer at a California beach soon realizes most people are not there to swim.

Suggested Writing Assignments

As a part of each writing assignment write a detailed analysis of your audience and specify the characteristics they would have that you need to keep in mind as you write, the problems that such an audience might present, and what the audience would expect to get from reading your paper. Also analyze your purpose in writing, specifying what you hope to accomplish in the paper. If appropriate, include an accurate and descriptive title for your paper.

Topic 1:

An organization to which you belong is going to have its annual convention in your city, and you have been asked to serve as local arrangements chairman. Among other things, that means that you must write a letter of invitation to the convention that will go out with announcements of the convention. In that letter you want to convince people that they would enjoy visiting your city and to give them information that would help them to make up their minds about coming to the convention. You do not need to mention about hotel rates since that information would be in the announcement. You would want to point out what special events might be going on in the city at convention time, major points of interest such as art museums or zoos, shopping areas close to the hotel, well-known restaurants, and so on. If you want to keep your letter to one page, you could add a separate sheet with specific information. Probably your letter should not run to more than 350 or 400 words. Remember that the opening paragraph is particularly important.

Topic 2:

You are a married person with a young child and you and your spouse want to move into an apartment nearer your job. In looking for apartments, however, you have discovered that landlords in the neighborhood you want to live in do not allow children. Write a letter to the city council pointing out that such exclusion by landlords is grossly discriminatory and may be unconstitutional. Ask for an interpretation of current city law and suggest that an ordinance against such discrimination needs to be passed if it does not already exist.

Topic 3:

As part of your duties at the County Social Services Bureau you have the assignment of writing informative pamphlets that will be available to any clients who come into the office. Your supervisor is particularly eager to have such a pamphlet about the options that are open to young unmarried women who have problem pregnancies, because women who would not want to ask for such a pamphlet would probably pick one up if it were displayed. She asks you to write the pamphlet, specifying that it must be direct but neutral language and be simple enough for young people to understand. The brochure should not be more than 600 words.

9 *Revision*

Experienced writers who care about doing good work plan on revising almost everything they write. Like John Kenneth Galbraith, they realize that "all first drafts are deeply flawed by the need to combine composition and thought. Each later draft is less demanding in this respect." [1] They know that a writer produces polished work by spiraling through a series of stages, making changes at every stage. And each of these changes is a revision, so revising becomes part of writing itself, not a separate last step in the sequence of operations that make up the composing process.

These professional writers revise because they have a *revision* of what they have written after they have put their thoughts on paper.[2] They make changes because when they take a second—or third or fourth or fifth—look at what they are writing, they are not satisfied with what they have done, and want to alter their work in progress to match the *vision* they had when they started to write. To achieve that goal they often make both major and minor changes, sometimes rethinking and reordering substantial portions of their drafts as well as deleting, adding, and making substitutions on the word, clause, and sentence level.

In contrast, many student writers seem to have a poor grasp of what it means to revise their writing. They don't see revising as an important part of writing, and they haven't mastered the strategies for doing constructive revising.

If you are an apprentice writer who wants to learn revising strategies, you can start by imitating the revising habits of professional writers. The first step is to get help when you revise. Professionals don't try to solve all their writing problems by themselves, and neither should you. They ask colleagues to look at their work and make suggestions, and usually they get feedback from their editors before a piece goes into print.

1. John Kenneth Galbraith, "Writing, Typing, and Economics," *The Atlantic,* August 1978, p. 79.
2. Donald Murray, "Internal Revision: A Process of Discovery," *Research in Composing* (Urbana, Ill.: NCTE, 1978), p. 85.

If you are currently a student working on your writing with the help of an instructor or other students, you may already have people who will read a first draft for you and point out places where you have strayed from your point or where your writing has swelled up with unnecessary or pretentious words. Talking with such people cannot only help you get a fresh viewpoint, a "revision" on your writing, but it may also help you to generate intellectual energy to develop your ideas. So get feedback on your work in progress when you can. Don't make the act of writing any lonelier than it must, by its nature, be.

All writers, however, both amateurs and professionals, have to develop their own revision strategies and become their own editors. They cannot afford to depend on other people to help them make choices about words and structures or to help them tinker with sentences or make decisions about what to expand or omit.

One reason writers should not depend on other people to evaluate their writing is that frequently one cannot find a qualified reader who is willing to read and comment on a piece of writing. Reading a draft carefully is time consuming, and often the most qualified critics are the ones who have the least time to spare. Sometimes you can't wait.

But the main reason that you have to learn to be your own editor is that your writing is more important to you than to anyone else. It's your creation. It represents you. It has your name on it, and you have to take the final responsibility for what it contains and how it looks. And though you can and should get advice from others—particularly experts if they're available—people who write frequently have to develop their own revising strategies. You are really the only one you can depend on.

Strategies for Revising

When writers revise, they make their changes in four ways: they *delete*, they *add*, they *substitute*, or they *rearrange* and they do it on all levels—word, phrase, clause, sentence, paragraph, or larger units of discourse. But just as different kinds of writers approach the task of writing in different ways, so they also approach revision in different ways. Some writers—the sprinters—turn out first drafts at top speed and do little revising the first time through. They do not stop to change words or worry about order or sentence structure. If they hit a snag, they "island hop" around the trouble spot and keep moving. They do not let their internal censors interfere with the flow of their thoughts although at one level they know even as they write a phrase or sentence that they are going to change it later. They do stop frequently to reread what they have written and may make a mark in the margin at spots about which they feel uncomfortable.

Professional writers who work like this plan to do their revising in several stages and usually do at least three or four complete drafts, each substantially different from the one before. They do more mulling and reflecting about their writing *between* drafts than they do while they are composing them.

The other type of writers—the plodders—begin their revising almost as soon as they begin writing and seldom get down more than three or four sentences without deleting words or phrases and substituting others. They pause longer between spurts of writing because they often pause to work sentences out in their minds before they write them down. They may cross out whole paragraphs and sections and rewrite them before going on to the next section. They are constantly weighing their options and trying to anticipate the effect their words will have on the reader. They also stop frequently to reflect on what they have written and what they want to write, and they try to combat wordiness or dullness as they go. Though they plan to write a second or third draft, they make important revisions in the first one.

Both kinds of writers may do their first drafts in longhand or by typing; they may even tape-record the first draft. Almost all writers agree, however, that whatever method they use for writing the first draft, it helps to have a typed, double- or triple-spaced copy when they begin work on their second draft. A typed draft helps the writer see overly long sentences, wordy phrases, and unnecessary repetitions; it is also easier to see when a stretch of writing needs to be broken into paragraphs or sections, and where internal headings would be helpful. Also, typed copy seems to give writers the distance they need in order to take a fresh and critical look at their work. So if you do your first drafts in longhand, type out what you have written, and if at all possible, let some time elapse before you go to work on the second draft.

A Plan for Revising

When you sit down to revise you need at least three things: a pencil to write with, a felt-tip pen or china-mark pencil to cross out with, and some kind of plan or sense of priorities. Probably the first time through you shouldn't try to focus on everything that might need changing. If you try to pay attention to organization, sentence length, punctuation, pronoun reference, word choice, spelling, and five or six other features as you read, you are going to overload your critical faculties. You will have too many problems competing for your attention at one time, and they will start interfering with each other like radio signals competing for a frequency. You'll be more efficient if you approach each draft with some specific priorities in mind.

First Revision

On the first reading start out by asking these major and inclusive questions that focus on *content* and *organization*.

1. Does the piece carry out my purpose? Does it *report* or *argue* or *persuade* or *amuse?*
2. Is it right for the audience? Are the tone and language and the kinds of examples I've used suitable for the reader I've envisioned?
3. Is my commitment clear and have I met it?
4. Is there a clear plan or organization with good signals and links to keep the reader on the track? Is there any place the reader could get lost?

Probably you will do your most substantial deleting, reorganizing, and rewriting at this stage because these are the crucial questions about any piece of writing. When you have revised in response to them, you may have quite a different paper. And that is one good reason not to make changes in sentence structure or word choice on your first revision.

Revising for Purpose.

Checking your work to see if you have carried out your purpose probably means looking back at the assignment you were given or the prewriting summary you made of the main points you intended to make. People who forget to keep those guidelines in mind as they write are sometimes quite surprised to find that their readers do not get the message from the paper that they intended to give. And you cannot afford that. So on your first rereading, stop ahead of time to think of what you intended to do and then check to see if you did it.

Revising for Audience.

Rereading your paper with the intended audience in mind takes a special effort of imagination for students because most students have not learned to project an audience other than their teacher. So go back and reread your audience analysis, then look at your word choices, your arguments, and your style. Are they going to work with your intended audience?

Revising for Commitment.

Next, ask yourself, "Did I do what I committed myself to do?" To find out, go back and check that commitment. What promise did you make in the first paragraph or two? Did you carry out the promise as fully as you contracted to do? For a long paper you may have to write out the general commitment as well as subcommitments that grew out of it. If you started with a fairly detailed outline, you should go back and check to see if you developed it adequately. If you worked from a list, go back over the list to see if you left out any points that should have been included.

When you compare your draft with your plans, you may find that in the process of writing you generated new ideas and changed direction. You may also have focused on your topic more narrowly than you thought you would and left out some of the material you had planned to use. No problem, if as you revise you delete extraneous examples and material that do not fit into the new focus. You also need to check over your introduction to be sure that it doesn't contain material that you failed to develop.

Revising for Organization.

As you are reading over your first draft, ask yourself, "Now if someone were to ask me how I went about organizing this paper, could I give them a quick answer?" For instance, if you had written a paper about pawnshops you might have used the popular journalism questions: *What* are pawn shops? *Why* do they exist? *Who* uses them? *Where* can they be found? *How* do they operate? A paper on stress might be organized on a cause and effect and solution pattern, and one on ski areas could be organized on a deductive pattern in which you generalized about what makes a good ski resort and then described resorts that meet those criteria. Try not to agonize about whether you have the *right* plan of organization; there may be several good ones. The main need is to have one your reader can follow.

On this same reading, consciously look for the links between your sentences and paragraphs. Have you put in enough hooks? Are you momentarily confused or lost as you move from one paragraph to another or one page to another? If so, check to see what the problem is. If you need to insert a link to make your writing more coherent, you might want to check back to p. 91, to see what terms or phrases might help express the relationship you want to show.

Second Revision

On the second revision ask these questions that focus on *economy* and *readability*.

1. Can I trim out words and make the writing more economical?
2. Can I make it easier to understand by lowering the reading level? improving sentence structure? adding examples or illustrations?
3. Can I make it easier to follow by improving visual presentation?

Cutting Your Writing.

Most of us use too many words in our first drafts. We pad the beginnings of our sentences with useless phrases like "It is the case that . . ." or "There exists a need for . . . ," and we use long noun and verb phrases instead of plain nouns and verbs. We repeat ourselves, we overexplain, we depend on adjectives instead of a noun to convey our meaning, and we search for a third item to complete a series even if we only need two. But overwriting in the first draft is not necessarily bad. It is probably better to get everything down that comes to mind and not worry too much about economy at first. You must, however, be ready to start cutting ruthlessly the second and third times around if you want to produce economical prose.

One way to start paring excess words out of your writing is to find spots where you could substitute one or two words for long phrases. For example:

> The reason the forefathers understood one-man rule to be so undesirable was that it allowed that man to make the norms for society all by himself.

could be revised to:

> The forefathers rejected one-man rule because it allowed that man to set social norms single-handedly.

One vigorous verb, *rejected,* does the work of seven words strung together in a flat phrase, and substituting *because* for *the reason for* emphasizes the cause-and-effect structure of the sentence. Here is another example:

> I will attempt to present a tone that will reveal that I know what I am talking about, but assume such a manner that the audience will not be offended by my argument.

could be revised to:

> I will strive for an authoritative but not offensive tone.

The revision not only substitutes one word, *authoritative,* for 15 words in the original, but it gets rid of the bunched-up, choppy phrases and clauses of the original. Don't be surprised if you have to rewrite the original twice to get a satisfactory revised version.

A second way to make your writing more economical is to combine sentences into more efficient packages. For example:

> Presently it is illegal for individual business firms to collude and set prices. By the same token, I suggest that the labor of different companies should not be allowed to work together to set wages.

could be revised to:

> Since individual business firms cannot legally collude to set prices, I suggest that neither should workers from individual companies be allowed to work together to set wages.

Notice the revision not only saves words, but presents the writer's ideas more forcefully. (See pp. 136–39 for more guidelines on sentence combining.)

A third effective, although sometimes painful, way to condense your writing is to cut any examples or explanations that you don't really need. That exercise can be good practice for the time when someone asks you to cut a speech from 20 to 15 minutes or to make your report no longer than two pages. Notice, for example, that this paragraph from a student's biographical statement for medical school would benefit by deleting the sentences that are bracketed.

> [My life, however, has not been completely committed to preparing for a medical career. I have tried to become as well rounded as possible.] In high school I was involved in the Bnai B'rith Youth Organization and was able to reach many responsible positions, including vice-president. I also contributed to my high-school newspaper and literary magazine. [Some of my poetry has even been published in a few smaller publications.] I also took part in school and community plays. Since my freshman year in college, I have been in Beta Beta Tau fraternity. [Being in a fraternity has allowed me to come in contact with many types of people and all kinds of activities. These include sports, social activities, and public service programs.]

And when you are cutting, take an especially hard look at sentences that particularly delighted you when you wrote them. Too often they are precisely the ones that should go because they were written to satisfy the writer rather than instruct the reader.

Finally, you should get in the habit of questioning some common constructions that often contribute to inflated prose: passive verbs, prepositional phrases, verb phrases, noun phrases, and *doubling,* the practice of using pairs of words that mean almost the same thing. I will point out ways of handling the first four problems in later sections. Doubling, however, is almost entirely a redundancy problem, and thus one the writer should try to cure on the second revision.

Here are some examples of doubling:

> The agency will *control* and *regulate* the dairy industry.
> We must find more *efficient* and *effective* ways to meet this need.
> Donavan brings remarkable *insight* and *perception* to the task.
> You should *check* and *verify* each finding before you act.
> They were able to salvage all that was of *value* and *worth*.

One might argue that sometimes a writer needs both words to convey a precise meaning; that *control* and *regulate* do not mean exactly the same thing. Or one could argue that sometimes a writer needs both words for emphasis, that including both *check* and *verify* strengthens the warning. Both arguments can be legitimate and a writer should not go through a draft automatically deleting one word from every pair of apparent synonyms. But you should take a look at those pairs, and if the doubling comes from carelessness, get rid of one of the words.

Lowering the Reading Level.

In recent years many states have passed laws requiring that business and government documents be written in "plain English," that is, in language that the average reader can understand without the help of a specialist. Such requirements, as well as publishers' concerns about the reading level of the material they publish, have caused writing theorists to recommend certain strategies that writers can use to increase the readability of their prose. The first two are:

1. Try to hold your average sentence length below twenty words.
2. Use comparatively few words of more than two syllables.

Simplistic? Yes. Anyone who wants to challenge such advice could quickly think of some very short sentences that are not easy to understand. And, as pointed out in chapter five, the readability of a sentence often depends less on the number of words than on how they are arranged. Nevertheless, roughly speaking, long sentences are more apt to be difficult to read than short ones. Consequently, when you are reworking your prose, you should take a careful look at sentences that run to more than twenty or twenty-five words. If they are not carefully arranged, they may be difficult to understand, and perhaps you should divide or condense them. For example:

With Einstein dead, is there another figure who has taken his place as a sort of World Conscience, someone who would be willing to listen to the plight of a distressed intellectual patiently and sympathetically, who would hearten him and his family, as Einstein heartened and comforted William Frauenglass and his family, and who would move into the public arena and put his prestige on the line to uphold principles of dissent?[3]

The sentence is not impenetrable, but a reader could follow it more easily if it were condensed and phrased in three questions instead of one.

With Einstein dead, is there another figure who has taken his place as a sort of World Conscience? Is there someone who would be willing to listen to the plight of a

3. Lawrence Cranberg, "Intellectual Independence," *Austin American-Statesman.* 13 May 1979, p. C12.

distressed intellectual patiently and sympathetically and comfort and hearten him as Einstein did for William Frauenglass and his family? Is there someone who would move into the public arena and put his prestige on the line to uphold the principles of dissent?

Look also at your word choices. If more than half of your words have three or more syllables, you may be making your writing unnecessarily difficult. Probably you could find shorter synonyms in many cases.

Improving Subject-Verb Patterns.

Recently professionals doing research on readability have demonstrated that word order in a sentence strongly affects its readability. They contend that one of the most common sentence patterns in all languages is that of subject (actor) + verb (action). Readers intuitively expect to encounter sentences in which the subject is an agent that is doing something and the verb describes that action; therefore they understand such sentences more easily than sentences in which the subject is a phrase or an abstraction.

This research strongly reinforces the advice given in earlier chapters: when possible use a concrete subject, preferably a personal subject. You stand a much better chance of constructing an actor-action sentence if you begin with a concrete subject. And in revising for readability, you can bring about almost immediate improvement by converting sentences with nonacting subjects into a specific subject-active verb pattern. Here is an example:

> The government's investigation into the shipment of the wheat by the exporter was met by his refusal in regard to an examination of his method of payments for its domestic transportation.

can be changed to:

> The government investigated how the wheat was shipped by the exporter, but he refused to let the government examine how he paid to have the wheat transported domestically.[4]

By making "government" and "he" the subjects instead of "investigation" the writer gets rid of the passive verb and the prepositional phrases that make the first version so ponderous.

Of course no writer wants to cast all or even most sentences in the same pattern. To do so might make prose easier to understand, but it would also make it boring. Nevertheless, in most cases writing sentences with actor subjects not only makes writing more readable, but makes it both livelier and tighter.

I believe that many of us do not have the habit of writing actor-action

4. Joseph Williams, "Defining Complexity," *College English,* February 1979, p. 597.

sentences in our first drafts; they come when we revise. And if your chief goal in revising is to make a document more readable for a general audience, changing your sentence patterns may be the most important rewriting you do.

You should also keep the reader moving. Do you have enough directional signals to nudge the reader from one point to the next? Have you illustrated and explained difficult or abstract points as you went along so that the reader does not have to reread to understand what you are saying? Have you composed your sentences in word groups that don't overtax your readers' short-term memory? Don't ask readers to hold more than five or six separate ideas in suspension while they wait for the clause or phrase that will make sense out of what has come before it. Notice what a strain the following sentence by a Supreme Court justice puts on the short-term memory.

> If it is the individual who is entitled to judicial protection against classifications based upon his racial or ethnic background because such distinctions impinge upon personal rights, rather than the individual only because of his membership in a particular group, then constitutional standards may be applied consistently.[5]

The sentence is also too long, but if it were rearranged so that readers could grasp the meaning as they read it would be relatively readable.

Sometimes one can make hard-to-process sentences more readable by rearranging clusters of phrases into a series of clauses that allow the reader to come to closure more often. For instance, this sentence is ponderous and difficult to follow.

> When the secrets of infantile sexuality were apparently being unearthed, Freud and his first disciples were still insufficiently aware of the great power of transference on the tendency of patients in the rather authoritarian setting of early analyses to please their analysts by providing them with the kind of material which the latter seemed eager to hear.[6]

Redoing it with more clearly defined clauses helps the reader.

> When the secrets of infant sexuality were apparently being unearthed, Freud and his disciples were not sufficiently aware that because of the great power of transference, patients in the rather authoritarian setting of early analyses tended to please their analysts by providing them with the kind of material they were eager to hear.

Here is another sentence that is hard to follow because it is clogged with phrase clusters.

> To the degree that the individual is open to all aspects of his experience, and has available to his awareness all the varied sensings and perceivings which are going on

5. Lewis Powell, Jr., quoted in "Verbatim," *Student Lawyer*, October 1978, p. 16.
6. Paul Chodoff, "Feminine Psychology and Infant Sexuality?" in *Psychoanalysis and Women*, ed. Jean Baker Miller (New York: Penguin Books, 1973), p. 196.

within his organism, then the novel products of his interaction with his environment will tend to be constructive for himself and others.[7]

Revising the sentence with clauses makes it much easier to read.

The individual who is open to all aspects of his experiences and aware of what he senses and perceives is most apt to turn out constructive new products from his interaction with his environment.

Notice that in the process of substituting clauses for noun clusters, one almost automatically substitutes one-word verbs for inflated verb phrases.

Adding Examples or Illustrations.

When writers revise they also have an opportunity to clarify their ideas by putting in examples and illustrations. Sometimes they may see a need to use more concrete and specific language or to add the visual touches that help to hold the audience's interests. When you are dealing with highly abstract theory, as one might be in a scientific paper, for example, such downshifting becomes particularly important. For instance, notice how much a student writer improved this paragraph about space colonies by adding the concrete details at the end.

Conditions on Model I would resemble conditions on Earth in other ways. The Earth's familiar cycle of night and day, for example, could be duplicated on Model I by changing the angle of mirrors running the length of both cylinders to create eight hours of darkness in every twenty-four hour period. The angle of these mirrors would also determine the temperature inside Model I, so the space colonists could choose to have the same moderate weather every day, or they could elect to vary the temperature to correspond to Earth's winter, spring, summer, and fall. Model I would be, in short, a rather nice place to live. Enriched lunar soil would grow lush crops, animals would graze beside the fish-filled lakes, and only harmless insects would be released.

Improving the Visual Presentation.

In previous chapters I suggested a number of strategies for holding your reader by making your writing *look* attractive, but most writers do not want to worry about external appearance at the first or second draft stage. Probably that is just as well because it is difficult to make final decisions about paragraphing or about divisions and headings until you have done almost all of your adding, deleting, and rearranging. But when you are reasonably well satisfied with content, you need to think about how you can arrange your words on the page in a way that will help your reader.

7. C. R. Rogers, "Toward a Theory of Creativity," in *Creativity: Selected Readings,* ed. P. E. Vernon (New York: Penguin Books, 1974), p. 142.

Unfortunately, people who do primarily academic writing—term papers, grant proposals, scholarly articles, and so on—do not usually pay enough attention to the visual impact that their writing makes. Their paragraphs are too long, they crowd too many words on a page, they do not think in terms of subdivisions within a section or chapter, and they use headings and subheadings only infrequently. But appearance does affect the impression that your writing makes, and even if you are still doing most of your writing for professors, you can learn a great deal about word arrangement from the writers and editors who work in business, industry, and public relations. These communication specialists have devised a number of techniques that you can use to guide a reader through your writing. Most of those techniques fall into three categories: dividing, highlighting, and forecasting.

DIVIDING.   As I pointed out in the last chapter, the most important decisions you make about dividing your writing are those about paragraphing, and at the revising stage you should be ready to make final judgments about this. Look over your typed manuscript to see if it gives the impression of being chopped up into two- or three-sentence paragraphs or whether it has long stretches of unbroken type that run for 15 or 20 lines. In either case, you need to reread what you have written to see if you can rearrange it into more manageable divisions. While you don't want to upset the unity of a tightly constructed paragraph just for the sake of appearance, you may be able to detect a dividing place that wasn't apparent before.

After you have made most of your decisions about paragraphs, skim your text to see how you can break it into larger sections and subsections. In a fairly long piece of writing, your argument or presentation probably divides naturally into steps or stages; perhaps you anticipated or planned for those stages in the list or outline you made when you were getting ready to write. If so, you might look back at your preliminary notes and check on the divisions you had planned, and then mark off those divisions as you developed them in your writing. They should make logical points at which to double your spacing, add marginal headings or one-word headings at the beginning of paragraphs. You can also use Roman numerals to separate stages in your paper, with or without accompanying descriptions.

In a piece that runs for several pages, you might want to assist your reader by adding two brief sections: an introduction that tells your reader what to expect, and a conclusion that summarizes the main points you have made. Writers of scientific and technical papers frequently include these extras that can be immensely helpful in keeping the reader on the track. For instance, at the beginning of a paper called ''The Facilitation of Significant Learning,'' psychotherapist Carl Rogers put this paragraph:

In this chapter I would like to describe two types of learning, two possible aims for education, and two sets of assumptions upon which the educational process can be based. It will be clear that for me the second member of each of these pairs seems more suitable for today's world. I shall then try to indicate some of the ways in which this second view might be implemented.[8]

At the end, Rogers gives a five-paragraph summary of his points, beginning like this:

In this chapter I have tried to present something of what would be involved if a new aim for education were adopted, that of achieving openness to change, and if focus were on that type of learning in which the whole person is involved, a meaningful experience of emotional as well as cognitive learning.[9]

In a shorter paper, you can settle for just an introductory paragraph that catches readers' attention and tells them what to expect. For example:

The most effective weight-loss plans are those that require the least change in customary eating habits. You probably stand less chance of losing weight, and keeping it off, when you resort to crash or fad diets than when you develop a diet plan based on the foods you normally eat.[10]

You can make your opening statement more emphatic by centering it at the top of the page or by using a different typeface.

HIGHLIGHTING.   As you revise your writing, you may see certain words or phrases that you want to emphasize and make stand out for the reader even if the only tools you have are a typewriter, a pen, and a ruler. Here are some techniques:

Indent and make a list. Separate your items and number them or provide some kind of marker. For instance:

No one reducing diet is suitable for everyone. Look for a diet that:
- provides all necessary nutrients but supplies fewer calories than you're now consuming
- includes foods of every food group
- doesn't leave you continually hungry, tired, and irritable
- is easy to follow both at home and away from home
- helps you learn eating habits you can continue for life.[11]

TYPE THE WORDS IN CAPITAL LETTERS.

Underline the words.

Mark off the words with lines both above and below.

8. Carl Rogers, "The Facilitation of Significant Learning," reprinted in *Instruction: Some Contemporary Viewpoints,* ed. Lawrence Siegel (San Francisco: Chandler Publishing Co., 1969), p. 37.
9. Ibid., p. 53.
10. "Successful Dieting," *Diet and Exercise* (Des Moines: Meredith Corporation, 1978), p. 14.
11. "Reducing Diets," *Diet and Exercise,* p. 13.

Put a box around the words.

SEPARATE YOUR LETTERS.

****Use special markers before and after words.****

→Use traditional pointing devices.←

In general, draw attention to material you want to stress by separating it, leaving space around it, or using lines or indicators. Don't try to skimp on paper; leave good margins and double-space. Hold your finished copy at an arm's length and see how it looks. Would you want to read it? And unless paper is as precious as gold, don't use both sides of a sheet of paper—most readers hate to have to turn over a typed sheet.

FORECASTING.   In addition to using divisions and visual attention getters to hold your readers' attention, you may want to keep feeding them signals to focus their expectations. Headings and subheadings can be expanded to give more information, or you can highlight key phrases. Forecasters are especially helpful if you're writing informative material such as brochures, handbooks, or instructions. For that kind of writing, you can not have too many signals to guide the reader.

Third Revision

On the third revision ask these questions that focus on *style*.

1. Can I add vigor and color to my writing by selecting better verbs?
2. Can I make my writing more pleasant to read by improving sentence structure?
3. Can I streamline my style by cutting prepositional phrases and reducing the number of derived nouns?

Selecting Better Verbs.

Verbs are a writer's most important tools. Thus when you are thinking about better word choices, whether you are working with sentences, paragraphs, or entire drafts, look first at your verbs. Watch for these potential problems.

TOO MANY PASSIVE VERBS.   If you know you have a tendency to lapse into the passive voice, go through your draft underlining or bracketing all the passive verbs that you find. If you are averaging several to a page, almost certainly you have more than you need, and you could tighten and invigorate your writing by substituting active verbs. For hints on ways to get rid of passive verbs, see pp. 112–13.

TOO MANY *IS* VERB CONSTRUCTIONS.   Check your writing to see if you rely too heavily on *is*-plus-an-adjective-or-noun sentence patterns to carry your meaning rather than finding one-word verbs to convey your meaning more economically and vigorously. Why write "Drinking is the cause of many accidents" when you could write "Drinking causes many accidents"? Why write "The movie is reflective of a new attitude about the Vietnam war" when you could write "The movie reflects a new attitude about the Vietnam war"?

TOO MANY VERB PHRASES.   Although I touched on this problem in chapter 6, the warnings I gave there bear repeating. Verb phrases not only use more words than simple one- or two-word verbs, but they also slow the pace of writing and devitalize it. Frequently the kind of writing that leaves a flat, "it-just-lies-there" impression is writing that is loaded down with verb phrases: For example:

> We should *give consideration to* those areas of the city that *are in need of* renovation. If we *are not in compliance with* urban-renewal laws by June 1, we will *experience the loss of* federal funds. Our failure *to take action on* this this matter *will result in a lowering of standards* of health care for that neighborhood.

Comprehensible, but wordy and dull. Notice the improvement if we substitute real verbs for the verb phrases and condense some adjective phrases.

> We should consider those city areas that need renovation. If we do not comply with urban-renewal laws by June 1, we will lose our federal funds and lower health-care standards for that neighborhood.

Train yourself to be verb-conscious. Get into the habit of checking the verbs in your sentences to see that they are easy for the reader to find because that reader follows your argument chiefly through your verbs. So make them conspicuous; don't bury them among a welter of nouns and prepositional phrases.

Cutting Prepositional Phrases.

The chances are that if you are a wordy writer, you are using too many prepositional phrases. These extremely common word groups, which usually function as modifiers, are useful and often necessary, but writing overloaded with them drags for two reasons. First, they slow down a sentence by making it choppy, and second, they often take the place of stronger, more economical modifiers. Look at this student example:

At this university there is a need for a high-quality day-center for the children of students and faculty. The Regents should authorize the funds for the establishment of such a facility even though opponents claim that the university should not be in the business of providing baby-sitters for anyone.

Nine prepositional phrases in two sentences. Now let's try a revision:

University faculty and students need a high-quality day-care center for their children. The Regents should authorize funds to establish such a facility even though opponents say the University should not provide baby-sitters for anyone.

The revision says the same thing more efficiently with only two prepositional phrases.

Here are two sentences from professional writing.

The fact of orality also generates whatever meanings any participant in orality has learned to attach to associations with other humans and to the processes of sustaining them by means of speech and listening. Quite apart from the persons involved, these learned meanings of speaking and listening may be supportive or destructive of wishes to influence or be influenced through speech; in any case the meanings of orality in consequence of the attitudes projected on it as an action are seldom insubstantial.[12]

Seventeen prepositional phrases in two sentences! Notice too the dense and abstract quality of the writing. There is a correlation; writers who are partial to prepositional phrases also tend to use too much abstract language and write overly long sentences. So if you prune out the phrases, you will probably prune other dead wood.

Reducing the Number of Derived Nouns.

Using too many derived nouns, those made from adding suffixes to a verb or an adjective, can make your writing flatter and stodgier. Some typical derived nouns are:

Noun	Original Verb or Adjective
cancellation	cancel
admiration	admire
visitation	visit
production	produce
derivation	derive
encouragement	encourage
employment	employ
conformity	conform
reliability	reliable/rely
significance	significant/signify
possibility	possible

12. Carroll C. Arnold, "Oral Rhetoric, Rhetoric, and Literature," in *Contemporary Rhetoric*, ed. Douglas Ehninger (Glenview, Ill.: Scott, Foresman, 1972), p. 63.

Notice first that all these nouns are abstractions and that most of them are general, so writing that relies heavily on them is not likely to be vivid or concrete. They are also the kind of nouns that, when used as subjects, join naturally with inert verbs; they cannot move or speak or act. They also seem to attract prepositional phrases: "cancellation of plans," "admiration for cowboys," "conformity to a standard," and so on. So if you can prune several derived nouns from your writing, you will almost certainly correct other problems as you do it.

Not that you should set up a mental taboo against derived nouns any more than you should decide to stop using prepositional phrases. You must have both. But if you realize that they can drag your writing down, and thus learn to watch for them when you are *revising*, you will probably improve your writing. For example:

ORIGINAL: Jones had made a contribution to the community.
REVISION: Jones has contributed to the community.

ORIGINAL: The possibility of becoming a doctor never occurred to her.
REVISION: She never thought about becoming a doctor.

ORIGINAL: The queen's admiration for Raleigh was well known.
REVISION: Most people knew that the queen admired Raleigh.

ORIGINAL: Brian got strong encouragement from his father.
REVISION: Brian's father encouraged him strongly.

Checking the Rhythm of Your Prose.

People who want to write well must become sensitive to the cadences and tempo of their writing, and learn how and why certain practices and patterns in writing affect its rhythm. They must also develop an intuition that tells them how that rhythm will affect readability and tone. Probably the best way to develop that intuition is to develop the habit of reading aloud your first or second draft, even if the audience will probably never read it that way.

Some of the elements that affect prose rhythm are

sentence length	frequency of closure
word length	punctuation
number of clauses	number of abstract words
number of prepositional phrases	number of concrete words

Almost every choice a writer makes affects prose rhythms, but revising gives a writer time to rethink some of those choices and improve spots where the rhythm sags or gets monotonous. Here are some of the features that you might look at in your writing to decide if you need to make changes to improve the rhythm.

SENTENCE LENGTH.   A series of long sentences slows down writing, and usually forces the reader to read more carefully in order to process the information. This is particularly true of long periodic sentences, the kind that are not intelligible until one reaches the last clause; it is less true of long sentences with frequent closure. An unbroken sequence of several long sentences also creates a monotonous, sing-songy effect. For that reason, a writer needs to consciously vary sentence length and occasionally break up a group of long sentences with a short, simple sentence. But if you want your writing to have a leisurely pace, using long sentences is a good way to achieve it.

WORD LENGTH.   Comparatively long words—three syllables or more— also slow prose rhythms down. If you need long words, you should use them, but if you could use either short words or long words, make your choice partly on the basis of the kind of pace you want to set in your writing.

NUMBER OF CLAUSES.   Several clauses in a sentence will inevitably slow down a piece of writing simply because they will add up to a long sentence; they may, however, also create a pleasant rhythm that enhances some kinds of writing. For instance,

> In recent years, of course, doubt has replaced many people's righteous glow as the price of the gallon of gas that will propel a T-bird about nine or ten miles down the pike edges up toward six bits, erstwhile desert raiders grow richer than Texans, heat sometimes fails to gush from heating ducts, rivers and even breezes smell bad, and fish sticks arrive at the table impregnated with tasty carcinogens. Our tenure in sinless Eden begins to seem less assured, and here and there among the fruit trees stand prophets calling themselves environmentalists, ecologists, postindustrialists, and other things, who assert loudly that there really is guilt after all. They cry out, these spoilsports, for a return to thriftiness on a grand scale—for husbandry of resources, for scrimping and patching and saving, for salvage and reuse, which in current prophet language are known as recycling.[13]

If, like John Graves, you want to create a leisurely pace and a contemplative tone, don't shy away from working several clauses into one sentence. If, however, you want to create a fast-moving pace and give the impression of being straightforward, stick mostly to one- or two-clause sentences.

PREPOSITIONAL PHRASES.   As suggested earlier in this chapter, a paragraph loaded with prepositional phrases is going to be choppy, harsh, and monotonous. Here is an example from a student paper:

> The rebirth of ship cruises has evolved from several factors, the most important of which have been the removal of the exclusivity of cruises and the affordability of

13. John Graves, "All That Litters," *Texas Monthly,* May 1979, p. 152.

today's ship trips. It is possible today to be in the middle income bracket and still be able to enjoy a junket by ship to exotic ports.

Notice, however, that other problems such as derived nouns—"exclusivity" and "affordability"—and abstract subjects contribute to the slow pace of these sentences. Again, one bad writing habit leads to another.

FREQUENCY OF CLOSURE.   You also help your readers to move along at a good tempo if you construct your sentences and paragraphs in patterns that allow them to come to frequent closure. Stringing together a number of phrases or dependent clauses can cause a mental traffic jam that disrupts the flow altogether. Furthermore, if we are reading something out loud we usually pause for breath at the points of closure; thus, having them occur fairly often sets up an easy-to-follow rhythm. A sentence in which we can hardly find the points of closure, like the one quoted earlier from Supreme Court Justice Powell, can leave us panting at the end if we have to read it aloud.

PUNCTUATION.   Since a crucial function of punctuation is to divide writing into units and establish a pattern that moves the reader along, it follows that the way in which a writer uses punctuation dramatically affects rhythm. The three most important marks of punctuation—the comma, period, and semicolon—are interrupters. Where you put them and how frequently you use them partially control how quickly your writing moves, and how often your reader pauses. Furthermore, the marks affect rhythm to different degrees; the comma indicates the shortest pause, the period the longest one.

If you write a series of short sentences with few commas and frequent periods, you will create a fast-moving, sometimes staccato rhythm in your prose. If that suits your purposes, fine. If, however your writing seems uneven, you probably need to rethink your punctuation. Probably you can join some of your sentences with conjunctions or semicolons, or combine some of them. As you do, you will reduce the number of periods and probably smooth out your writing.

When you are using commas to punctuate within a sentence, you can sometimes choose whether to use several or just a few. As I pointed out in chapter 7, today most editors have relaxed their views on punctuation and use only as many commas as they think are necessary for clarity. But if you want your writing to have a conspicuous, measured rhythm use as many commas as strict rules of usage allow. For example:

If, once the decision had been made, Thompson had been willing to cooperate, he would have had little trouble in getting his associate, Mary Hardy, accepted for the project.

is almost identical to:

> If once the decision had been made Thompson had been willing to coop-
> erate, he would have had little trouble in getting his associate Mary
> Hardy accepted for the project.

Notice how much more quickly the second version moves.

ABSTRACT/CONCRETE WORDS.   As several examples throughout this book
have already demonstrated, writing made up mainly of abstract nouns and
passive verbs almost always has a flat and monotonous rhythm to it. Because
we have more trouble processing abstract language, we read more slowly; and
because the verbs we encounter show no action, we don't feel any movement
to what we are reading. But if we revise a colorless and abstract paragraph to
include some concrete words, some people, and some active verbs, it comes
alive and moves more quickly. Notice how this actual example of a paragraph
of flat, cumbersome, bureaucratic prose can be transformed.

> An increasing number of staff in physical education, health, driver education and
> coaching have expressed a need and desire for Red Cross certification in first aid as
> well as instruction in CPR. A recent staff-development day activity (CPR) made avail-
> able to instructors in these curriculum areas resulted in a positive reaction by staff
> toward the value and primacy of CPR as well as first-aid training. Due to the higher
> student-injury-risk factors associated with instruction in the physical education and
> coaching areas, currency in knowledge and application of first-aid practices by staff is
> essential both from a legal and practical standpoint. Health and driver-education staff
> members should similarly be knowledgeable since first aid/CPR units of instruction are
> included in the curriculum of each area. Consequently I would like to recommend that
> all current and future staff employed by the school district be required to attain and
> maintain current Red Cross certification and to receive CPR instruction while em-
> ployed as an athletic coach and/or instructor in health, physical and driver education.

This can be revised as follows:

> Because teachers in physical education, health, and driver education and coaches
> who recently took CPR training at a staff-development day thought the instruction was
> valuable, an increasing number of people working in those areas say they would like to
> take such training. Because so many students are injured in physical-education classes
> and in athletic activities, those teachers and coaches need such training for both prac-
> tice and legal reasons. Health and driver-education instructors should also know first
> aid and CPR because the courses they teach include units in that instruction. Con-
> sequently, I recommend that this school district require all persons who are or will be
> coaching or teaching health, driver education, or physical education to take CPR in-
> struction and to get and maintain Red Cross first-aid certification.

Revising this paragraph into plain English not only makes it more rhyth-
mic and much easier to read, but it brings out the relationship between the
ideas in the paragraph, a relationship that is buried under the stiff jargon of the
original. When I revised, I used several strategies. I cut out excess words (the

doubling with "value" and "primacy" for instance), I substituted active verbs for passive ones, changed the sentence pattern in four of the five sentences to an actor-action pattern, changed "staff" to "teachers" and "coaches," and got rid of more than half of the prepositional phrases and a few of the derived nouns. And a supervisor could read and understand the new version in half the time the old one would take.

Final Check-up

After you have revised your paper for content, economy, and style, you can put it in final form by following through with two more steps.

First, read your paper through to see that you have corrected what you know are the most common problems in your writing. Most of us know we have certain bad writing habits: for example, I have a tendency to "double," I overuse the semicolon, and I am too fond of the phrases "of course" and "a lot." So I try to watch for these lapses when I do my final corrections.

Second, proofread your paper. Look for typical kinds of usage problems such as disagreement between subject and verb, dangling modifiers, or faulty pronoun reference. Now, *before* you get time and money invested in a clean copy, is the time to catch such lapses and revise them or mark them in the margin with the traditional proofreader's symbols. People who expect to write extensively in their careers need to know these symbols. You can find them in any standard dictionary.

If you are a poor speller, this final revision stage is probably also the best time for you to go through your paper systematically and flag any words you think you may have misspelled. When you know ahead of time that you will be doing that, you can stop worrying about your spelling as you write and free yourself to choose the best words you can think of, not the ones you think you can spell.

Realities about Revising

Like everyone else, writers have to do the best they can given the limitations under which they work, and sometimes three or four drafts are not possible. They also have to set their priorities, and some writing projects are less important than others. Writing a 500-word autobiography to accompany an application to law school surely justifies more effort than writing a 2,500-word history term paper. The first may warrant five or six drafts, the second may warrant two. The writer who does not make those distinctions is unrealistic.

Writers also need to be candid with themselves about their attitudes toward writing. How much do you care about doing really first-rate work? Are you willing to put in the extra eight or ten hours that may be necessary to raise the grade on a paper from a B to an A? Are you willing to write and rewrite, get advice, rewrite once more, and perhaps once more again? Is your writing so important to you that you are willing to make it your top priority?

Competent student writers who face these questions are often dismayed when they realize how much time and effort they will have to invest to turn satisfactory writing into good writing, and they settle for doing satisfactory work. Competent writers who make that decision—and sometimes the pressures of school or a job make such a decision necessary—should do so consciously, aware that they could improve their work. Most satisfactory writers *can* become good writers. Whether they have the time, energy, and *will* to do so is another matter. But if they decide they want to be really good, they are going to have to work at revising.

Revising under Pressure

But all of us occasionally—sometimes frequently—find that we must write under pressure, and that we don't have time to write three or four drafts and tinker with our sentence structure and word choice as we would like to. It is impossible to set a draft aside for 24 hours when your deadline is tomorrow. What happens to revising under such circumstances? Do you give up and resign yourself to turning in a sloppy piece of writing?

Not necessarily. First, no matter how pressed you are, you should plan on doing two drafts. You can do them separately in quick succession, or you can in effect be writing a second draft even as you compose the first one by stopping to change, delete, and add as you write. Then when you make your clean copy you can make a few more changes as time allows. Also, before you make the final copy, check for paragraphing and spelling. That task won't take much time, and those are important concerns for the reader.

Second, try to internalize the most important criteria for clear, readable prose so that when you have no time to revise, you won't allow certain constructions to get onto the paper. For instance, try not to write jargon. If you're tempted to throw in terms like *interface* and *viable* and *aspect,* don't. Try not to use passive verbs. And when you get ready to start a sentence with an abstract subject, stop and ask yourself whether you could use a personal or concrete one instead. If so, use it. Finally, try to keep your worst writing habit in mind so you can avoid it.

Third, keep your audience in mind constantly. As you go along, ask yourself these questions: ''Am I telling my readers what they want to know?''

"More than they want to know?" "Do I have a design that will help them follow what I'm writing?" "Am I using words they understand?"

Fourth, unless you are going to have to turn in your very first draft, don't worry about spelling or punctuation. If you do, you may block your flow of ideas and not get through at all. Also, when you are doing the first draft, don't start worrying about luxury concerns such as too many prepositional phrases, derived nouns, and varying sentence length. By itself, none of them is a major concern, and you can't afford to stop to think about them when you are pressed. If on the second reading they seem to be a problem, you can change them if you have time.

Finally, read through and see what you can cut. If you are like most writers, that is the revising technique that will do most to improve your writing. And have confidence in your ability to turn out good work under pressure. The more you write, the more your subconscious mind is apt to come to your rescue in an emergency. Many writers do creditable work against tight deadlines, and you can too. And remember too that the more often you do careful revision when you have time, the more skillful you will become at revising under pressure.

When to Stop Revising

Writing teachers and writing textbooks stress the conventional wisdom that all good writing is rewriting, and for the most part they are right. Everything we know about the writing process suggests that writing is developmental and evolutionary, and that writers grow and learn to make increasingly good choices among words and patterns by writing several versions of the same passage.

For most writing tasks, however, I think one can reach a point of diminishing returns with revising. For the average writer, that point probably comes at about the fourth or fifth draft. If you have put substantial effort into those drafts, and made significant changes as you worked, I suspect that writing another two or three drafts isn't going to appreciably improve your manuscript, at least not in proportion to the time those drafts would take. Some writers would claim otherwise; Hemingway talked about rewriting one manuscript 38 times, and presumably he thought each version was an improvement. But for the following reasons I would suggest that you think twice before you go on to draft five or six.

First, when you have read and reread a manuscript over a dozen times, you are liable to lose your sense of perspective about it. If there are still flaws in it, you are so familiar with them that you probably can't see them by this time. You can get bogged down in trivia, and like the blocked writer in

Camus's novel *The Plague,* you could debate endlessly over whether you should call the horse "brown" or "chestnut." At some point you have to realize that minor changes don't really make a great deal of difference.

Second, you may be blocking your own growth as a writer by investing too much in one piece of writing, worrying too much over the problems that the piece presents. Instead of continuing to wrestle with something that won't come out right, you might learn more by moving on to another kind of writing and another challenge.

Third, you run the danger of becoming a perfectionist who is not willing to turn loose of a piece of writing because he or she is still not satisfied with it. This kind of refusal to stop writing can become a form of protection. As long as you don't admit that the piece is finished and ready to be judged, you can shelter yourself from criticism. But finally you have to take your writing out of the drawer and make it public in order to find out if it works. That makes you vulnerable, but you cannot improve your writing until you are willing to expose yourself to criticism.

Finally it comes to this. Writers work at revising in order to make their finished product match, as far as possible, the ideal product they had in mind when they began to write or the ideal that they created as they wrote. They almost never succeed completely because they learn as they rewrite. As George Orwell said, "As soon as we perfect a style, we outgrow it." [14] In some ways, that is a discouraging comment, but in other ways it is optimistic because it suggests how much we can grow as writers.

EXERCISES

All of the examples provided for revision here are taken from the papers of students in advanced writing classes.

1 Revise these two paragraphs to improve organization.

Buying a used car from an individual is your best bet. An individual wants to sell his old car as bad as you want to buy it, which is a 180-degree turn from the motives of a dealer. A common place to start looking for personal sales is in the classified section of most newspapers. These numerous ads provide a wide variety of cars in all shapes and sizes. And if you look hard enough, usually you can find a good running machine for a reasonable price. Buying a car from an individual rather than a dealer might take more time and effort, but will be well worth it.

14. George Orwell, "Why I Write," in *The Orwell Reader,* ed. Richard Rovere (New York: Harcourt Brace Jovanovich, 1956), p. 395.

Halfway through a hard five-mile run all those nagging worries and minor frustrations seem to evaporate like the sweat pouring down your face. Running is the perfect cure for those brief attacks of anxiety that everyone experiences occasionally. It gives a person the opportunity to escape from the pressures of everyday life and literally run away from one's troubles. Psychologists no doubt have elaborate theories on tension and its cures, but it seems that the main reason running is so beneficial is simply that when you are running at a good pace for more than a couple of minutes the only thing you can think of is how good you'll feel when it's all over. A sincere runner can only concentrate on survival and just isn't bothered by the trivial problems of a marriage or a career.

2 Revise these examples to improve readability; focus particularly on sentence length and sentence patterns.

In some cases the student will have to deal with people who get very emotional, especially on those occasions where the test taker has taken the exam several times because he/she has failed over and over, and this is the last time the person will be permitted to take the exam in six months.

The mere hiring of persons previously discriminated against on the basis of that discrimination could easily produce animosity within the organization possibly making the feelings of discrimination deeper and the burden harder to overcome.

This means that the underground supply of heroin would no longer attract the addict, he could get it from the government, and without anyone to sell heroin to organized crime and dealers would be forced out of business for there would be no profit to be made by illegal suppliers.

In many cases, the only way a professor can know about a student's personal attitude, motivation, and effort is if the student tells him and the inference of these factors is not always possible in that performance levels vary with the student and the circumstances.

3 Revise these examples for economy.

One part of the reasoning behind the Federal Trade Commission's ruling is that individuals should be aware of a doctor's services and charges so that they can more easily choose a physician based on these factors.

If you could eat only one meal in Lake country, try to eat it at Robert's House of Pancakes. If you can pick the time and the season, wait for an unusually frosty morning in January, when a pile of pancakes chased down with a few dozen cups of coffee feels the most appetizing. The House of Pancakes is in Wauconda, a town of about 7,000 within an hour's drive of the Loop. The most central real estate in the community is devoted to the palace of starch; the northwest corner of Main Street and a major highway, Route 176, which bisects the town on its path between urban areas north of Chicago and the regions far to the west.

Because this article is intended for publication in an airline magazine, its audience is necessarily very diverse. However, several assumptions can be made about airline customers. First, they are probably more highly educated than the average American and therefore have a slightly higher socio-economic status. Second, it can safely be assumed that the average airline passenger is well traveled.

4   Reorganize these samples to improve readability.

On the 15th of this month, Representative John Anderson, a Republican from Illinois, will present to the House a bill which will institute a 50-cent per gallon federal tax on gasoline, raising 50 to 60 billion dollars per year in revenue. This money would be redistributed to the public largely by cuts in the Social Security tax. Employees' contributions, now 6.13 percent, could be shaved to 3 percent. Employers' contributions could be cut back from 6.13 percent to 5 percent. The bill also provides for income-tax credits to businesses for the use of motor fuels. The impact on the elderly would be softened by using part of the revenue to increase Social Security benefits. We expect the tax to reduce the consumption of gasoline by some 5 to 10 percent—an effect obviously in conflict with the goals of oil companies. Nevertheless, we feel that this bill is not only necessary but fair. Fair to the consumer and fair to you—the oil company. It is now certain that our dependence on foreign oil must end. America has already made that commitment. We must now devise a fast, equitable plan for carrying it out.

The Law School Admissions Test, the LSAT, plays a large part in choosing tomorrow's lawyers. I recently endured that LSAT and performed well enough to be admitted to the law school of my choice. Although I support its use, my experience has shown me that the LSAT is far from perfect. The test is a necessary screening device for law schools when one considers the large number of applicants for each opening. Nevertheless, the LSAT must be revised if it is to be effective.

5   Revise these passages to give them more vigor.

Careful selection of foods containing all the various nutrients is important for maintaining health and adequate energy. Whether you prepare your own food or eat in a dorm, you can maximize your resistance to disease and increase your energy by selecting foods with the most nutrients. The following selected nutrients are listed here with their corresponding importance for body functions and major sources. This will assist you in selecting a daily balance for a healthy diet.

There must also be more emphasis on physical activity and nutrition education throughout the high-school years. This means more than just classroom discussion. It means requiring health and physical education in all four years of high school and eliminating as much as possible access to artificially produced foodstuffs. We must give our children more graphic demonstrations and presentations of the side effects of various drugs and chemical substances as well.

6 Revise these passages to get rid of excess prepositional phrases and derived nouns.

Schools are visibly reacting to the threat of law suits by limiting the activities of coaches and restricting the use of school facilities. The American Association of Health, Physical Education, and Recreation has published a coach's handbook. This manual is now employed by many schools. It spells out the activities and limitations for a "prudent and careful" coach. Now coaches are instructed how to limit their liability. School facilities are similarly limited. Gymnasiums which were used for community recreation are now closed. There is an increase in general apprehensiveness among athletic directors and the promotion of more austere relationships between instructors and students.

My ultimate goal is the obtainment of a judgeship.

Anxiety caused by the fear of succeeding in her chosen field can greatly inhibit a woman's ability to achieve. Conversely, most young men see success as the key to security and happiness and grow in assurance about their capabilities. They retain a negative attitude toward successful women. These attitudes can prevent women from getting equal pay and retard their upward mobility, as well as create hostility and further anxieties. Lack of success causes fear of achievement, which in turn lessens chances of success.

7 Revise these passages to get rid of unnecessary passive verb forms and verb phrases constructed with *is*.

The number-one industry in New Orleans is tourism. Therefore, preservation of the city's unique old charm is a productive investment for all concerned. Protection of the city for the sake of beauty and interest should also be of great consideration. St. Charles Avenue should be observed as an area equally as important as the Vieux Carré, in beauty, interest, and need for protection. Organizations such as the Live Oak Society should be supported in their protection of the trees that line that avenue. Other groups should be encouraged to help support the preservation of historical homes along the street.

Your service organization is well known for doing successful projects aimed at aiding youth and we would like for you to help us. The need for this type of service is well supported. In the future more blind students will have higher educations and they will be able and more willing to support themselves rather than being dependent on family and friends. Your help is wanted and needed. Your time is greatly appreciated.

Windy Point is not the only place where good diving can be found, but its importance comes from its close proximity to the city. There is coolness, quietness, solitude, and adventure only seventeen miles from the city. It is these characteristics that make Windy Point a viable alternative to the city's parks and bars.

First, building medical schools is a capital investment made only one time, and except for costs such as staff salaries and utility bills, a sole payment results in a continuing stream of service; by it, the yearly use of medical schools and lab equipment is provided for. In contrast, payments for socialized medicine are made year after year, and additional costs of government administration and regulation have to be paid for. In short, capital investment is cheaper than socialized medicine.

8   Proofread the following two passages, marking them with the standard proofreading symbols.

Living in a small west Texas town, the problem of where to go on a Saturday night is easy. I use to wait impatiently for the long-hangin sun to go down each Saturday. Once it did I would make a mad dash from work to the shower to dinner table and to my girlfriends house. We always agreed on where to go to dance, the only hotspot was a dancehall 20 miles away called the Stagecoach Inn.

In the past strong racial and sexual prejudice have made obtaining desired jobs impossible for some because the employer had his own prejudice as the deciding factor. This does not make good bussiness sense, however, neither does the movement of today which forces employers to hire stricly on the basis that women and minority people have been discriminated against in the past and should be hired to compensate for those past wrongs, paying no attention to whether or not they are more qualified for the job than the next man. (or woman) . . . It makes no sense to hired someone if they are not qualified for the job, irregardless of who they are. Common bussiness logic would indicate this to be the solution. In hiring fact not emotion should be the deciding factor.

Writing in College

Writing Papers for College Courses

Almost all college students are writers whether they want to be or not. Writing is an essential part of their educational experience because most college instructors believe that if students are really to understand concepts and master a body of information they ought to be able to express this information in writing. Thus instructors call upon students to write papers or essay exams in order to demonstrate how much they have learned in a course.

This testing function of college writing is usually the one that looms largest in students' minds and causes them the most anxiety, but another function of college writing may, in the long run, really be more important. That is its value as a tool for active learning. The process of writing on a subject stimulates one to think about that subject and to generate ideas and make connections in a way that one is not likely to do simply by reading about the subject. Moreover, even if a person is writing only an analytical report, that person must read and reread the material out of which the paper will come; that process also enhances learning. And students whose writing assignments call for them to apply concepts they are learning, or to find data to illustrate or test principles in their field of study learn far more than those who simply memorize those concepts and principles.

Writing also helps retention. Learning psychologists estimate that people forget from 80 to 90 percent of the material they learn in a course within a year. The material most likely to be retained is that material learned while writing for the course.

Special Problems.

But though students get major benefits from writing for classes, they also face special writing problems, problems that the average business or professional writer seldom encounters. These problems stem in part from the special nature of a student's audience; they stem also from the kinds of topics and format prescribed for most student writing.

The most vexing of the problems relating to the audience may be that usually the person for whom the student is writing already knows more about the assigned topic than the writer. Thus college writers often despair of being able to write anything that might interest their audience. And thinking about that audience frequently causes student writers to worry about another problem: they fear that instructors always read papers or exams with a preconceived idea of what their content should be. Sometimes they are right, but often they are not.

A third audience problem for student writers is that the persons reading their papers grade them, and thereby have power over them. How well one writes a paper affects the grade in the course; the grade in the course affects the grade point average; one's GPA can affect the chances of getting into graduate or professional school, keeping a scholarship, or being interviewed for a job. Worrying about this power of the reader can stimulate writers to do their best, but it can also intimidate them and create a frame of mind that promotes poor writing.

These problems of audience are aggravated by the special criteria set for most writing students are asked to do. Often the first direction instructors give when assigning a paper concerns length: "write a five- (or fifteen- or thirty-page) paper on . . ." And students are so conditioned to thinking about writing in those terms that if the instructor does not mention length, the first question they will ask is "How long does it have to be?" This kind of arbitrary stipulation often makes a writer feel that the number of words in a paper is more important than the satisfactory development of a thesis. Such instructions can hamper students unless they can learn to translate numbers of pages into terms that mean something specific.

Instructors who may be very specific about the length of a paper may not be specific enough about the topic for that paper. They may present student writers with a situation seldom found outside the classroom: that of trying to find something worth saying on a general and perhaps vague topic. Maddening as such assignments may be, students have to learn ways to cope with them. And the experience of being forced to carve a limited and manageable thesis out of a large general topic can be useful for the person who later must write professional papers or talks.

Successful Strategies for College Writing.

Although the category "college writing" is a broad one that includes graduate theses as well as research papers and technical and business writing, the suggestions I am going to make here apply principally to essay exams and to papers written for liberal arts courses such as history, philosophy, government, economics, English, sociology, or classical civilization. Usually the kinds of writing that professors assign in such courses are enough alike for students to use similar approaches and writing strategies. And usually the expectations of professors in these courses are also enough alike so that students are warranted in making certain generalizations about their audience that will help them to write successful papers.

First, you should realize that although professors know a great deal more about their paper topics than you know as a student, they are not necessarily bored with that topic. Experts though they may be, experienced teachers always hope to learn from their students; thus you can reasonably assume that your teacher is interested in what you have to say. And if you give your own supported opinions, interpretations, or conclusions rather than second- or third-hand views, probably at least some of what you write will be enlightening to your readers. They probably will be bored, however, if you just rehash what someone else—even your professor—has already said.

Second, when professors begins to read student papers, they probably do have certain expectations about the content that they expect to be fulfilled, but those expectations may be broad. Seldom do they think there is only one right response to a paper assignment. As long as you stay on the topic and can make a good case for the thesis you have chosen, most professors will give you good marks for original ideas well expressed. But you do have to support your conclusions; your opinion is *not* as good as the professor's unless you can make a reasoned defense of it.

And of course successful student writers also try to analyze their audience's character. Predictably, the professor who maintains an open mind and flexible attitude in class discussion will also welcome varied approaches and diverse opinions on papers or exams, and the professor who discourages dissent in class will probably also expect students to take an orthodox view in their papers.

You can, however, be sure that all professors, regardless of their temperament, are concerned not only about the ideas of papers, but about the way those ideas are developed and expressed. In a 1975 survey conducted by Professor James Sledd among 1500 professors at the University of Texas at Austin, nearly 1,300 complained of poor organization in student papers, over 1,100 about poorly supported assertions, almost 1,000 about failures in logic, and more than 800 about lack of significant content. More than 1000 professors also complained about poor grammar, punctuation, and spelling.[1] These data suggest that the student who wants to do well on a paper for any course should do at least the following:

- If you have a choice, pick a topic in which you are interested and that you think is worth spending your time on. You are much more apt to write a paper your professor finds significant if you are not bored with your subject.

1. These results were published in *ADE Bulletin,* Feb. 1977, p. 3.

- Make a plan. Read the question or assigned topic carefully, work out your thesis, and decide how many points you have to make and in what order you should present them. Check your list as you write, and stay on the track. By numbers, headings, or some other kind of highlighting, draw your reader's attention to your plan of organization.
- After you write an assertion, downshift to illustrate or explain your point. Give examples or textual references. You don't need to give a detailed explanation that will waste your reader's time, but you should show grounds for your conclusions.
- Be careful to show the relationship between your ideas. Help your reader follow your reasoning with pointers such as *consequently, nevertheless, although, for this reason,* and so on. People think logically by making connections; they write logically by showing those connections.
- Proofread! Or get someone else to proofread if you don't recognize your own spelling and punctuation errors. If you are writing an essay exam, try to leave yourself enough time to reread and correct glaring errors. And if you know you are a poor speller, see if you can get permission from your instructor to bring with you a card on which you have written out key words spelled correctly. If the exam is open book, tape the list to your book.

Anticipating Problems.

The anxiety you may feel about writing for a person who has the power to judge you is not only natural but is common to many writing situations. If you become a lawyer in a firm, people above you will be reading your briefs, and if you become a social worker or school counselor, your supervisor will be reading your case studies. What makes such situations nerve-racking, however, is not so much the knowledge that you are being evaluated, but uncertainty about the criteria the evaluator is using. And as a student, if you can get professors to specify what they value in a paper, you greatly improve your chances of writing good papers. If you can get them to put their criteria for grading in writing—and many departments require their faculty to do so—you improve your chances even more. Persuading them to bring in a successful paper from a previous class can also be instructive.

If you get an unmanageable or confusing assignment, don't wait until the last minute and then flail around trying to decide what the professor wants. Try to pin him or her down ahead of time with some tentative suggestions such as, "I interpret this assignment to mean that you want us to analyze the way Shakespeare uses language to create an atmosphere of despair in *Richard III.* Is that valid?" If it isn't, try to find out why, and then try again. Or if your problem is trying to isolate a manageable topic from a deliberately broad assignment such as "Write a term paper on some problem in our county judicial system,'' you might draft a tentative thesis and ask your professor to look at it. For example: ''The investigative powers of the Harris County grand jury have sometimes been used to repress civil liberties.'' Most professors are willing to give their opinion about whether proposed topics are workable and worth pursuing.

Inevitably, you must make your decisions about topics and theses partially on the basis of the length of paper you have been asked to write. You have to translate ''3–5 pages'' or ''18–20 pages'' into terms that tell you something about the scope and depth of treatment you should attempt to achieve in your paper. Here is a guide to help you interpret the typical specifications about the length of papers.

3–5 PAGES.   A very short paper, probably one of several that you will be asked to write during the term. If read aloud, it would take no more than 10 minutes, so don't tackle a topic that you don't think you could explain clearly to an audience in that time. Focus on one major point that you can articulate and support. For example, the development of one character in a play or at most the contrast of two characters. In a short economics paper, you might be able to describe the unique features of credit unions or analyze the effects of increased gasoline prices on suburban real-estate sales.

8–10 PAGES.   A fairly short paper, 2,000—2,500 words or about as long as a 20- to 25-minute talk. In a paper of this length you should be able to state, illustrate, and discuss the implications of a limited thesis. You would not want to commit yourself to develop a proposition with several parts to it, or one that needed to be supported with frequent quotations. You could, however, probably write an effective comparison of the New York and Paris subway systems, or explore the effects on high schools of large numbers of teen-aged students holding night jobs at fast-food restaurants.

18–20 PAGES.   A moderate-length paper that allows the writer to treat a limited topic in some depth and complexity. The professor who assigns a 20-page paper usually plans for it to be the major paper in the course, and thus expects students to write about some important issue in a way that uses information or concepts that have been learned in the course. To do so the students may need to cite references, compare trends, establish and apply criteria, or give evidence and draw inferences from it. In a 20-page paper one could probably employ one or more of these strategies to develop a single but fairly comprehensive thesis. For example: ''In the past three years the Supreme Court has handed down several decisions that have restricted the freedom of the press,'' or ''Unless Congress passes comprehensive legislation to help private farmers, agribusiness will probably take over food production in this country within 10 years.''

30 PLUS PAGES. Few professors assign 30-page papers in undergraduate courses. If they do, however, they are apt to base the student's grade in a course primarily on that paper because they expect such a paper to be significant and comprehensive. In a paper of this length one could make fairly detailed comparisons of two theories, trace the development of a theme through several novels, analyze the effects of a falling birth rate on private colleges, or discuss the intrusion of Marxist ideology into the women's movement. A 30-page paper gives a writer room to research a topic, bring in pertinent background material, formulate hypotheses, and explore implications. Done well, it is a demanding project and a rewarding learning experience.

Finding Your Purpose.

Whatever their length, most expository papers or essay exams written for general college courses fall into one of two categories: informative or argumentative. Frequently the categories overlap and a writer may seek to inform and persuade in the same piece of writing, but students have a special need to know the main purpose of a paper before they begin to write. Professors who expect the writer to make an objective analysis of forces contributing to a drop in worker productivity in the United States don't want to read an argument, and professors who expect a writer to take and defend a position on using price controls as a tool to combat inflation don't want a paper analyzing how price controls work. So decide on your purpose when you begin to write and keep it in mind as you plan the development of your paper.

If you are writing an informative paper, you may be repeating material your instructor already knows in order to demonstrate that you have mastered the content being taught in the course, or you may be writing to teach your instructor something he or she didn't know before. In either case, you need to keep two cautions in mind as you write. First, use neutral language. Avoid loaded words and expressions of opinion; keep adjectives to the necessary minimum. Second, cite your sources. Let your reader know where and how you found your information by describing your procedures in the introduction of the paper and by footnoting references or citing them in the body of the paper. (More on how to do that in the section on reports.)

Try to anticipate when your reader might ask "How do you know that?" and never let that question go unanswered for more than a few lines. Writers who document their work as they go not only give their readers the information they need if they want to learn more about the topic, but they also strengthen their own credibility. The reader is much more inclined to read a paper with a favorable attitude if it is evident from the beginning that the writer's statements are solidly based.

You also need to document your sources when you are writing argumentative papers because in college you are seldom called on to write the kind of political or commercial persuasion that depends primarily on emotional appeal. Rather you are being asked to write a logical argument based on facts and reasoning, and for that kind of writing you must present evidence. Since I have already discussed approaches to logical argument in chapter 4, I will add only one hint here. When you are writing academic papers in which you want to be persuasive—for example, a criticism of the state's Aid to Dependent Children program—imagine yourself in the role of a defense attorney who is presenting a case to an intelligent and alert jury. State your main assertion at the beginning, marshal the evidence to support that assertion, and present it clearly and forcefully. If the paper is long, summarize your points at the end and restate your assertion; if it is short—an answer on an essay exam, for instance—simply make your case and stop.

Good Qualities for College Papers.

Finally, although the readers of academic papers are a difficult audience to write for, student writers can be fairly confident that those papers will be sympathetically read if they meet these criteria:

- The paper has a clear thesis, a discernible plan of development, and an accurate title.
- The thesis of the paper is supported with substantial evidence and reasoning.
- The paper is tightly focused and thoroughly covers a limited and specific topic.
- The language of the paper is clear and objective.
- The paper is well documented.
- The paper is economical—no puffing or padding.
- The paper is legibly and neatly written or typed.

Those standards are the basic ones. Two bonus qualities that most professors hope to find and will usually reward when they do are

- Original thought.
- Graceful and vigorous writing.

Not every college writer can achieve those last two goals, but most writers can, with practice, learn to write papers that meet the first seven criteria.

The Research Paper

The task of writing a substantial research paper should hold no particular terror for people who can handle other kinds of college writing assignments. The ways in which one chooses topics, gathers material, generates ideas, and works out a plan of organization are much the same for research papers as they are for term papers, grant proposals, or extensive case studies. In fact, all these kinds of working writing mingle and overlap; in important ways, they are more alike than they are different.

There is, however, an approach especially suited to research papers, whether it be for a course, a journal, a company, or an agency, and this approach includes these steps:

- Identifying a topic
- Defining the purpose of the paper
- Defining the audience for the paper
- Setting up search strategies
- Taking notes
- Choosing a plan of organization
- Mastering the conventions of documentation.

Identifying a Topic.

If you have a choice of topics, you should probably try to identify one that you are interested in and for which you already have some information. Also, start thinking immediately how you can narrow your topic so that you will be able to focus your search and concentrate on doing a thorough job on a sharply limited area.

If you are writing on an assigned topic, you also need to decide on your limits. *Exactly* what are you supposed to research? Which industries in Washtenaw County, Michigan, are contributing to air pollution? What are the differences between the way the plea-bargaining system works in Boston and Chicago? What is causing the dispute between ranchers and the federal government about grazing on lands managed by the Bureau of Land Management? Pinpoint the issue, and then set the boundaries of your project and abide by them. Try to give your readers precisely what they want to know, no more and no less.

Defining the Purpose of the Paper.

Perhaps even more than other kinds of papers, the research paper requires that you know *why* you are writing. Like reports, research papers are usually data-based; in most instances when you write a research paper you do so primarily to give information. If that is your purpose, you should dig out your facts, present them as objectively as possible, and finish the paper by summarizing your findings. You might want to add some background information to put your findings into context, but that information should also be presented objectively.

At other times, however, the person who asked you to do the research might want not only your findings, but the inferences that can be drawn from those findings. Then you could employ the inductive method (pp. 61–64) by first describing the data you have found and then moving to a conclusion about it, or you could use the Toulmin method of reasoning (pp. 65–70) by making your claim, giving your data, and explaining the warrant between them.

Finally, writers sometimes use research to persuade as well as to inform as did the author of the sample paper on black history that follows this section. In such cases, writers present and document the results of their research and then use it as the basis for argument. They may still present their evidence objectively, but the tone of a persuasive research paper is usually more personal than that of a strictly informative research paper.

Defining the Audience for the Paper.

The audience for a research paper that you write in college and the audience for a research paper that you write on the job are different, and you need to keep those differences in mind when you plan your paper. However, in both cases, you need to begin by asking yourself, ''What does my audience want to get from this paper?''

If your reader is your professor, that reader probably assigned the research paper for two reasons: first, to help you to learn more about some important topic in the course you are taking, and second, to find out how well you have mastered the content and methodology of the course by having you investigate and report on a topic that is related to the material you are studying. The professor would also like to learn something from your paper, but doesn't count on doing so. That would be a bonus.

The audience for a research paper written for a business or an institution has different priorities. That audience is reading to learn; those readers assume that you know how to gather information, organize it, and document it. They are interested in the result of the research more than the method by which it was done although they want the report well documented so that they can look up a reference if they need to. They want the research findings presented briefly and clearly in a way that will answer the questions raised by the person who asked you to do the report. In business, research projects are expensive, and you should not waste your time or your readers' with unnecessary comments or proofs that you might feel your professor expects.

Setting up Search Strategies.

USING BOOKS AND PERIODICALS.   Only when you have chosen a topic and identified your audience and purpose are you ready to start your search. And you should start it early because doing careful research requires a surprising number of hours in the library. Take with you a working list of books chosen from references and bibliographies in your textbook or from suggestions made by your professor and start checking them out in the card catalog. You can supplement your list with additional references you might find in the subject-card index. Read the brief descriptions on the library cards to see which books seem to suit your purpose, and, using separate three-by-five-inch index cards for each book, write down the information you will need to find the book and to refer to it in your footnotes and bibliography. For example:

Martin Luther King, Jr.
The Trumpet of Conscience
New York and London: Harper and
Row, 1968

Making complete notes at this stage will save you time later even if you end up not using all the books you've listed on your cards. Remember also to get more references than you think you will need because inevitably you won't be able to find all the books that look useful.

Next, check the periodical indexes. The one most useful for general subjects and most apt to be found in even small libraries is *The Readers' Guide to Periodical Literature,* which you probably learned to use in high school or as a college freshman. If you didn't, ask the reference librarian to explain it to you. Other useful but more specialized guides to periodicals that could be helpful are: the *Applied Science and Technology Index, Book Review Digest, Business Periodicals Index, The Education Index, New York Times Index, Public Affairs Information Service,* and *Social Science and Humanities Index.* Most libraries have a list of periodicals they subscribe to, and checking it can be helpful. You can also ask the reference librarian about specialized periodicals and encyclopedias.

When you find an article in a periodical that you think you may want to use, make a three-by-five-inch card for it too. For instance,

Robert G. Mogull
"The Pattern of Labor Discrimination,"
Negro History Bulletin, 35,
No. 3. (March 1972), pp. 54-57

USING THE COMPUTER.   Ask your reference librarian if your library has facilities for doing a computer search of the literature about your topic, and if it
does, whether you can learn how to make the search yourself. Many libraries
run regular, short training sessions to show their patrons how to use the computer for research. You can learn the rudiments in an hour. If your institution
has an extensive library that will enable you to follow up on the leads you get
from the computer, you will have an abundance of material to work with. But
be sure to find out ahead of time how much a computer search costs, and who
pays for it. If you have to pay dearly for thirty minutes of computer time, you
may choose to dig in the library stacks instead.

However you do your search, remember the Law of Serendipity. The
word _serendipity_ means "the faculty of making desirable discoveries by accident" and comes from the fairy tale about the three princes of Serendip. In
the course of their search for a fortune, they found that the accidental discoveries they made during their journey were more important than the prize they
found at the end. Because experienced researchers know the value of such
lucky accidents, they stay alert for them, glancing at the titles of books
shelved next to the ones they are seeking, or running their eyes over the table
of contents in a periodical that has the article on their prepared list. Your best
piece of information may be the one you stumble onto while you are looking
for something else.

Taking Notes.

Sometimes the chore of taking notes for a research paper looms so large
that you are tempted to photocopy everything you find, then worry about mak-

ing sense out of it after you get out of the library. That procedure is probably not a good idea, though, not only because it is expensive, but because it is slow and only delays the selective skimming that you will finally have to do in order to decide which material is usable. So when you think you have enough references collected on 3″ x 5″ cards, get another stack of cards, preferably larger, and start taking notes. Cards work much better than note paper because you can write one entry to a card and then organize them later. Also, cards are easier to sort and read than notes on loose paper.

Begin *every* card by writing your source on it; put the full citation on the first card—e.g., Donald Murray, *A Writer Teaches Writing,* Boston: Houghton Mifflin, 1968. You can abbreviate on successive cards—e.g., Murray, *A Writer*—but having the complete information on the first card will save you trouble later. And get in the habit of *always* writing the page number of a reference or quotation on each card; if you don't, you will find yourself going back to the library to hunt for the page.

In general, your notes will be of two kinds: summaries and quotations. You can write the summaries in the abbreviated form you might use for taking notes in class, but don't condense them so much that you will be puzzled when you try to read them a week later. The time you take to put your information into a sentence instead of a phrase might save you a trip back to the library. And you should put quotations in exact form and use quotation marks around them so that you will remember to document them in the paper. Remember also to put in the ellipsis points (see p. 267) if you leave out any part of the quotation.

You also need to set up a system for organizing your notes. At the very

---

Black leaders   3

Black nationalists -
    Roy Innis & Ron Karenga
    leading spokesmen -
Appeal to black pride, push black
studies - Blacks should control their own
communities - must increase economic &
political power ——.

Time, special issue on Black America
        pp. 14-22
                4/6/70

least number them as you work so you will be able to arrange them in the same order in which you did your research. Usually, however, you need more information than simple numbers will provide; you need some kind of code word on each card to remind you which part of the paper it will fit into. For example, in the sample paper at the end of the chapter, "Climbing History's Mountain," the divisions might have been M. L. King, civil rights movement, black leaders, economic inequality, and educational problems. Having your notes arranged in such divisions will help you to see how the parts of your paper are going to develop and may help you decide on a plan of organization.

Choosing a Plan of Organization.

If you haven't decided on a plan of organization by the time you have finished taking notes, you can scarcely delay any longer. You have all those cards and you have to impose some order on them before you start to write. And because a research paper is usually longer than other papers—perhaps 20 to 30 pages—a careful, detailed plan is especially important. You need more control to keep the parts of your paper in balance and to keep your reader from getting lost.

You can start your planning by thinking about what some of your options might be. For instance, you could write your paper chronologically, simply telling the history. A variation of this plan is to start by giving background material, and then move on to current happenings. You could also use a comparison/contrast format: for instance, you could compare how blacks and whites view integration. Or you could compare the ideal of racial equality with the actual situation. Or you could start with an anecdote that illustrates your thesis and then develop the thesis as an argument.

Probably the best way to get all of your material under control is to make a rough outline based on the categories you have set up for your note cards. If you do this, you will establish the broad classifications that you are going to cover in your paper and find a logical way to order them within the paper. Write those classifications down. Then make notes about subpoints you want to cover in each category. As you work, develop a series of general assertions that can serve as the framework for your paper. And as you outline, think about what subheadings you might use to keep your writer on the track.

You can also create a plan of organization by capsuling, summarizing, or writing an abstract for your paper. If well done, an abstract or summary can give you substantial guidance for organizing your paper. Notice, for example, that the abstract of the proposal for a day-care center on p. 21 is a kind of outline. Each sentence could be separated out as a main heading and points to support it brought in as subheadings. Supplemented by a list of secondary points you want to make, a comprehensive abstract will serve you just about as well as an outline. And it gives the added advantage that after you finish, you can polish it and include it with the paper in order to give your professor advance signals about what he or she will be reading.

Mastering the Conventions of Documentation.

You need to learn how to document a research paper accurately for two important reasons: first, to let your readers know where you found your material, and, second, to make it possible for them to locate and use that material if they wish. Keeping those two purposes in mind is more important than worrying about whether you use a comma or a colon after the name of a city. Your main concern should be to let your readers know the *author, title, date, publisher,* and *page numbers* of any writing you cite. With that information, they should be able to trace any of your references. When you are referring to a radio or television show or to a movie, give as much information as you can so that a person who wanted a print or transcript of the program would be able to request it.

So common sense is the chief guide to documentation. You will, however, probably want to decide on a system of documentation and stay with it throughout your paper. The two most common systems are these: internal documentation combined with a bibliography at the end of the paper or chapter; and full documentation for each source in footnotes or endnotes.

If you use the internal documentation, you can cite your source within the text of your paper by giving the reference in parentheses immediately after you make your point. For example:

This approach corresponds to the frequently cited theory that scientific revolutions come about through paradigm shifts. (Kuhn, p. 79)

You then list Kuhn's *The Structure of Scientific Revolutions* in the bibliography at the end of the paper; the reader can turn to the bibliography to check the source if desired. If you are using more than one book by the same author, you can designate them in the bibliography and reference by giving the date for each one. This internal method is simple and quick, and it saves you the trouble of keeping the numbers of your notes straight and of writing out each note in full form; however, it is probably not quite as efficient for the reader as full documentation for each note.

If you choose the full documentation system you should settle on the form prescribed by one of the standard style sheets—*The MLA Style Sheet* or the *New York Times Style Manual,* for example—and be consistent throughout your paper. The MLA-endorsed form for the most common kinds of documentation are as follows:

A book with a single author:
1. Martin Luther King, *The Trumpet of Conscience* (New York: Harper and Row, 1968), p. 17.

A book with two authors:

1. Kenneth Clark and Harold Howe, *Racism and American Education* (New York: Harper and Row, 1971), p. 84.

An unsigned magazine article:

1. "The Saga of Boston," *Ebony,* Oct. 1974, p. 113.

Periodical article with author:

1. Wendy Watriss, *"Pupils Blame Parents for Busing Problems,"* *Christian Science Monitor,* Oct. 20, 1972, p. 54.

An article in an anthology:

1. James Britton, "The Composing Processes and the Functions of Writing," in *Research in Composing,* ed. Charles Cooper and Lee Odell (Urbana, Ill.: NCTE, 1978), p. 13–28.

A translation:

1. Lev Vygotsky, *Thought and Language,* trans. Eugenia Hanfmann and Gertrude Vakar (Cambridge: M.I.T. Press, 1962), p. 91.

After you have referred to a work once, you can abbreviate your next reference to it. For example,

2. Galbraith, p. 92.

If you need to check on the right form for some other kind of entry, you can find a copy of the *MLA Style Sheet* in almost any library.

Endnotes or Footnotes.

Traditionally, a footnote appears at the bottom of the page on which the citation is made, and readers can refer to it immediately if they want to check a reference. In some ways, then, the footnote serves the reader better than internal notes or notes that are placed at the end of a chapter or paper. But footnotes can become a nuisance, particularly if there are a great many of them on one page. They cause problems for the typist and printer, they sometimes seem to overbalance the text, and they can be distracting to the reader. For these reasons many publishers prefer to put notes at the end of chapters or sometimes even at the end of a book. Your professor may allow you to use endnotes; if so, that is probably your best choice, particularly if you are doing your own typing. The form of the notes is the same whether they appear at the foot of the page or at the end of the paper.

Bibliographies.

Writers who use internal documentation in their papers must include a bibliography at the end of their papers or their system will not work. However, authors who are using standard MLA documentation may also want to include a bibliography at the end of their paper for several reasons. One is that a good bibliography can serve as a guide to further reading. Another is that it is easier to look for a particular reference in a bibliography than to search through the footnotes. And student writers should include a bibliography to show their professor the scope of their research.

In your bibliography, the documentation changes slightly. Author's last name is listed first and punctuation is usually different. For example:

> Rooney, Roger C. *Equal Opportunity in the United States.* Austin: University of Texas Press, 1973.

Bibliographies are arranged alphabetically by author and the revised form makes it easier for readers to find the work they are looking for. If the author is unknown, arrange the entry by the first word of the title (excluding *A, An,* or *The*). All entries are listed together, not by categories such as books, articles, or pamphlets. For magazine articles give the page numbers.

Other Aids for Research Papers.

If you must write a complex and important research paper, you may want more help than you can find in this comparatively short section on the forms of documentation. If so, in almost any library you can get books that treat the topic comprehensively and will give you additional sources that you can consult. Perhaps the best complete and useful book is:

> Jacques Barzun and Henry Graff. *The Modern Researcher.* 3d ed. New York: Harcourt Brace Jovanovich, 1977.

Another good and comparatively inexpensive paperback that has an especially good specialized bibliography is:

> James D. Lester. *Writing Research Papers: A Complete Guide.* 2d ed. Glenview, Ill.: Scott, Foresman, 1978.

Sample Research Paper

CLIMBING HISTORY'S MOUNTAIN

In the late 1960s, the American black had high hopes; Martin Luther King had instilled a new faith in the American black with his program of nonviolent resistance. Unfortunately, King, the one person who most blacks believed could lead them to their desired equality, was assassinated on April 4, 1968, by a sniper in Memphis, Tennessee.[1] Martin Luther King's death severely hindered the use of nonviolent resistance that King believed must guide the Negro in race relations. Reverend King firmly held that with nonviolent resistance, no individual or group need submit to any wrong, nor need anyone resort to violence in order to right a wrong. As King put it:

> If we are arrested every day, if we are exploited every day, if we are trampled over every day, do not let anyone pull you so low as to hate them. We must use the weapons of love. We must have compassion and understanding for those who hate us. We must realize so many people are taught to hate us that they are not totally responsible for their hate. But we stand in life at midnight; we are always on the threshold of a new dawn.[2]

Through this course of action, King thought the Negro would be able to oppose the allegedly unjust system while loving the perpetrators of the system.[3]

The Kerner Commission and the Three-Way Split

With the death of King, many Americans turned their attention to a report by the National Advisory Commission on Civil Disorders, the Kerner Commission, which had been published on March 1, 1968. The report's basic message—that white racism supposedly underlay the ghetto system and must be overcome—finally made its way into the heart of America upon the death of Martin Luther King. Hundreds of local groups began discussing ways of implementing reforms, perhaps because of one statement in the report:

> What white Americans have never fully understood—but what the Negro can never forget—is that white society is deeply implicated in the ghetto. White institutions created it, white institutions maintain it, and white society condones it.[4]

During the course of compiling their report, the Kerner Commission studied America's racial history, investigated the causes of riots, and talked to thousands of ghetto dwellers. As the eleven members took to the streets of the ghettos, they found that ghetto dwellers wanted some very simple things: more police protection against crime in their own communities; more and better jobs, schools, and housing; improved public facilities and services, and also an opportunity to elect people of their own choosing to public office. They also requested a decisive voice in planning their own communities, and an end to disrespectful treatment from white

America.[5] Ghetto inhabitants said that their desires for these reforms were justified because there was a striking difference in environment from that of a white, middle-class neighborhood and their neighborhood. In 1968, crime rates in the ghetto, which were consistently higher than in other areas, reportedly created a sense of ghetto insecurity. Poor health and sanitation conditions in the ghetto resulted in higher mortality rates for nonwhite babies under the age of one month; the rate for nonwhite babies of this age was 58 percent higher than for white babies. For nonwhite babies from one to twelve months, the mortality rate was almost three times as high. Also, ghetto dwellers complained that their garbage collection was often inadequate. Of an estimated 14,000 cases of rat-bite in the United States in 1965, most were in ghetto neighborhoods.[6]

All things considered, the basic conclusion of the National Advisory Commission was that the United States was moving toward two societies, one black, one white—separate and unequal.

Over the last decade, black Americans have fought the movement toward these two unequal societies. More than in the past, the assault on inequality after the death of Martin Luther King was taking place on the community level. The lack of national voices made the decibel level of black protest seem lower when it had actually intensified. Most blacks seemed to realize that they would never again have a leader of the magnitude of Martin Luther King. This realization contributed to a new mood among blacks who led the drive for racial progress in the late sixties and early seventies. Black leaders, who had developed a new sense of pride and self-reliance, seemed angrier than ever with social, economic and political conditions. These leaders seemed even more determined to revolutionize race relations and achieve full equality in society. But disputes concerning how equality should be achieved resulted in a three way split. The three prominent factions in the drive for racial equality were the integrationists, best symbolized by Martin Luther King; the black nationalists, of whom Roy Innis and Ron Karenga were leading spokesmen; and the revolutionaries, represented by the Black Panthers.[7] The nationalists appealed to black pride, pushed for black studies, insisted upon local control of black communities, and also argued that blacks must increase their political and economic power. The integrationists advocated the classic technique of progress through the courts, the Congress, and the government. This leaves the radical element, the Black Panthers, who said that they were fundamentally interested in one thing, which was freeing all people from all forms of slavery in order that every man will be his own master.[8] The Panthers held that people should collectively decide what they need, and should share fully in the wealth they produce. To this end, the Panthers thought the whole government should be subject to the dictates of the people. From the Panthers' point of view, the government and its subsidiary institutions were illegitimate because they failed to relate to the people, and they failed to meet the needs of the people. Therefore, they had no right to exist.

Some specific things that the Panthers asked for were full employment for black people, and the exemption of all black men from prison and military service. The Panthers wanted exemption from military service because they felt that blacks should not be forced to defend a "racist" government that did not defend them; the Panthers also thought blacks now jailed were unfairly tried and should be released.[9]

Economic Inequality

One goal that all three divisions of the equal rights movement had in common was economic equality. Over the years, blacks have maintained that there is socioeconomic inequality in these fields. This inequality supposedly spawned black disillusionment and dissatisfaction for the "white system."

Economically, blacks have made considerable progress, but this, they add, is most impressive in comparison with the black's past condition, not in comparison with white achievements. The median income for whites continues to be 35 percent higher than for blacks. In absolute terms, the real median income of the average black family roughly doubled in the sixties; rising as a result of expanding opportunities in employment and education, increased numbers of wives entering the labor force, and government welfare programs. In 1960, only 13 percent of nonwhite families had annual incomes over $10,000 a year; by 1972 this proportion had increased to 35 percent. But the absolute dollar gap between blacks and whites actually widened between 1960 and 1972. Meanwhile, in 1972, over seven million blacks still lived in poverty, with another two million on the poverty threshold. Together, the poor and the near-poor were 42 percent of all blacks.[10]

Negroes, in contrast to whites, are primarily employed in blue-collar and service occupations. A much larger proportion of Negroes than whites are working in the fields. Furthermore, research indicates that blacks are mainly employed at the bottom levels of the blue-collar fields, as operatives and laborers where education and skill prerequisites are minimal, rather than at the upper levels. These occupations in which blacks are concentrated are precisely the ones that have the highest rates of unemployment. Blue-collar and service workers have the highest rates of job loss and also account for most of the unemployed.[11] In general, blacks earn less than whites, and often complain that they are forced to work irregularly, have trouble finding jobs, and are more frequently discouraged from even looking.

Granted, as noted above, the type of employment most blacks receive is not always desirable; however, blacks still have probably made more progress in employment than in any other socioeconomic category. The proportion of black people employed as managers and administrators, professional and technical workers, and craftsmen—the three highest-paying occupations—almost doubled between 1958 and 1973.[12] The mean annual earnings of black males increased from 53 to 66 percent of those for whites between 1959 and 1971, and average black female earnings moved very close to equality with the earnings of white females. The percent of black males earning less than $3,000 annually (in 1969 dollars) dropped from 40 to 22 percent between 1954 and 1969, while females declined from 75 to 52 percent. The proportion of earnings over $10,000 rose from three to nine percent for black males and from one to five percent for

black females; these figures are steadily rising each
year.[13]

Much of the occupational/earnings shift is traceable
to the affirmative efforts of such corporate giants such
as United Air Lines, Avon Products, Inc., Chase Manhattan Bank, Prudential Insurance Company, Aetna Life Insurance Company, and the General Motors Corporation,
which all began minority hiring programs. The trend set
by these companies were later followed by other companies, and this helped ease some of the tension at a time
when black/white relations were reportedly at a critical
point. Legislation by Congress has made it easier for
blacks to get jobs because a certain number of minority
representatives must be present. However, while blacks
have achieved more equal entry into better jobs, they
say that the critical issue is whether they will continue to advance in these jobs and move up into responsible positions.

The Educational Battlefront

Another pressing issue in contemporary race relations pertains to education and segregation. Blacks say
that the historical reality of race relations in America
is that whites have never altered their institutions
primarily for the benefit of blacks. Blacks also argue
that school systems have not been an exception to this
rule. There has been progress made since the halt of the
"separate but equal" schools, but there is still work to
be done. As the Kerner Commission put it in 1968:

Education in a democratic society must equip children to
develop to their potential and to participate fully in American life. For the community at large, the schools have dis-
charged their responsibility well. But for many minorities,
and particularly the children of the ghetto, the schools have
failed to provide the educational experience which could
overcome the effects of discrimination and prejudice. This
failure is one of the persistent sources of grievance and resentment within the Negro community. . . . The black record of
public education for ghetto children is growing worse.[14]

There have been black gains at all levels of education. A larger proportion of black than white children

are enrolled in preschool programs and the proportion of nonwhites with fewer than five years of education fell from 33 to 13 percent between 1960 and 1972, while those with high-school diplomas increased from 14 to 37 percent. In both categories, the nonwhite gain was faster than the white.[15] Although blacks are still less likely to complete high school, their drop-out rate is declining. In 1967, 23 percent of blacks between age 14 and 24 had dropped out of high school without finishing, compared to 12 percent by whites.[16] Though blacks are less likely than whites to be attending college, they are narrowing this gap also. Between 1960 and 1973, the number of blacks enrolled in college increased by approximately 540,000, a gain of 370 percent, which raised the ratio of blacks to whites from one to 20 to one to 12. Blacks are slightly more likely to attend public and junior colleges, and to go to school part-time.[17]

Meanwhile, progress in achieving public school desegregation continued during the late 1960s and early 1970s, with the percentage of blacks in majority black schools dropping from 77 percent in 1968 to 63 percent in 1972, while blacks in all black schools declined from 40 to 11 percent. The greatest desegregation process has occurred in the South. Ironically, there has been little change in the North and West, reflecting a hands-off policy in areas where segregation is caused by housing patterns. One exception to this has been Boston, which was a battleground in the busing war in 1974. Boston was boiling on September 12, when school authorities began busing more than 18,000 students under orders of a federal court.[18] Resistance to the integration program divided the city and resulted in more than 100 injuries to blacks and whites and at least 160 arrests.

Many psychologists attribute much of the racial unrest involved in desegregating schools, like the situation in Boston, to meddling parents whose ignorance and fear have led to explosive situations. To illustrate this point, it might be helpful to look at some comments of individuals involved in the racial disorders in Savannah, Georgia, during the 1971-72 school year.

How can you say busing is the issue when busing has been going on for so many years? It's not busing. It's integration, and everyone worries whether the kids are ready for integration. It's the parents and administrators who are not ready.[19]

The preceeding quote was the opinion of a black senior—class president named Pat Washington. Two other students, Eric Williams, a white football player, and Sandra Mitchell, a black sophomore, expressed sentiments:

I don't think busing will work. We have been thrown together too fast. But I'll tell you one thing: if we didn't have parents bugging us, it wouldn't be so bad.

Parents are the problem. They should leave the kids alone and let us go to school together in peace.[20]

What Can Be Done?

In sum, much can be said about race relations over the last decade. On the positive side, blacks can sit at lunch counters, sit downstairs in movie theaters, ride in the front of buses, register to vote, work, and go to school where once they could not. But in a great many ways, blacks argue, nothing has changed. A careful look at all the facts and figures that measure how well or poorly a group of people are doing—the kinds of figures that measure infant mortality, unemployment, median family income, life expectancy—demonstrates that there is some basis to their argument. The average black American, while better off in comparison to his father, is actually worse off when his statistics are measured against similar ones for white people.

Perhaps the insight of President Lyndon Baines Johnson says it best. In 1973, Johnson, in a symposium on civil rights at the University of Texas at Austin, made the following statement:

To be black, I believe, to one who is black or brown, is to be proud, is to be worthy, is to be honorable. But to be black in a white society is not to stand on level and equal ground. While the races may stand side by side, whites stand on history's mountain and blacks in history's hollow. We must overcome unequal history before we overcome unequal opportunity. That is not, nor will it ever be, an easy goal for us to achieve. . . . We know there is injustice, we know there is intolerance, we know there is discrimination and hate and suspicion. And we know there is division among us. But there is a larger truth. We have proved that great progress is possible. We know how much still remains to be done. And if our efforts continue and if our will is strong and if our hearts are right and if courage remains our constant companion, then, my fellow Americans, I am confident we shall overcome.[21]

Reggie Rice

Notes

1. Martin Luther King, Jr., <u>The Trumpet of Conscience</u> (New York: Harper and Row, 1968), p. 27.
2. King, p. 43.
3. Coretta Scott King, <u>My Life With Martin Luther King,Jr.</u> (New York: Holt, Rinehart and Winston, 1969), p. 17.
4. <u>The Report of the National Advisory Commission on Civil Disorders</u>(Washington D.C.: 1968), p. 17.
5. <u>Report,</u> p. 32.
6. Samuel F. Yette, <u>The Choice: The Issue of Black Survival in America</u> (New York: Putnam's 1971), p. 181.
7. <u>Black America 1970, Time</u> special issue, 6 April 1970, p. 13.
8. William H. Grier and Price Cobbs, <u>Black Rage.</u> (New York: Holt, Rineheart and Winston, 1968), p. 97.
9. Grier and Cobbs, p. 117.
10. Robert G. Mogull, "The Pattern of Labor Discrimination," <u>Negro History Bulletin,</u> 35, No. 3 (March 1972), p. 54–57.
11. Mogull, p. 57.
12. <u>A Decade of Struggle, Ebony</u> special supplement, Jan. 1975, p. 27.
13. <u>Decade,</u> p. 56.
14. <u>Report,</u> p. 19.
15. Kenneth Clark and Harold Howe, <u>Racism and American Education.</u> (New York: Harper and Row, 1971), p. 84.
16. Clark and Howe, pp. 86–87.
17. Clark and Howe, p. 89.
18. "The Saga of Boston," <u>Ebony,</u> Oct. 1974, p. 113.
19. Wendy Watriss, "Pupils Blame Parents For Busing Problems," <u>Christian Science Monitor,</u> Oct. 20, 1972, p. 54.
20. Watriss, p. 55.
21. Roger C. Rooney, <u>Equal Opportunity in the United States</u> (Austin: Univ. of Texas at Austin Press, 1973), p. 128.

Selected Bibliography

Clark, Kenneth and Howe, Harold. <u>Racism and American Education.</u> New York: Harper and Row, 1971.

<u>A Decade of Struggle, Ebony</u> special supplement, Jan. 1975, p. 27.

Grier, William H. and Cobbs, Price. <u>Black Rage.</u> New York: Holt, Rinehart and Winston, 1968.

King, Coretta Scott. <u>My Life With Martin Luther King, Jr.</u> New York: Holt, Rinehart and Winston, 1969.

King, Martin Luther, Jr. <u>The Trumpet of Conscience.</u> New York: Harper and Row, 1968.

Mogull, Robert G. "The Pattern of Labor Discrimination." Negro History Bulletin, 35, No. 3 (March 1972), 54–57.
The Report of the National Advisory (Kerner) Commission on Civil Disorders. Washington, D.C., 1968.
Rooney, Roger C. Equal Opportunity in the United States. Austin: Univ. of Texas at Austin Press, 1973.
"The Saga of Boston." Ebony, Oct. 1974. p. 113.
Watriss, Wendy. "Pupils Blame Parents for Busing Problems." Christian Science Monitor, October 20, 1972, p. 54.
Yette, Samuel F. The Choice: The Issue of Black Survival in America. New York: Putnam's, 1971.

EXERCISES / *Prewriting Activities*

1 Narrow these topics to ones that might be adequately covered in papers of three to five pages.

The economics of shopping malls
Future trends in cattle raising
The problems of teaching the hyperactive child
Getting ready to look for a job

2 Narrow these topics to ones that might be adequately covered in papers of eight to ten pages.

The class structure in American high schools
The myth of romantic love
The origins of punk rock music
The effects of diet on aging

3 In a paragraph of about 100 words, write out the purpose a writer would probably have in writing a paper with one of these titles.

Sociology: Changing Sex Roles among Blue-collar Workers
Economics: Causes Underlying the Fluctuating Price of Gold
Philosophy: An Analysis of the Allegory of the Cave in Plato's *Republic*

4 Write a short paragraph analyzing what the reader of a paper with one of the following titles would expect to get from the paper.

English: An Analysis of Women Characters in Hemingway's Short Stories
Psychology: A Comparison of the Learning Patterns of Six- and Eight-Year-Old Children
History: The Effects of Lincoln's Assassination on Southern Reconstruction

CHAPTER 11

Writing on the Job

Grant Proposals

In recent years a kind of writing that must be both informative and persuasive has become increasingly important, the grant proposal. Most scientific researchers find that they must know how to write grant proposals if they expect to get their projects funded; so do educators who want to improve the teaching of writing, welfare workers who want to help their clients practice better nutrition, or librarians who want to encourage reading in their community. In fact, in many fields, almost any person who wants to start a project that involves more than routine activity will find that he or she can do so only by successfully applying for a grant.

A small industry has even grown up to help people master the art of "grantmanship." Self-styled experts contract to write grants for people, professional journals advertise expensive two- or three-day seminars on writing grants, and bookstores stock manuals with detailed instructions and indexes to a variety of funding agencies.

But you do not have to be an expert or a specialist to write a satisfactory grant proposal. The format is not mysterious, and the information you need is generally available from libraries or institutional offices. The agencies and foundations that give grants usually provide specific instructions about what you should include and provide a checklist and cover sheet to help you put the proposal together. So all the applicant really needs to have, besides patience and determination, is the ability to write clear, well-organized prose and some appreciation of the psychology of grant writing.

Purpose of the Proposal.

When you write a grant proposal, you have one overriding purpose: *to persuade someone to give you money*. In order to do that, you are going to have to convince the reviewers at the foundation or agency to which you are applying that you have a good idea for solving an important problem, that you have or can get the facilities and equipment for handling the task, and that significant benefits will result when you do solve the problem. In short, you have to do a major selling job, but you have to do it with rhetorical restraint and with an abundance of evidence and sound reasoning to support your request. Your task is made easier, however, because the conventions for grant proposals are well established and not difficult to follow.

Preliminary Planning.

Your first concern in writing a grant proposal should be to give yourself plenty of time. The research, legwork, writing, budget preparation, and so on will take longer than you think. Next, find out what kind of agency or foundation might be interested in funding it. If you are going to apply to a local organization, you need only get its application form and instruction booklet, but if you are unsure about where you should send the proposal, go to the library and ask for a directory of organizations that award grants. Not only the names are listed, but also the specific areas of interest and special requirements of the grant-awarding agencies. If you are connected with or close to a university or college, you can also get an abundance of information from its office for research.

Narrow the list of possibilities by noting the kind and size of grants that foundations make, and choose the funding organizations whose records show that they have been supporting projects similar to yours. Learn as much as you can about those organizations because their reviewing committees are going to make up the audience for which you will be writing.

Your next step should be to rough out a plan for your proposal. Although the sequence of items for the proposal is probably prescribed by the funding institution, write yourself some notes about how you are going to present that sequence. The key items you should think about are 1) the description of and rationale for the project, 2) the procedures to be followed in carrying out the project, 3) a description of facilities available for working on the project or research, 4) the credentials and experience of the people who will work on the project, and 5) the budget. You are not ready to start writing the proposal until you can draft a paragraph or two for each of those items, and until you can summarize what other people have already done in the specific area you plan to work in. And you should have done the research for such a summary before making your decision to apply for the grant. This planning is important because even though you will undoubtedly be doing some creative thinking and revision as you write the proposal, grant proposals must be carefully structured documents. One cannot depend on inspiration to guide their development.

The Body of the Proposal.

Although the forms provided by most grant giving agencies specify that your proposal should begin with the title and an abstract, you will probably want to postpone writing those items until later. (Suggestions about both will come later in this chapter.) Begin your proposal with the description of your project, your reasons for proposing it, and a discussion of what you hope to accomplish with it. Obviously this introductory section of the proposal needs to make a good impression on your readers so as you write it keep in mind those cardinal virtues of good writing: significance, unity, clarity, economy, and vigor. Get to the point immediately by stating what you intend to do. Follow up with an explanation of why you think it is worth doing, what other people have done in similar work, and what you expect your project to accomplish that has not previously been done. You may need several paragraphs or several pages to cover all these points adequately, but try to write as succinctly as possible.

Suppose, for example, that you are an architect who has joined with a historian, an engineer, and a landscape architect to get funds to restore an old deteriorated market-area to its original condition. In the introductory section of your proposal you would identify and objectively describe the building you want to restore, describe the work that needs to be done and the approximate cost, give reasons for restoring the building—historic value, effect on surrounding area, attraction for tourists, and so on—describe and cite the effects of similar projects in other cities, and explain your belief that a restoration project that emphasizes the city's heritage can become the focus of an economic renaissance of the inner city. You should strive for a vigorous and confident tone in this section, and should include enough pertinent details and enough references to previous or similar projects to sound competent and knowledgeable.

If the first section of the proposal is important because it describes what you want to do and explains why you want to do it, the second section is equally important because it must explain *how* you plan to accomplish your goal. Now you need to prove that you are competent and knowledgeable by outlining practical procedures for carrying out your plan and giving a realistic timetable for the work. If your proposal involves research, specify how you are going to collect your data, how you will control variables, and what analytical methods you will use. Experienced reviewers will take a particularly close look at this part of the proposal because they do not want to waste money supporting a project that sounds worthy but is poorly designed.

When you describe the facilities available to you for working on the project or carrying out the research, and give the credentials and experience of your coworkers, you are also establishing your credibility as an applicant. This section needs to be written carefully and honestly to show that you have the qualifications to spend the foundation's money productively. It is a good idea to include a biographical data sheet for each person who will be working on the project.

How you conclude your proposal depends on the kind of format prescribed by the organization giving the grant. If it gives no specific guidelines use your best judgment. If the proposal runs to 15 or 20 pages, you may need to help your reader by reiterating the key points in a summary section and stressing the innovative features of your proposal. Reviewers of such proposals tend to favor projects that explore new territory or suggest fresh approaches. If, however, the instructions for writing the grant proposal are very specific, abide by them and do not add a separate justification section at the end.

Making a Budget.

The first time you estimate a budget for a grant proposal you should seek help if you can because such budgets must include hidden costs that are easily overlooked, items like contributions to retirement funds and to the operating expenses of the institution whose facilities you will be using. Almost every college has employees whose job it is to help applicants with their grant proposals; don't hesitate to use them. If you are drawing up a complicated budget and you do not have access to such people, try to find a professional consultant and pay for an expert opinion. At the very least, get a book on preparing grants and look at sample budgets.

But no one else can actually make a budget for you. Only you can estimate how long your project is going to take and consequently what the outlay for salaries will be; how much computer time you may need and how much should be allotted for travel expenses; what kind of equipment you will need and what it costs to operate it. And don't make vague estimates. Finding out what things cost takes leg work and lots of phone calls, but you need to figure all your expenditures as accurately as possible before you take your tentative budget to a consultant. Remember too that you should explain and justify any large item that does not seem self-explanatory.

Resist the temptation to underestimate your costs because you feel that an accurate statement seems so high that you would not have a chance of getting the grant. The people who review grants have a good idea what expenses on a project should run, and if you turn in a budget that is unrealistically low they will question your professional competence. If necessary, it would be better for you to scale down the scope of your proposal than to look financially naive.

Writing the Abstract and Title.

When you have finished the budget and finished any other sections that the grant announcement may specify, you are ready to write your abstract and title. Since they will introduce your proposal to the reviewers, you need to write them very carefully so that they will succinctly and accurately state your case. The title should be as brief as you can make it and still be explicit. For instance, "A Proposal to Make an Authentic Restoration of the Farmers' Market and Surrounding Square in Dayton, Ohio," or "A Study of the Effect of Syntactical Arrangement on the Readability of Nonfiction Prose."

The following excerpt from a 1977 grants announcement pamphlet from the National Institute of Education sums up the guidelines you should follow in writing your abstract.

> Abstract: The narrative should be succinct, non-technical description of the research. It should not exceed 250 words, and should be so clearly written that the following questions could be answered by reading it.
>
> Paragraph (a) What is the specific purpose of this study? What information is being sought?
>
> Paragraph (b) Who needs it? Why is it desirable to do this?
>
> Paragraph (c) How is the study to be conducted (a non-technical description of the general methodology).
>
> Paragraph (d) What difference might the results make?—to whom?

See pp. 233–37 for more detailed information about writing abstracts.

Getting a Second Opinion.

When you have finished writing the proposal and have revised it into a second draft, give a copy of your proposal to a knowledgeable person whose judgment you trust. Ask that person to put himself or herself in the role of a reviewer and to read your proposal with a skeptical eye, looking particularly for omissions, oversimplifications, or unwarranted claims. Also ask that person to mark any places where the language is vague or confusing or where the writing is biased or inflated. If you can get two qualified and patient people to read the proposal, so much the better.

The Final Draft.

When you have the proposal in final form, have it professionally typed, leaving good margins, making sure to follow to the letter the instructions provided in the grant application. Mark the internal divisions with headings and subheadings and make sure charts and diagrams are labeled. Proofread the final copy meticulously to be sure that it looks as good as it can, and get the necessary number of copies made by a reliable service so that they will not be streaked or dim. In other words, make sure that the packet of paper that is going off to represent you makes the best possible appearance.

Evaluation Criteria.

Reviewers for granting agencies and foundations judge proposals they receive on these criteria:

- Is the research or project proposed relevant to the goals of the agency?
- Is the proposal innovative?
- Is the problem the proposal addresses important?
- Do the applicants show knowledge of previous work in this area.
- Is the proposal project adequately designed?
- Are the people who will work on the project competent?
- Can the project be carried out in the estimated time?
- Is the budget accurate and reasonable?
- Are the facilities and equipment for the project adequate?

If your grant proposal meets all these criteria and is clearly and carefully written, you stand a good chance of getting your money.

Nontechnical Reports

Just as scientists, architects, or anthropologists who thought they were going into non-writing professions often find themselves spending a surprising amount of time writing grant proposals, so nurses, social workers, bankers, or psychiatrists—in fact, perhaps the majority of professional people—find that they spend an unexpected amount of time writing reports. The report is the essential document of the business and professional world, the instrument used to inform and instruct colleagues and customers and to furnish data on which people can make decisions. So important are business and technical reports that many specialists give courses and write textbooks on technical report writing; if you think you will do a great deal of that kind of writing, you will probably want to take such a course in college or after you go to work in your profession. But people who are called on to write occasional nontechnical reports such as a summary of a public opinion survey or an analysis of customer complaints can learn to write successful reports by following the ordinary procedures for writing good prose.

Characteristics of Reports.

Reports are about facts. The person who reads the report you have written does not expect to find out what you feel, think, believe, fear, or hope; he or she expects to find out what you have investigated, observed, experienced, or read about. Meteorologists giving a weather report to a pilot do not say that it's a "nice day." Rather they say "Clear skies, visibility unlimited, no turbulence in this area." From those facts they may draw an inference and add, "Should be a good day to fly," but strictly speaking, that inference is not part of the report.

Reports are based on data; we use them as we use reference books to find out information. Consequently the person who writes them should keep these points in mind:

- The writer should focus on the material under discussion.
- The writer should not express personal emotions or opinions.
- The writer should not argue or seek to persuade.
- The writer should not use a literary style that calls attention to itself.[1]

Writing a good report becomes an exercise in restraint. It also becomes an exercise in practicing subtle communication skills because although writers must seem not to be thinking about their audiences, they must be acutely aware of the audience. Equally, though they must not draw attention to themselves directly, in an indirect way they must convince their readers that they are conscientious and reliable reporters.

The Audience for Reports.

People who write reports usually do so on assignment and for a specific audience. For example, a biologist might write a report on an environmental study for the state Fish and Game Commission; a nurse might write a report on her study of a pregnant diabetic woman for the instructor of her course in clinical practices; a navy officer might write a report on needed ship repairs for the head of the United States Bureau of Ships. Or a report might be as simple as a one-paragraph summary of snow conditions at Taos written for people who want to go skiing. The authors of any of these reports need to identify the intended audience as precisely as possible to decide just what it is they want to get from reading these reports. Because writers do not want to waste their audience's time by telling them more than they need to know, they need to assess carefully their audience's level of expertise. They also need to think about how much specialized vocabulary they can use; for the right audience it can act as a kind of shorthand, but for the wrong one it can impede communication.

Moreover, a writer needs to think about how many people will read the report and how much influence they have, how long it will last, and what actions might be taken on the basis of its contents. The snow report becomes useless after a day and is thrown away; the environmental study will reach readers at several levels of power, will serve as the basis for recommending action, and will almost certainly be filed and stored. For those reasons it should be comprehensive, documented, and written in a language nonspecialists can understand.

The language of the report should have an objective tone that puts con-

1. Guidelines adapted from James Kinneavy, *A Theory of Discourse* (Englewood Cliffs, N.J.: Prentice-Hall, 1971), p. 88.

siderable distance between reader and writer and avoids the pronoun *you* unless it seems required by the context. But writing this way should not mean writing stuffy, dull, or pedantic prose, nor should it mean writing an inflated and passive style loaded down with derived nouns and prepositional phrases.

The writer stays in the background with this kind of fact-centered, objective style. This effect is enhanced by using neutral language and by using few adjectives. But writers who try to sound objective simply by not using the pronoun *I* may create more problems than they solve. For one thing, they can wind up with a contrived and awkward style; for example, "This investigator visited Padre Island on June 25" or "The author of this report interviewed the patient." The writer trying to avoid *I* may also fall back on passive constructions and abstract subjects that can confuse the reader; for example, "The feasibility of the study was determined by the investigator" or "This material was decided to be relevant." Nearly any reader would prefer that an author write, "I interviewed the patient" or "I collected the data."

Moreover, using *I* in a report identifies you as a writer who deserves credit for having compiled and written a good report. And you can strengthen that impression by routinely citing and consistently documenting all your sources. You can furnish your documentation either with footnotes written according to the style prescribed by a reputable style sheet or by giving your references in parentheses within the body of the text (see pp. 210–12).

The Structure of Reports.

Reports usually function as documents that are meant to convey information to readers so that those readers can do a job. Therefore, the report should be organized to serve the reader.[2] How can you put it together so that the reader can grasp the contents as quickly and efficiently as possible? When you are writing reports on assignment, often the reader has already decided on a plan of organization and gives you specific instructions on how to carry it out. For example, the instructions for major term reports in one school of nursing stipulate that those reports must be organized as follows:

Abstract
Introduction, including statement of the problem
Review of the literature
Clinical application
Conclusions
Recommendations

A business firm or government bureau might insist that writers reporting to them follow this kind of plan:

2. Gordon H. Mills and John A. Walter, *Technical Writing,* 4th ed. (New York: Holt, Rinehart and Winston, 1978), p. 292.

Abstract
Introduction
a. Statement of the problem
b. Purpose of the report
c. Description of method used
Body of report
a. Detailed description of procedures carried out
b. Explanation of findings
Conclusions
a. Detailed summary of results

Such formulas can simplify your task and serve as useful models for many kinds of report writing assignments.

Sometimes, however, you must develop your own pattern of organization for a report. When you do, start with a comprehensive and accurate title that lets your reader know precisely what to expect from the report. (Remember also that the title controls how the report will be filed.) Immediately after the title page, many readers expect to find an abstract that summarizes the content of the report. Even if an abstract is not required, it is a good idea to include one for a long paper, as it helps to focus the reader's attention and makes it easier for him or her to follow your report. (See pp. 233–37 on writing abstracts.)

Begin the report itself with an introduction that states the issue or problem to be addressed, the purpose of the report, and the method used for carrying out that purpose. Such a businesslike opening may seem dull, but it is important nevertheless. Readers want to know from the start why they should read the report and where and how you got your evidence.

How you organize the body of the report will depend on your purpose for writing and the kind of material you are dealing with. If you are writing a research report about a diabetic pregnant woman, you would probably want to use a narrative form to recount the woman's case history, give the results of your interviews with her, and document the clinical symptoms as the pregnancy advanced. Then you would want to review the literature of what is known about the complications that diabetes causes for pregnant women, apply that information to the case you are writing about, and give your findings. In the conclusion of your paper, you would summarize what you learned.

In other kinds of reports writers usually begin by stating the most important information in the report. Although this kind of organization may not work well for persuasive or entertaining writing because it takes away the writer's chance to build to a climax, it does work well for factual explanatory writing. Readers for that kind of writing do not want to be intrigued and kept in suspense; they want to know results. If those results are important to them, they will probably read on to find out how they were obtained; if they are not, they do not have to spend any more time on the document.

After you have given the crucial information, you must then go on to discuss your procedures and findings in detail. Not everyone who is interested in the main content of your report will read the detailed discussion, but it should be written carefully nevertheless so it can be referred to if needed. Finally, most reports that run to more than a few pages should conclude with a summary that restates the main idea.

Case Studies:
A Special Kind of Reports.

Professionals in many fields must spend substantial time writing reports that deal not with impersonal data but with the behavior of people. Those reports are called *case studies* or *case histories,* and the methodology for education and research in a number of disciplines depends heavily on the case-study method. Some of these fields are clinical and experimental psychology, social work, speech therapy, medicine, and the social sciences such as anthropology, sociology, and linguistics. People working in any of these fields of study need to know how to write case studies; so do nurses, policemen, and emergency medical technicians.

Because most case studies are not highly technical, people who must write them usually do not have to take special training. They can manage quite well if they do their best to write clear, concise, economical, and unpretentious prose and keep in mind a few extra guidelines that apply particularly to case studies. The first is to learn to write objective, concrete descriptions of behavior without expressing personal opinions or biases and without judging; the second is to learn to write comprehensive reports that include all pertinent information; the third is to learn to anticipate the specific questions that the case study is expected to answer.

The first guideline is probably the most difficult to follow because most of us have trouble being neutral when we watch or talk to other people. We like or dislike them, approve or disapprove of their behavior even when we don't know them. Yet a linguistic researcher or social worker or clinical psychologist cannot afford to let emotion or bias appear in a case study that is supposed to be only a description. The professional responsibility of these people is to record what they observe, are told in an interview, or learn through a test. So a child-guidance counselor should write "Philip is below normal weight and height for his age and expresses fears about being attacked by larger boys in his grade," not "Philip is pathetically thin and intimidated by larger boys." And a cultural anthropologist should not describe an Indian tribe as "brave and proud," but should instead describe the behavior of the tribe. When a person is collecting and recording data, even data about human beings, that person must take great care not to prejudice the reader with connotative language.

Inexperienced report writers sometimes also have trouble deciding how much information they should include in their case studies. A writer does not want to waste the reader's time or mix irrelevant information with important data, but good case studies must include all *pertinent* facts. So the question becomes "What is pertinent?" and the answer must depend on the purpose of the case study.

In the case study of the diabetic pregnant woman, the nursing student needed to include information about the woman's weight, diet, economic circumstances, educational level, family history, marital status, and previous pregnancies, as all these matters affected her ability to control her diabetes. On the other hand, in behavioral psychologist Stanley Milgram's study of destructive obedience in a laboratory situation, the author gives only this much information about the subject:

> The subjects were 40 males between the ages of 20 and 50, drawn from New Haven and the surrounding communities. Subjects were obtained by a newspaper advertisement and direct mail solicitation. Those who responded to the appeal believed they were to participate in a study of memory and learning at Yale University. A wide range of occupations is represented in the sample. Typical subjects were postal clerks, high school teachers, salesmen, engineers, and laborers. Subjects ranged in educational level from one who had not finished elementary school, to those who had doctorate and other professional degrees. They were paid $4.50 for their participation in the experiment. However, subjects were told that payment was simply for coming to the laboratory, and that the money was theirs no matter what happened after they arrived.[3]

For the rest of the case study, Milgram reported only the subjects' actual behavior in the laboratory. Any other information about them was not relevant to the study.

Your ability to select data that is appropriate for your case study and to exclude information that is irrelevant or peripheral reveals a great deal about your competence in your field. If you cannot discriminate between useful and irrelevant data or judge how much evidence you need for a particular study, you signal to your reader that you probably don't know what you are doing. As one expert puts it:

> As to pertinence, the report writer should not collect data for its own sake, use it indiscriminately, or use it to pad or make the report appear to be more professional.[4]

Finally, people write case studies in order to answer questions that someone has asked or will ask about their work. You should be able to figure out what those questions will be if you know *why* they are being asked. For ex-

3. Stanley Milgram, "A Behavioral Study of Obedience," *The Norton Reader,* revised, shorter edition, ed. Arthur Eastman et al. (New York: W. W. Norton, 1965), p. 195.
4. Jack Huber, *Report Writing in Psychology and Psychiatry* (New York: Harper and Row, 1961), p. 13.

ample, the emergency medical technician who is writing a case history of a patient brought in from an automobile accident knows that the doctor wants information that will help in treating the patient, so the technician reports on blood type, location of injuries, temperature, blood pressure, treatment given, and so on. However, a rehabilitation counselor who is writing a case history in order to help that same person qualify for a state training program knows that the screening committee wants to know whether the person can be helped and why the state should subsidize rehabilitation. To answer those questions the counselor needs to include information on the person's injuries, educational level, financial status, and so on. The kind and amount of information the audience needs will vary with the task; thus people who write case studies may need to develop their sense of audience and purpose even more highly than other writers do.

Abstracts

The Uses of Abstracts.

People who write regularly in business, industry, technology, medicine, or the academic profession learn to write abstracts early in their careers because the abstract is an essential part of the communication system in their field. A good abstract summarizes an article or report so succinctly and accurately that readers can quickly infer from the abstract the essential content of the longer work. Ideally, an abstract should have the same relationship to an article or report that an architect's model of a building has to the completed building. Just as one should be able to tell from an architect's model what a building is going to look like, one should be able to tell from an abstract what a report is going to say. And both the model and the abstract should be self-contained units, independent miniatures that make sense even when separated from the piece of work they represent.

Promissory Abstracts.

Abstracts are important because they can serve both writers and readers in a number of different ways. First, a writer can draft a preliminary abstract of a paper as a way of beginning to think about the topic and as a device for organizing those ideas. This kind of abstract is preliminary and flexible, more like a working sketch for a building than like a model, and usually it will be substantially revised or discarded altogether when the paper is completed.

Second, a person may write an abstract that is a kind of promissory note to a program chairman or an editor. In this kind of abstract the writer sketches out the paper or report he or she plans to write and submits it for consideration. If the editor or chairman thinks the projected piece of writing is worth publishing or presenting, and if the person submitting the abstract has good credentials for writing such a piece, the abstract may be accepted, and the writer is then committed to produce the paper. People who submit abstracts of this kind must follow them faithfully when they write their final paper because they have made a contract on the basis of the abstract.

People who will be working in fields in which one earns rewards by publishing or presenting papers should master the art of writing these promissory abstracts as part of their professional training. For one thing, you can often meet a deadline for papers or program proposals if you can submit an abstract by that deadline rather than a completed paper. Second, once an editor or program chairman accepts your proposal on the basis of an abstract, you have made a comitment and established a deadline that will force you to write the paper. Many of us need that kind of motivation.

Summary Abstracts.

Abstracts written after a report has been completed can also serve several purposes. First, they may appear at the beginning of a report and function as a kind of preview that lets the reader know what to expect; this is particularly useful for long reports. Second, they can serve as a summary that will give an administrator or executive necessary information in a capsule form. Third, the abstract can be separated from the paper and serve as its representative. In this capacity it can be filed so that someone wanting information about the report can consult it quickly. It could also appear in the program for a professional meeting to help participants decide if they want to hear the full paper, or it could be published in a journal or catalog of abstracts so that people searching for material on the topic could determine whether they want to read the full-length paper.

Since an abstract serves so many functions, you can see why it is so important that it be well written. One authority claims that it is the most important part of a paper:

> The first significant impression of your report is formed on the reader's mind by the abstract; and the sympathy with which it is read, if it is read at all, is often determined by this first impression.[5]

Writing the Abstract.

Good abstracts are hard to write precisely because they must accurately compress so much information into compact form, and because they should be written in easy-to-understand, nontechnical language. Moreover, your method of writing an abstract will differ when you are writing a promissory

---

5. Christian K. Arnold, "The Writing of Abstracts," in *The Practical Craft,* ed. Keats Sparrow and Donald Cunningham (Boston: Houghton Mifflin Co., 1978), p. 264.

abstract and when you are writing a summary abstract. The first is creative, the second analytical.

WRITING THE PROMISSORY ABSTRACT.   When you are writing a promissory abstract, you need to go through a process similar to the one you use at the preparatory stages of writing a paper. First write down the main idea or thesis that you want to present; then brainstorm and take notes on all the possible points you might want to make about that thesis. On a new page jot down sources and examples that you might use to illustrate your thesis. Finally you might write down why you think the paper you propose is worth presenting or why an audience would be interested in reading or listening to what you have to say.

Then beginning either with a statement of your main idea or a listing of the main evidence on which you base your thesis, write a first draft that answers these questions: What are you going to say? What is the basis for your assertion? Why is it worth saying? Who needs to know it or what is the information good for?

Don't worry too much about length on this first draft. Get down as much information as you think the program chairman or editor needs in order to make a judgment about the paper. You can trim it to size later. In the second and third drafts cut if necessary, and simplify and polish your writing because this abstract will represent not only the content of your paper but it will also be a sample of your prose style. You can present your credentials for giving the paper on a separate sheet or in a letter.

Here is a sample of a promissory abstract that I turned in for a conference on composition:

Working from available research on the writing process, from authors' accounts of how they write, from comments on writing by Jacques Barzun, John Kenneth Galbraith, and Albert Kazin, from analysis of my own writing habits and those of other professionals, and from general accounts of the creative process, I have drawn some inferences about the composing processes of working writers. From the evidence I have also made 12 generalizations about the habits and attitudes of effective writers. Teachers of composition can make use of this information because as Shaughnessy points out in her book, *Errors and Expectations,* beginning students need to know how writers work. (The completed paper will be no longer than 3,000 words.)

The program chairman accepted the paper, and four months later I wrote it.

WRITING THE SUMMARY ABSTRACT.   In writing a summary abstract, you need to start by carefully rereading your paper and underlining the main points. Write brief summaries of each section in the margins as you would if you were studying for an exam on the paper; star the most important points you make. Then make a rough outline of the paper so that you see your plan of development at a glance; you may realize, for instance, that although you spent twice as long developing point one as you did in developing point two, the points are equally important and you do not need to give twice as much space to point one in the abstract. It is because of concerns of this kind that you should not try to write an abstract by stringing together sentences that summarize each paragraph.

One way to write an analytical abstract would be to put down the most important idea in your paper in the first sentence and in two or three more sentences develop that idea. Then describe how you arrived at your thesis giving specific details if it seems useful. Finally, summarize the implications of your thesis or hypothesize about what its value might be. Another approach might be to begin by stating the problem you are writing about, then describe the approach you used to work on it, and finally give your results. And there are other ways to write an abstract. You do not have to organize abstracts in the same way that you organize your papers, but that method may be easier when you first start to write them.

As you write the abstract, think of the audience that may read it. Use terminology that an intelligent nonspecialist could understand and try to make your summary so complete that someone outside your field could understand what you are talking about. Keep reminding yourself that this abstract should be a self-contained piece of writing that can stand on its own when it is separated from the paper it represents. And when it is separated, it represents your thought, so you want it to be an intelligible, cohesive piece of writing.

For example, here is how a summary abstract of the proposal for the university day-care center mentioned in chapter 2 might look.

The university needs to sponsor and subsidize an on-campus day-care center for the children of university faculty and students for several reasons. Such a center would help the university to attract more of the large number of women who are returning to school to finish their educations or improve their professional credentials. It would also help the university to attract and hold young men and women faculty who favor working for institutions who offer good family-related fringe benefits. In addition, providing good on-campus child care would improve the performances of both students and faculty by reducing their anxiety about their children not being adequately cared for.

The university should provide funds for this facility on a prorated basis because doing so would help to compensate for its not providing paid maternity benefits or leaves of absence for faculty. Further, data from countries that provide this kind of care indicate that such facilities contribute to better infant health and to an increase in scholarly productivity among women faculty. The cost of such a center would be approximately $250,000 for the first year, and $120,000 a year after that. These costs would be met partially by tax money and partially by user fees.

Length of Abstracts.

Although one might think that the length of a finished paper would control the length of the abstract that represents it, such is not usually the case.

More often the length of an abstract is limited by the directions a writer receives from an editor, a supervisor, or a program director. Sometimes directions specify that the abstract must not exceed 100 words; then a writer has to
reduce content to the essence. More often, direction will say that abstracts
should not exceed 250 words; that is, one double-spaced page typed in pica
type. If the directions say "no more than one page" rather than give the
number of words, you can squeeze in another 50 words by using elite type.
Probably it is best not to single-space an abstract.

Even if you have no specified limit for your abstract, as a rule you should
try to keep it to one page. A reader who intends to read both the abstract and
the report doesn't want to go through a three-page preliminary. Also one-page
abstracts are filed more easily and go onto microfiche or microfilm more easily.

When you begin writing abstracts you will continually face a conflict between keeping the abstract short enough and putting in everything that you
think should be included. Inevitably you compromise and probably your abstracts will never come as close to being perfect miniature reports as you
would like for them to be. Neither do anyone else's. But as you continue to
write them and to realize what a necessary professional tool they are, you will
develop an instinct about what to include in an abstract, and your task will
gradually become easier.

Papers for Oral Presentation

Many young professionals find early in their careers that they must often write
papers for oral presentations. When they give such papers, they are not necessarily giving speeches; rather they are apt to be reading a paper to explain a
concept or theory, offer a solution to a problem, or present the results of their
research. They want to make a good impression, but too often they do not
succeed because they have written their papers for a reading audience rather
than for a listening audience. The needs of the two audiences are significantly
different.

Length of Papers.

The first concern of any person writing a paper to be given orally should
be its length. How much time are you going to have? 10 minutes? 25 minutes?
You need to find out and take the limit very seriously. If you are asked to be
on a 90-minute panel with two other speakers, don't assume that you will
have 30 minutes to read your paper. Almost certainly the panel will start late,
the moderator will need time to introduce the panelists, and time should be

allowed for questions and discussion. You should really count on only 20 minutes to present your paper, and you should plan accordingly. And even if you are the only person who will be delivering a paper at a meeting, usually you should condense what you have to say into 30 minutes or less. Only the most charismatic speakers can hold their audience's attention much longer than that.

The best way to be sure your paper is not too long is to read it into a tape recorder, and time it as you play it back. That way you can judge the pace to decide whether you are reading too quickly. Probably you will be. Most of us tend to forget that the audience needs time to absorb our points as we make them. If you don't have a tape recorder, read your paper out loud and time it. Then start cutting if you have to. If, however, the paper doesn't quite fill up your allotted time you should probably resist the temptation to expand it.

When you are writing a paper for oral presentation, you should figure on *at least* two minutes to read one double-spaced, 250-word page in pica type. (For elite type, adjust accordingly.) If you can read 125 words in a minute— and that's a fairly brisk pace—you can plan on 20 minutes for a 2,500-word, 10-page paper. And if your finished paper runs 11½ pages, you should not plan to rush through it to meet your deadline. Better to cut it back to the proper length and read it effectively.

Structure for Oral Presentations.

Once you know the time allotted for your paper, you can decide how to restrict your topic to one that you can treat adequately in the 2,500 or 3,000 words to which you are limited. You have to make your points clear the first time; therefore you should have fewer points. Because an oral presentation usually requires that you explain and illustrate your points more fully, you need to insert signal sentences to preview or summarize for your audience or to keep them headed in the direction you want to go. Remember that your audience cannot go back and reread earlier paragraphs.

Whether you choose to begin your oral presentation with a lead-in paragraph to catch your audience's attention, or with a direct statement announcing your thesis depends partially on the occasion and partially on your personal style. I usually prefer a direct opening statement that announces my thesis and starts my audience off in the right direction. For example:

Students who are struggling to become writers can profit in several ways from learning about the behavior of professional writers.

I would then go on to list those ways in order to give my audience a preview of what they are about to hear. After the preview I would work my way through my points, being careful to use words such as *first, second,* and *next,* and strong signal words such as *therefore* and *consequently* to help my audience anticipate what is coming. And I would downshift frequently, particularly when I wanted to illustrate an abstract statement.

By using these obvious devices you help your listening audience move with you through your paper. You map it for them and provide directional signals. You can even reinforce your signals by writing your main points on a blackboard as you go. You can also punctuate your presentation with slides or charts shown with an overhead projector. These visual aids not only reinforce the content of your paper, but they give your listeners intermittent breaks in which to absorb the content.

Oral Style.

When you begin to work on the second or third version of a paper that you will be reading aloud, try to think in terms of an oral style. As one authority points out, that means several things:

> In other words, a style adapted to the ear instead of the eye means that the language will be simpler to grasp; unusual terms will be used more sparingly, and when they are used will be spoken more clearly and defined more fully; ideas will be paced more slowly; and the development will be less condensed than in writing.[6]

Three more strategies that will make your prose more listenable have already been discussed in earlier chapters as ways of making your writing more readable. The first is to construct sentences in which there is frequent closure. That is, try not to write long strung-out sentences for which the meaning cannot be grasped until one reaches the end (see page 140).

Second, when possible rearrange many of your sentences into the agent/action pattern (see page 177). Since that pattern gives readers strong signals about what to anticipate, it should also help listeners. If your agent is a concrete or personal subject, so much the better.

Third, check your writing to see if it is overburdened with derived nouns—words ending in *-ity, -ness, -tion,* and so on—or with a disproportionate number of prepositional phrases.

In addition, a listening audience will particularly appreciate a speaker who uses metaphors and analogies as explanatory devices. Probably nothing helps an audience grasp a vague or elusive concept as quickly as having a writer clarify it by a graphic comparison. In fact, listeners may remember the central point of a paper primarily because of the visual image triggered by an apt analogy. Thus if you were to form an image for your listeners by comparing the process of transmitting documents over telephone lines to someone transmitting braille impressions through the fingers you help them to understand a complex process.

6. Roger P. Wilcox, *Communication at Work* (Boston: Houghton Mifflin Co., 1977), p. 454–55.

Finally, it seems useful to point out that "reading a paper" should not mean that you stand before your audience with your eyes focused only on your paper. People do not like to feel that they are being read to. To counteract that impression, you should study your paper ahead of time so that you can look up from it frequently. Make eye contact with your audience to let them know that it is important to you that they understand what you are saying. And if you have written your paper specifically with that listening audience in mind probably they will.

EXERCISES / *Prewriting Activities*

1   In a paragraph of about 100 words, analyze the audience you would have for the following writing tasks. How knowledgeable would they probably be, and what would they want to get from reading your writing?

A.   A grant proposal to the National Endowment for the Arts to ask for $165,000 to support a project to give dancing lessons to children whose families cannot afford such lessons.

B.   A report to the commanding officer at the Air Force Academy on cadets' attitudes toward the honor code of the Academy.

C.   A case study to the probation officer about a thirteen-year-old child who is on probation from the juvenile court for stealing a car.

D.   A speech for the California Bar Association on the possible effects of legislation to limit liability in medical malpractice suits.

2   Choose articles from three magazines that vary widely in their focus, for instance, *National Geographic, Psychology Today,* and *U.S. News and World Report.* Read the articles carefully and take notes on points in each one that should be included by a person writing a summary abstract of the articles.

3   Analyze the purpose you would have in writing a promissory abstract for a paper you propose to give with one of the following titles.

The Declining Use of Migrant Labor in the Food Processing Industry.

Existential Despair in the Novels of Joan Didion.

Using the Care of Pets to Raise Self-Confidence in the Mentally Retarded.

4   In a paragraph of no more than 150 words, analyze the specific problems you would anticipate in giving an oral presentation under the following circumstances:

A.   Presenting a report on the effect of high interest rates on real-estate sales in your area.

B.   Presenting the results of a psychological experiment on factors found to produce writing anxiety in high-school students.

C.   Presenting to the directors of a corporation an oral report on new underwater oil drilling operations completed in the past year

Suggested Writing Assignments

For each paper, begin by defining and analyzing your audience and your purpose. Specify the characteristics of your audience that are important to keep in mind as you write, and state the specific points that your audience would want to get from reading your paper. Also state clearly and in some detail what you hope to accomplish by writing the paper. When appropriate, give your paper an accurate and descriptive title.

TOPIC 1:

Choose a foundation or government agency that gives money for research projects that will contribute to knowledge in a particular field or help to solve a serious problem. Some of the best-known foundations are these:

Ford Foundation   National Institute for Education
Rockefeller Foundation   National Endowment for the Humanities
Exxon Corporation   National Endowment for the Arts
Sloan Foundation   National Science Foundation

Write a grant proposal for one of these projects:

A.   A film on nutrition for young mothers in poverty areas.

B.   An expedition to New Mexico to record oral history of a tribe of Indians.

C.   An educational film on the most effective methods of birth control. Specify a particular audience.

D.   Outreach project to teach illiterate adults to read.

E.   Research project to develop a chemical to eradicate mesquite from pasture land.

F.   A film to teach high-school students how to establish and use credit.

TOPIC 2:

Write a report in response to one of these assignments:

A.   A credit report on a family applying for a home loan. Give the wife and husband's ages, employment, income, education, and what ever other features you think may be pertinent.

B.   A report for an urban planning class showing how population patterns in your area have changed in the past ten years.

C.   A report for the state legislature showing the comparative salaries and ranks of men and women in higher education in your state.

TOPIC 3:

Write a case study about one of these individuals. Specify the purpose of the study:

A.   A 21-year-old man who was blinded in an industrial accident on his summer job is applying for a tuition grant and financial assistance in order that he may return to college.

B.   A family who wants to adopt a child from an ethnic group different from its own.

C.   A 45-year-old displaced homemaker whose husband has died, leaving her with no insurance and only a small income. She has no marketable skills so she is applying for admission to a city retraining program offered for women who want to return to school. The program offers subsidies to ten such women each year.

TOPIC 4:

Choose an article from a magazine in which you are particularly interested and write a 250-word abstract that reflects the tone and emphasis of the original article and functions as a miniature model of the original. Attach a copy of the original to your paper.

TOPIC 5:

Write a promissory abstract to go with one of the oral presentations suggested under Topic 6.

TOPIC 6:

Write a talk on one of these topics, to be presented under the circumstances specified for each one.

A.   Write a talk for a summer orientation meeting on campus. Try to get incoming students interested in working in campus organizations and politics.

B.   Prepare a radio talk to persuade young people of the benefits of individual exercise programs (not competitive team sports)

C.   Prepare a talk for a local service club—Rotary, Optimists, Altrusa, or American Association of University Women—and outline your plan for increasing voter participation among 18- to 25-year-old people.

D.   As education officer for your corporation, give a talk to a group of executive trainees on the value of learning to write clearly and effectively.

E.   Present a 10-minute summary of the results of your research on how the typical middle-income family in your area spends its food budget.

CHAPTER 12

A Brief Review of Grammar

As long ago as the first chapter, I included acceptable usage among the most important qualities of good writing. Indeed, some professionals seem to be bothered almost as much by shaky grammar as by shaky thinking. Benjamin DeMott, not only a fine writer but an English teacher, recalls one rock-ribbed senior partner in a law firm who was obsessed with what he thought was the misuse of the comma. Obviously such quirks are impossible to predict. But are there any particular errors that most managers and professional people find especially troublesome? Oddly enough, there has been little research into this question. In September 1979 I decided to try and find out.

In September of 1979, I sent a questionnaire to 101 professional people, asking them how they would respond to lapses from standard English usage and mechanics in each of 63 sentences if those sentences appeared in a business document that came across their desks. The 84 people who responded to the questionnaire represented a broad range of professionals: engineers, judges, bankers, attorneys, architects, public relation executives, corporation and college presidents, tax analysts, investment counselors, and a U.S. Congressman, to name just a few. They ranged in age from 30 to 70, but most were in their late 40's and early 50's. 22 were women, and 62 were men. No English teachers were included in the survey.

Each of the 63 sentences on the questionnaire contained one error in usage or mechanics, and the respondents were asked to mark one of these responses for every sentence: Does Not Bother Me, Bothers Me a Little, Bothers Me a Lot. The last question asked for an open-ended comment about the most annoying feature they encountered in writing they had to read.

After tabulating all the responses to the sentences and reading all the comments, I came to these conclusions about how professional people react to writing that they encounter in the course of their work.

1. Women take a more conservative attitude about standard English usage than men do. On every item, the percentage of women marking "Bothers Me a Lot" was much higher than the percentage of men.

2. The defects in writing that professional people complained of most were *lack of clarity, wordiness,* and *failure to get to the point*. They also complained strongly about poor grammar, faulty punctuation, and bad spelling.
3. The middle-aged, educated, and successful men and women who occupy positions of responsibility in the business and professional world are sensitive to the way people write. Even allowing for the strong possibility that they were more than normally conservative in responding to a questionnaire from an English teacher, most professionals seem to believe that writers should observe the conventions of standard English usage.

Responses to the individual items on the survey indicate, however, that these professional people clearly consider some lapses in usage and mechanics much more serious than others. Here is the way in which they ranked items on the questionnaire:

Extremely serious lapses from the standard:

Incorrect verb forms. E.g., "he brung," "we was," "he don't."

Double negatives.

Sentence fragments.

Subjects in the objective case. E.g., "Him and Jones are going."

Fused sentences. E.g., "He loved his job he never took holidays."

Failure to capitalize proper names, especially those referring to people and places.

A comma between the verb and complement of the sentence. E.g., "Cox cannot predict, that street crime will diminish."

Serious lapses from the standard:

Faulty parallelism.

Subject-verb disagreement.

Adjectives used to modify verbs. E.g., "He treats his men bad."

Not marking interrupters such as "However" with commas.

Subjective pronouns used for objects. E.g., "The Army sent my husband and I to Japan."

Confusion of the verbs "sit" and "set."

Moderately serious lapses:

Tense shifting.

Dangling modifiers.

Failure to use quotation marks around quoted material.

Plural modifier with a singular noun. E.g., "*These* kind."

Omitting commas in a series.

Faulty predication. E.g., "The policy intimidates applications."

Ambiguous use of "which."

Objective form of a pronoun used as a subjective complement. E.g., "That is her across the street."

Confusion of the verbs "affect" and "effect."

Lapses that seem to matter very little:

Failure to distinguish between "whoever" and "whomever."

Omitting commas to set off interrupting phrases such as appositives.

Joining independent clauses with a comma; that is, a comma splice.

Confusion of "its" and "it's."

Failure to use the possessive form before a gerund. E.g., "The company objects to *us* hiring new salespeople."

Failure to distinguish between "among" and "between."

Lapses that do not seem to matter:

A qualifying word used before "unique." E.g., "That is the *most* unique plan we have seen."

"They" used to refer to a singular pronoun. E.g., "Everyone knows *they* will have to go."

Omitting a comma after an introductory clause.

Singular verb form used with "data." E.g., "The data *is* significant."

Linking verb followed by "when." E.g., "The problem is when patients refuse to cooperate."

Using the pronoun "that" to refer to people.

Using a colon after a linking verb. E.g., "The causes of the decline are: inflation, apathy, and unemployment."

The Grammar of Sentences

Sentence Fragments /frag

For a discussion of sentence fragments and ways to treat them, see pp. 145–47 of the text.

Comma Splices /CS

Sometimes when writers are working in haste and not thinking about the relationships between the statements they are putting down, they may join two groups of words that could be read as sentences with a comma instead of with a conjunction that would show the relationship between those word groups. When they do, they produce a *comma splice* (sometimes also called a *comma fault* or a *comma blunder*). That is, they join independent clauses with a punctuation mark that is so weak it cannot properly indicate the strong pause that should come in such a sentence. Here is an example of a weakly punctuated sentence:

> The first part of the book gave Jim no problem, it was the second part that stumped him.

Notice that the reader does not get a strong sense of separation between the two parts of the sentence. The emphasis would come through more clearly if it were written like this:

> The first part of the book gave Jim no problem, but the second part stumped him.

or this:

> Although the first part of the book gave Jim no problem, the second part stumped him.

Either revision correctly de-emphasizes the first part of the sentence, and puts the stress on the second. In the original, the parts of the sentence appear to be equal.

Here is another example of a weakly punctuated sentence:

> Society is another strong force in shaping morals, people tend to have those values of the society in which they grew up.

This time by using a comma splice the writer has disguised the cause and effect relationship between the parts of the sentence.

For two reasons writers should usually avoid comma splices. First, independent commas that "tack" clauses together indicate that the writer is unsure or unconcerned about the relationship between the parts of the sentences. Second, commas that join independent clauses invite misinterpretation. A comma is such a weak interrupter that the reader is liable to slip right over it.

However, if you want to join several short independent clauses with commas to increase the tempo of your writing, you can probably do so without creating any problems. For example:

> She met him, she liked him, she married him.
> It's not smart, it's not practical, it's not legal.

Fused or Run-on Sentences /fs

Sentences in which two independent clauses have been run together without any punctuation are confusing and distracting to the readers. Here is an example of a fused sentence:

> The success of horror movies is not surprising some people have always enjoyed being frightened.

Without punctuation, a reader at first makes "some people" the object of "is surprising" and then has to go back and reprocess the sentence. Also, without punctuation, the reader at first misses the cause and effect relationship of the clauses. This sentence could be revised to:

> The success of horror movies is not surprising; some people have always enjoyed being frightened.

Dangling Modifiers /dg

Modifying phrases that don't fit with the word or phrase that they seem to be attached to can cause problems for readers. Usually those misfit phrases, which we call *dangling modifiers,* come at the beginning of a sentence as an introductory phrase. An example of a dangling modifier is:

> *After leaving Cheyenne,* the cost of living became a problem.

The reader expects to find out who left Cheyenne, and is frustrated. Here is another example:

> *Having worked all day,* mistakes were to be expected.

At first one gets the impression that the mistakes have worked.

Notice that writers increase their chances of beginning a sentence with a dangling modifier when they use abstract subjects and passive verbs. If the writers of both sentences had used an acting, concrete subject, probably they would have seen their mistakes immediately.

Parallelism ///

Practiced writers use parallel structures frequently in order to unify and tighten their writing. That is, they incorporate two or more points in a sentence by using a series of phrases or clauses that have identical structure. For instance:

> Country Western fans love Willie Nelson, jazz fans love Oscar Peterson, and ballad fans love Judy Collins.

or

> Stein hit Hollywood determined to live high, hang loose, stay single, and make money.

Sentences like these work by establishing a pattern that helps the reader to anticipate what is coming. It is like seeing groups of similar figures on a test sheet; circles together, triangles together, squares together, and so on. But when people see a figure that doesn't fit—a circle among the triangles, for instance—they find the exception jarring to their sense of unity. The same thing happens when readers find phrases or clauses that don't fit the pattern of the rest of the sentence. Here is an example of faulty parallelism:

> My purpose was to show what services are available, how many people use them, and *having the audience feel the services are significant.*

The reader does a double take after the second comma because the third point is not handled in the same way as the first two. Here is another example:

> The commission has two options: either they can recommend legislation to plug tax loopholes or *getting rid of the graduated tax scale altogether.*

The reader expects a second independent clause after ''or'' but gets confused because the structure changes.

Probably the time to check your writing for parallel structures is when you are doing the second draft. As you read over your sentences, try to see what patterns you are setting up, and be sure that you don't disappoint or frustrate your reader by making sudden switches.

Sentence Predication /pred

Every complete sentence must have at least two parts: a subject and verb. The verb, along with all of the parts that go with the verb to make a statement, is called the *predicate* of the sentence. Thus the portion of the sentence that completes the assertion that began with the subject of the sentence is called the *predication of a sentence*. Sometimes, however, people writing sentences try to pair up subjects and verbs or objects and verbs that just don't work well together. We call the problem caused by such mismatched combinations *faulty predication*. Most cases of faulty predication seem to fall into one of three categories.

1. Mismatched subject + active verb.

> The rape center will accompany the victim to court.
> Research grants want to get the best qualified applicants.

In each of these sentences the writer has predicated an action that the subject could not carry out; a "rape center" cannot "accompany" someone, and a "research grant" cannot "want." Notice that if the writers had used personal subjects instead of abstract ones for these sentences, they probably would have avoided the mistake. If you start your main clause with a personal subject, you are much less apt to join that subject with a mismatched verb.

2. Subject + linking verb + mismatched complement.

> The main trait a person needs is success.
> The activities available for young people are swimming pools and tennis courts.
> Energy and transportation are problems for our generation.

When people write sentences like these, they seem to have forgotten that the verb *to be* and other linking verbs act as a kind of equal sign (=) in sentences in which the complement of the sentence is a noun. Thus when they use a linking verb after a subject, they should be sure that the noun complement they put after it can logically be equated with the subject. In none of the sentences above could the reader make that equation. "Success" is not a "trait," "activity" cannot be a "swimming pool," and "energy" cannot be equated with "problem."

Again, if the writers of these sentences had started out with personal subjects, they probably would not have gotten into these tangles. These sentences could be rewritten:

> A person needs to be successful.
> Young people can use the swimming pools and tennis courts.
> Our generation faces problems with energy and transportation.

Writers who use the construction, "Something is when . . ." are getting tangled in the same kind of mistake.

> The worst problem is when motorists ignore these signals.
> Community property is when husband and wife share all earnings.

Although a reader is not likely to misunderstand these sentences, they really are substandard usage. The writers are actually saying "problem = when" and "property = when." The best way to avoid this difficulty is simply to make it a rule not to use the construction *is when*.

   3. Subject + verb + mismatched object.

     These theories intimidate the efforts of amateur players.

     The company fired positions which had been there only six months.

In these sentences, the writers have not thought about the limitations they put on themselves when they used the verbs "intimidate" and "fired." Both verbs have to apply to people (or at least creatures). You cannot "intimidate" an "effort" or "fire" a "position." Again, notice that if they had used concrete instead of abstract words as objects, they probably would not have gotten into the problem.

    Probably most writers who have problems with predication are not looking at the sentence structure of their first drafts as carefully as they should. One of your concerns when you read that draft should be checking your verbs to see that you have matched them with logical subjects and complements. And although there are no rules to follow to avoid getting yourself tangled in predication knots, I can suggest one guideline for avoiding problems: use personal and concrete subjects whenever you can, and connect your verbs to specific and concrete terms. If you do this and write agent/action sentences (see p. 177) you will eliminate most predication errors.

The Conventions of Verbs

You can check the definitions of the different kinds of verbs in the Glossary, p. 273.

Subject/Verb Agreement /agr

1. When a sentence has two or more subjects joined by *and,* the verb of the sentence should be plural.

   CORRECT: Building a savings account and lowering one's tax bracket *are* two benefits of a tax-sheltered annuity.

   INCORRECT: Continued inflation and a high interest rate affects the housing industry.

   CORRECT: John, Alan, and he *play* in the band.

   INCORRECT: Margery and she *goes* to the opera often.

Exception: If the subject is a group of words considered as a unit, use a singular verb.

CORRECT: Scotch and soda *is* a popular drink.
CORRECT: "Law and order" *was* the candidate's campaign promise.

2. When a sentence has two subjects joined with *or* the verb should be singular.

   CORRECT: Dr. Margaret Woods or Professor Janice Green *is going* to be our next president.
   INCORRECT: Either John or I *are* going to be nominated.

3. Any modifier that comes between the subject and verb of a sentence does not affect the subject-verb relationship; single subjects still take singular verbs and plural subjects still take plural verbs.

   CORRECT: Skiing or backpacking, two of the area's most popular sports, *is* sure to be included in the trip.
   INCORRECT: The best one among so many options *were* hard to choose.
   CORRECT: Students who come from another country *are* frequently *ignored.*
   INCORRECT: The arrangements that he made without my permission *was* not satisfactory.

4. In sentences that begin with *there* or *here* followed by a linking verb, the verb should agree with the subject that *follows* the verb.

   CORRECT: There *are* many pieces of evidence to consider.
   INCORRECT: There *is* numerous objections to his plan.
   CORRECT: *Are* there many opportunities for development there?
   INCORRECT: Here *is* the guidelines we should consider.

5. In sentences that follow a subject/verb/noun complement pattern, the main verb should agree with the *subject* of the sentence.

   CORRECT: The chief drawback of going to Paris *is* high prices.
   INCORRECT: Literary agents *is* a necessary evil.
   CORRECT: Bikers *are* a menace in that town.
   INCORRECT: One characteristic of the disease *are* headaches.

6. When the subject of a sentence is a collective noun, such as *team, majority, group, committee,* and so on, you should consider how you are using the word and make your decision about verbs accordingly. If the subject seems to act as a single unit, use a singular verb; if you want to indicate that the individual parts of the group are acting separately, the verb should be plural.

   CORRECT: The number of people involved *increases* every day.
   CORRECT: A number of the people *are protesting* the decision.
   CORRECT: The team *have voted* 11–14 to drop out of the conference.

CORRECT: The team *is headed* toward the conference championship.
CORRECT: The majority *indicate* that they are satisfied.
CORRECT: A two-thirds majority *is needed* to confirm.

7. In a sentence or clause in which the subject is a pronoun, the verb must agree with the pronoun in number. Those pronouns that sometimes give trouble are the ones that seem to refer to numbers of people, but technically refer to only one. For instance, *everyone, no one, anybody, anyone, nobody,* and *everybody.*

CORRECT: Everybody *is* responsible for the report.
CORRECT: She thinks that everyone *sees* her as a failure.
INCORRECT: Everyone at the meeting *are* agreed on two points.
INCORRECT: Nobody in the company *think* worse of him for it.

The pronouns *each, either,* and *neither* also take singular verbs.

CORRECT: Each of the participants *is* eligible for credit.
INCORRECT: Either Davis or Nelson *are* going.
CORRECT: Neither of the couple *admits* that he or she might be wrong.

The pronouns *any* and *none* may take either singular or plural verbs.

CORRECT: None of the problems *is* serious.
CORRECT: He decided that none of the contestants *were* right.
CORRECT: Any of my students *is* qualified to write the proposal.
CORRECT: *Are* any of the applicants women?

Controlling Verb Tenses /t

1. If you have more than one verb in your sentence, try to keep the tenses of all of them consistent.

CONSISTENT: As the day *progressed,* Jones *became* surlier.
INCONSISTENT: As the day *progressed,* Jones *becomes* surlier.
CONSISTENT: When the main event *was* over, the spectators *cheered.*
INCONSISTENT: When the main event *was* over, the spectators *cheer.*

Exception: If you are making a prediction in part of your sentence, you can mix present and future tenses.

CONSISTENT: When the war *is* over, James *will come* home.

2. In general, use the present tense consistently in writing about books or famous documents; this tense is traditionally called the "historical present."

The Magna Carta *guarantees* an individual's right to petition the king.

In *Middlemarch*, George Eliot gently satirizes the pretensions of the English middle class.

3. In general, keep your verbs in the same tense throughout a piece of expository writing unless the logic of your discourse requires that you shift.

The Subjunctive Mood /mo

Although fewer and fewer people seem to bother with using the subjunctive form of verbs in their writing, careful writers should at least know what the subjunctive forms are and when they should be used.

1. The subjunctive forms of the verb are used when one wants to express a point conditionally or to express wishes. For example:

If Castle *were* in charge, he *would* handle the protesters well.
I wish I *were* not involved in that proposal.
If that *should* happen, the admiral *would want* to know.
You *would be* a great help if you *were to join* us.

2. Occasionally *had* is combined with another verb to talk about events that didn't take place. For example:

Had I thought of it, I *would* have written.
Had he known what he was getting into, he *would* have been appalled.

3. The subjunctive form of a verb should be used in clauses beginning with *that* when the main verb expresses desires, orders, or suggestions. For example:

The lawyer requested that her client *be given* a new trial.
We suggest that there *be* a recount of the votes.

Pronouns

Look in the Glossary for definitions of the various kinds of pronouns: demonstrative, indefinite, interrogative, reciprocal, reflexive, and relative.

There are three key terms used in discussing conventions for the use of pronouns: *agreement, case,* and *reference.*

When a pronoun is substituting for the noun that is its antecedent, it must *agree* with that antecedent in gender, person, and number. So after the sentence "Mazie is our new neighbor," a pronoun referring to Mazie would have to be feminine, in the third person, and singular.

Pronouns have three *cases*.

Subjective pronouns serve as subjects and subject complements (*I, you, he, she, it, we, you, they, who*).

Objective pronouns serve as objects (*me, you, him, her, us, you, them, whom*).

Possessive pronouns show possession (*my, mine, your, yours, his, her, hers, its, our, ours, your, yours, their, theirs, whose*).

Except in idiomatic expressions like "It is raining" or "It will be a long time," a pronoun must refer to an identifiable antecedent in the same sentence or the previous one.

Problems with Agreement /agr

1. Pronouns that refer to singular subjects must be singular; pronouns that refer to plural subjects must be plural. Two subjects joined by *or* are considered single; two subjects joined by *and* are considered plural.

   CORRECT: The students are encouraged to submit *their* work.
   INCORRECT: Harvey or George will bring *their* cars.
   CORRECT: Harvey or George will bring *his* car.
   INCORRECT: Every individual should be given *their* rights.

2. The indefinite pronouns *anybody, anyone, everybody, everyone, each, nobody, no one, either,* and *neither* are singular, and any pronoun that refers to them should also be singular.

   CORRECT: *Everyone* believes *his* own ideas are best.
   INCORRECT: *Everybody* who came in brought *their* drawings.
   CORRECT: *Neither* of the children had a chance to tell *her* story.
   INCORRECT: *Anybody* who thinks *their* problems are unique is wrong.

3. The indefinite pronouns *both, all,* and sometimes *none* are plural, and any pronoun that refers to them should be plural.

   CORRECT: *Both* of the girls took *their* degrees in psychology.
   INCORRECT: *Both* of the women told *her* story.
   CORRECT: *None* of the customers expect *their* money to be returned.
   CORRECT: *All* of the graduates have received *their* diplomas.

4. Since collective nouns may be considered either plural or singular depending on the context of the sentence, choose your pronoun according

to that context. If the group named by the collective noun is acting as a unit, use singular pronouns; if it is acting as separate individuals, use plural pronouns.

CORRECT: The *tribe* moved *its* headquarters to a higher mesa.
CORRECT: The *tribe* asked for better schools for *their* children.
CORRECT: The *team* won *its* first game with no trouble.
CORRECT: The *team* voted 5–4 to buy a new car for *their* manager.

5. When you are using a relative pronoun in a clause, choose *who* or *whom* when referring to a person, *which* or *that* when referring to an animal or thing. Although many writers find *that* an acceptable pronoun for referring to people, conservative grammarians still prefer *who* or *whom*.

INCORRECT: The members of the first brigade are the ones *which* got leave.
ACCEPTABLE: The people *that* were recognized had more than 30 years' service.
CORRECT: It is the students on scholarship *who* will benefit.

However if you take the conservative view that *who* and *whom* should be used only to refer to people, you run into problems when you need an impersonal possessive pronoun. There is no possessive form of *which* or *that,* and saying "of which" sometimes gets awkward. For these reasons it is acceptable to use *whose* to refer to animals or objects.

ACCEPTABLE: That is the football field *whose* lights can be seen for ten miles.
AWKWARD: That is the football field the lights *of which* can be seen for ten miles.

Problems with Case /ca

You should decide whether to use the subjective, objective, or possessive case of a pronoun according to the function that pronoun serves in the sentence.

1. If a pronoun acts as the subject of a sentence use the subjective form.

CORRECT: McLaughlin and *I* will take care of getting permissions.
INCORRECT: Barton and *him* are going to be in charge.
CORRECT: The Watkins and *we* are going to be honored at the ceremony.
INCORRECT: The Maloneys and *us* were brought to court.

Notice that the plural subject is causing the problem in the incorrect sentences. Few people would say "Him is going to be in charge" or "Us were brought to court.'' Thus when you want to test your construction, try your sentence using just the personal pronoun as a subject.

2. If a pronoun acts as the subject of a clause, use the subjective form.

CORRECT: Jackson asserted that *she* will be the new chairman.
CORRECT: We will have to change our plans if *he* is not accepted.

It is when one must choose the right pronoun to use in a relative clause that the old *who/whom* problem comes up. Many people think the distinction is no longer important, but if you want to be sure you get the right form, use these guidelines.

Check whether you should use *who* or *whom* by rephrasing the clause with another pronoun. If your sentence is ''Carson is the man (who/whom) we have chosen for the job'' ask yourself, ''Would I write, 'we have chosen *he* or *him*'?'' Obviously you would use *him;* therefore use *whom* in your clause. If your sentence is ''One must admire a woman (who/whom) can be trusted,'' ask yourself, ''Would I write '*her* can be trusted or *she* can be trusted'?'' Since your answer is *she,* you should use *who* in the clause.

CORRECT: Carl is a person *who* has made a great impression.
CORRECT: Cochran is the woman *who* people believe will win. (Notice that inserting ''people believe'' does not affect the clause.)
INCORRECT: Carrington is the person *whom* we think will win.

3. If a pronoun is part of an appositive phrase or clause that modifies the subject, use the subjective case.

CORRECT: The originators of the plan, Bowden and *I,* are going to make a report.
CORRECT: Rogers, *who* is head of the firm, has three degrees.
INCORRECT: The committee members—Westbrook, Douglas, and *me*— have decided to resign.

4. If a pronoun is acting as a noun complement for a linking verb, or is part of the modifier of that complement, use the subjective case.

CORRECT: The winners of the contest are Jones and *she.*
CORRECT: This is *she* speaking.
INCORRECT: The qualified people are Hawkins and *me.*
CORRECT: Canfield is the person *who* belongs.

5. If a pronoun is acting as the object or indirect object in a sentence, or phrase, use the objective case.

CORRECT: McElroy decided to give Sheila and *me* another chance.
CORRECT: When you have finished, send the results to Fox and *me.*
INCORRECT: The army sent my husband and *I* to Japan.
CORRECT: Keats is the person *whom* you saw with the president.

6. If a pronoun comes after a preposition, use the objective case.

CORRECT: We have plenty of opportunities for both Walter and *her*.
CORRECT: The choice will be between Carlotta and *him*.
CORRECT: Kate is the person to *whom* I spoke yesterday.
INCORRECT: Hanson divided the work between Jerry and *I*.

Notice that problems with choosing the right pronouns here are probably caused by there being more than one object. A person would probably not write "The army sent I to Japan"; therefore, *I* should not be used as an object just because it is paired with another word.

7. If a pronoun is used as an appositive or modifier with a direct or indirect object, it should be in the objective case.

CORRECT: Coles blames the failure on three people: Marshall, Karen, and *me*.
CORRECT: We are going to see Justin, *whom* you know.
INCORRECT: Gifford loves his army buddies, Clark and *I*.

8. *If a pronoun comes before and modifies a gerund, use the possessive case.*

CORRECT: I hope they will not object to *my* leaving early.
CORRECT: *Their* buying another car was an extravagance.
INCORRECT: The professor did not object to *us* leaving early.

Problems with Ambiguity /amb ref

Readers should never have to guess about the antecedent of a pronoun. They should never have to say "What does the *it* refer to?" or "Who is *he?*" To avoid this problem, try to keep these guidelines in mind.

1. Keep your demonstrative pronouns—*that, this, those, these, it,* and *which*—close to their antecedents. Usually the antecedent for a pronoun should be in the same sentence or the previous sentence. If it strays much farther than that, your reader may become confused.

2. When you use *which, it, this,* or *that* as the subject of a clause, check what precedes it to be sure that the reader has a clear antecedent to fit with the pronoun. If the antecedent is missing or vague, you may have to rewrite the sentence. For example,

UNCLEAR: Didion is a very moralistic writer, *which* is the basic theme of her books.
CLEAR: The basic theme of all Didion's books concerns morality.

UNCLEAR: The general public worries about falling scores on achievement tests, but they don't want to pay for *it*.
CLEAR: Although the general public worries about scores on achievement tests, they don't want to spend money to improve those scores.
UNCLEAR: Plato wrote an elitist book about running a government, and I don't believe in *that*.
CLEAR: I do not believe in the elitist theory of government that Plato wrote about in his book.

3. If there are two possible antecedents for a pronoun, make it clear which word the pronoun refers to.

   UNCLEAR: The doctor told Jacques that *he* was a lucky man.
   CLEAR: The doctor told Jacques to consider himself a lucky man. Or, The doctor told Jacques, "You are a lucky man."
   UNCLEAR: My father knew Whitburn when he lived in New York.
   CLEAR: My father knew Whitburn when the latter lived in New York. Or, When Whitburn lived in New York my father knew him.

4. When the antecedent for a pronoun is the indefinite pronoun *one,* you have a choice of corresponding pronouns. For example,

   CORRECT AND FORMAL: When *one* is applying for medical school, *one* must have persistence.
   CORRECT AND INFORMAL: When *one* comes to Cornell, *she* had better be prepared for cold weather.
   COLLOQUIAL AND UNSUITABLE: When *one* takes a vacation, *you* need lots of money.

Reflexive Pronouns /refl

The accepted forms are *myself, yourself, himself, herself, itself, ourselves, yourselves,* and *themselves.* The forms *hisself* and *theirselves* are nonstandard. Reflexive pronouns have only two functions.

1. Reflexive pronouns can act as intensifiers; that is, they add emphasis to a statement.

   I did it *myself*.
   They took care of the problem *themselves*.

2. Reflexive pronouns can indicate reflexive action; that is they indicate the subject of the sentence is also the object of the verb.

   John injured *himself* severely.
   Claudia takes *herself* very seriously.
   The debaters talked *themselves* into a corner.

3. Reflexive pronouns should *not* be used as a substitute for pronouns used as objects.

INCORRECT: The mail brought Wayne and *myself* good news.
INCORRECT: She wants us to put Janice and *herself* on the program.

Mechanics

Numbers /n

   Editors' attitudes about numbers in a manuscript have become more flexible in recent years, and there are no longer strict conventions about how numbers should be written. Traditionally, numbers are not written out when they are used in the following circumstances.

1. Use figures for dates.

January 16, 1785.
October 1–5, 1981

2. Use figures to indicate page numbers, chapters, references and such.

Chapter 12   Corinthians 14:32
page 7 (or p. 7)   pp. 33–48

3. Street numbers.

1903 Harris Avenue   Route 1, Box 70
29310 Cayman Boulevard   Apartment 6A, 213 Cedar Street

4. Time

12:30 A.M.   1530 (military or European usage)
5:15 P.M.

Some people write out a number when it precedes *o'clock,* but the form is not mandatory.

5. Money, except when talking about round sums.

$24.95   five thousand a year
90¢   a million dollars
$13,500

6. Figures of three digits or more. Some people prefer to write out all figures under 100; others write out all figures below 20. Neither choice is necessarily right. The point is that a writer should be consistent about his or her method. Don't write *25* one place in a report, and *twenty-five* in

another. I prefer to write out only figures below 10 and to use figures for all other numbers whenever possible. My reason is that the reader can understand numbers more readily if they are written in numerals, and I think that the reader's convenience is more important than traditional forms.

Capitals /cap

Because only a few college students seem to have trouble deciding when they should capitalize words, a quick review of the most important rules should suffice here.

1. Capitalize the first word of each sentence.
2. Capitalize the days of the week, the months, and the name of official holidays: the Fourth of July, Memorial Day.
3. Capitalize proper names: Mary Carter, George Wills.
4. Capitalize the names of towns, cities, states, countries, oceans, rivers, and mountains, and the words derived from them: Denver, Mt. Ranier, Brazil, French class.

Italics /ital

When you underline a word in a paper or report you indicate that you would want that word to appear in italic or slanted type if your work were printed. Italics generally serve one of four purposes.

1. Use italics to highlight the names of books, plays, magazines, movies or plays, long poems, or musical compositions, and often for the name of special planes, or trains, or ships: Shaw's *Pygmalion,* Gershwin's *Rhapsody in Blue, The Christian Science Monitor, Queen Elizabeth II* Steinbeck's *In Dubious Battle,* Homer's *Iliad.*

   Increasingly, however, writers are putting titles in all capital letters rather than in italics; that seems quite acceptable: Tschaikowsky's SWAN LAKE, Miller's DEATH OF A SALESMAN

2. If you use foreign words or phrases that are not commonly used in English, put them in italics: *cuisine minceur, deus ex machina, angst, mano a mano, habeas corpus.*

3. You may use italics to highlight a word or phrase to which you want to call attention.

The women's movement has given a new meaning to the word *chauvinism*.

In England a lawyer is a *barrister* or a *solicitor*, not an *attorney*.

4. You may use italics to emphasize a word.

Affirmative action and equal opportunity are *not* the same thing.

Use the device of italicizing words for emphasis sparingly, or it will lose its effect.

Punctuation

Commas /,

Commas are the weakest mark of separation used in writing; thus we use them to indicate a slight pause that will help readers to better understand what they are reading. Ideally, writers should not have to think about the rules for commas but would insert one when they felt the need for a pause. However, the standard guidelines are fairly easy to remember.

1. Use commas to set off items in a series.

   She spent most of her money on food, books, and bus fare.
   France, England, Sweden, and Spain have all joined the Common Market.

2. Use commas to set off interrupting, nonessential phrases or clauses in a sentence. If a phrase is not necessary to the basic meaning of the sentence, set it in commas; if it is essential to the meaning of the sentence, omit the commas.

   NONESSENTIAL PHRASE: Johnson, for all his problems, was an effective president in many ways.
   ESSENTIAL CLAUSE: The person who is elected in November will be the 37th president.
   NONESSENTIAL CLAUSE: Commuting students, many of whom have full-time jobs, make up 90 percent of the student body.
   ESSENTIAL CLAUSE: Students who have jobs get better grades.

At times, though, you may have trouble deciding if a clause is essential or nonessential. For instance, a sentence like "Meats which have high fat content are forbidden on some diets" could be interpreted two ways. You will have to decide how to punctuate it in order not to confuse your reader.

3. Use a comma before the conjunction that joins two independent clauses.

The advertising whetted her interest, and she was determined to go.
Charles will finish his report tonight, and we will take a new case in the morning.
Either they sign the contract, or we close down the mill.

4. Use a comma to set off an introductory qualifying word or phrase in a sentence. However, if the meaning is clear without the comma, it is not necessary.

Unfortunately, John is not as bright as he thinks he is.
On the whole, the crowd took the bad news fairly well.
Nevertheless the cost spiral seems to continue.

This rule is no longer a strict one, and you may disregard it if you think the meaning would be clear without the comma.

5. Use commas to set off interrupting phrases or clauses within a sentence. Nonessential appositives, which clarify but do not change the meaning of the subject, are set off with commas.

Graham, *chairman of the board,* lives in Bermuda.
Mark Twain portrays Merlin, *Arthur's court magician,* as a comic figure.

So are transition words or phrases that point or qualify.

The salmon, *for instance,* is a game fish.
It can be said, *however,* that Eleanor never admitted defeat.

So are terms of address.

Miss Cinderella, your coach is waiting.
If you will pardon me, *Mr. Gulliver,* I'll cut these ropes.

6. Use a comma to set off a subordinate clause at the beginning of a sentence.

Although Jim had never earned much money, he enjoyed life.
When the touchdown was made, Molly kicked the extra point.

But a subordinate clause at the end of a sentence does not need to be separated by a comma.

7. Use a comma when you want to mark a contrast or separation point clearly.

Modern cowboys ride pick-ups, not broncos.
It is not independence he wants, but security.

8. Use commas to mark off divisions when you are writing titles, dates, and addresses.

The feast of the Great Pumpkin started on October 31, 1965.
Classes will begin on Tuesday, September 4.
Wright Morrow, Dean of Humanities, will address the club.
Rose lives at 13 Washington Square, Austin, Texas.

9. Use commas to mark off direct quotations in a dialogue.

"Take what you want and pay for it," Max said.
"Leave that where it is," Clark shouted, "and get out."

Don't Use Commas /omit comma

1. Commas are not used to join independent clauses. When you have two or more groups of words, each of which could be a separate sentence, you need to join them in some way that will show their relationship. A comma is too weak to perform that task, and you will wind up with a comma splice. See page 247.
2. Do not use a comma as a punctuation mark in the middle of a phrase or clause. A comma always interrupts, and thus you should not use it when you want an uninterrupted flow of thought.

Semicolons /;

The semicolon is a separating mark that is stronger than the comma but not quite as strong as the period. Used judiciously, it can tighten your writing and provide good transitions. Here are its chief uses.

1. Use a semicolon to join independent but closely related clauses.

Jane was disgusted; Jack was merely bored.
In 1920 women got the vote; now they want equality.
If nominated I will not run; if elected I will not serve.

2. Use a semicolon before a transition word that joins independent clauses.

James has no interest in buying the Taj Mahal; nevertheless, he will participate in the negotiations.
Joan was wearing a splendid new jogging suit; however, she collapsed during the second mile.

3. Use semicolons as separation marks when you want to connect several clauses or phrases that have internal punctuation.

The people who gathered at the swimming pool were Grant Rock, a former Harley-Davidson rider and bongo drum player; Mondy Koonz, who was a disco queen in the '70s; Sam Santos, who did great imitations of Woody Allen; and Lily Lopiano, the rodeo sweetheart from Laramie.

Colons / :

The colon is a device that gives the reader a signal to anticipate more information. It has six uses:

1. The colon signals an illustration at the end of an independent clause.

   One attribute is necessary for living in Mexico: patience.
   Our throw-away culture makes a mockery of old fashioned virtues: thrift and self-restraint.

2. The colon signals a list.

   To make gazpacho, throw the following ingredients in your Cuisinart: onions, tomatoes, green pepper, cucumber, garlic, and tomato juice.
   These clubs contributed to the relief fund: Rotary, Optimists, Kiwanis, Bluebonnet Belles, and the Thanatopsis.

However, do not use a colon after a linking verb that precedes a list.

   WRONG. The Texas towns listed are: Bug Tussle, Muleshoe, Honey Grove, Dime Box, and Roan's Prairie.

Do not use a colon after a preposition that precedes a list.

   WRONG. "Middle-aged Crazy" is a song about: 40-year-old men, 20-year-old women, disappointments, hangovers, and frustrations.

3. The colon signals an amplification of a statement.

   New Yorkers are mad for Texas chic: they love cowboy boots, chili parlors, Lone Star beer, and Texas performers like Willie Nelson and Jerry Jeff Walker.

4. The colon signals a subtitle that explains the main title.

   The Serial: A Year in the Life of Marin County.
   Creative Separation: The Dividends of Splitting.

5. The colon signals a quotation.

   One of Galbraith's statements illustrates my point: "Faced with the choice of spending time on the unpublished scholarship of a graduate student or the unpublished work of Galbraith, I have seldom hesitated."

6. Colons and double colons are used to indicate relationships in an analogy.

typewriter:author::brush:painter
exercise:body::thinking:mind

Dashes /——

Dashes are so handy for punctuating sentences that often writers are tempted to rely on them rather than worry over making decisions about commas and semicolons. But a writer who uses too many dashes gives the impression of being sloppy and undiscriminating; therefore, you should probably use dashes for only limited purposes.

1. Use dashes to set off a qualifying or contradicting segment of the sentence, either within or at the end of a sentence.

   Barrel racing—and the contestants are always women—is one of the most dangerous rodeo events.
   Charles is always willing to support a good cause—unless it is unpopular.

2. Use a dash to indicate a sudden shift in the direction of a sentence; used this way, dashes sometimes serve to emphasize irony.

   As a staunch country girl, Lucy loves barbecue, kicker dancing, beer in bottles—and air conditioning.
   The market for new novelists is overcrowded and underpaid—unless you are in science fiction.

3. Use a dash to indicate a statement that will summarize material already given.

   Too much sausage, too many jalapeños, too much beer—all contributed to his sleepless night.
   Danger, excitement, challenge, strenuous exercise—these are the attractions of white-water canoeing.

4. A dash is used to indicate that a sentence is breaking off.

   If one tries to reason with such people—well, we all know what happens then.

Remember not to mix dashes with commas, periods, or semicolons; if you are going to use them in a sentence, be consistent. Mixing them is like mixing a parenthesis with a quotation mark.

To write a dash, make a line about twice as long as a hyphen. To type a dash, type two consecutive hyphens and do not leave any space either before or after the dash.

Dots / . . .

Anytime you quote from someone else's writing and omit any part of it, you should use separated dots, or *ellipsis points,* to indicate that something has been omitted. If what you are omitting is within a sentence, signal the omission with three separated dots: . . . Use four separated dots to signal an omission at the end of a sentence or the omission of a whole sentence or paragraph.

PART OF A SENTENCE OMITTED: Watching television, you'd think we lived . . . surrounded on all sides by human-seeking germs, shielded against infections and death only by a chemical technology that enables us to keep killing them off.

Lewis Thomas, *The Lives of a Cell*

COMPLETE SENTENCE OMITTED: In 2000 B.C., when Ishmael found himself in need of a horse, Allah sent him a mare from the heavens. But King Hassan didn't call on Allah. . . . He called instead on Hugh Roy Marshall, who lives on the largest Arabian horse farm this side of Mecca—in suburban Houston. Now the royal stables are thriving again, thanks to five Houston-bred Arabians Marshall sold to Hassan for about $190,000.

The Texas Monthly, October 1978

Parentheses / ( )

Parentheses are used to separate out a portion of writing that is either explanatory or that adds information that is incidental to the main point being made.

At least it is usually possible in English to avoid the generic *he* altogether or to alternate *he* or *she* to strike a balance as Dr. Spock has done in the latest (1976) edition of *Baby and Child Care.*

Casey Miller and Kate Swift, *Words and Women*

Migraine is something more than the fancy of a neurotic imagination. It is an essentially hereditary complex of symptoms, the most frequently noted but by no means the most unpleasant of which is a vascular headache of blinding severity, suffered by a surprising number of women, a fair number of men (Thomas Jefferson had migraine, and so did Ulysses S. Grant, the day he accepted Lee's surrender), and by some unfortunate children as young as two years old.

Joan Didion, *The White Album*

Brackets $\Big/$ [ ]

Brackets are related to parentheses, but the two are not interchangeable. Brackets have the special function of signaling that the writer is inserting an explanation into a quotation and that the portion enclosed in brackets is not part of the original.

> Brooks said, "I think she [Emily Dickinson] was the finest poet of her time."

It is customary to use the term *sic,* set off by brackets, to explain that an error in a quotation is part of the original and not the responsibility of the person giving the quote.

> The researcher wrote, "This manuscript is attributed to Shakspeer [*sic*]."

When you need brackets and the typewriter you are using does not have them, you can either put them in by hand after you finish your paper or go through the awkward business of constructing them from the slash mark and the underlining mark on your typewriter.

Quotation Marks $\Big/$ " " or ' '

Quotation marks have two chief purposes: first, they enable writers to signal that people are speaking, and second, they enable writers to indicate that some part of their writing have been written by other people. There are also some other, less important uses for quotation marks.

1. *Spoken words.* To indicate dialogue or oral discourse, put quotation marks around all spoken words.

> "This has been a fabulous summer," Joannie said.
> Jimmy replied, "What in the world does that mean?"

When you are quoting within a quotation, use single quotation marks for the interior quotation.

> "I always remember your saying to me, 'Everything takes longer than you think it will,' " Carter said to his mother.

2. *Quoted sources.* Anytime writers use the actual words of material that is not their own, they are obligated to indicate that they are *quoting.* For short quotations (usually 25 words or less), the quotation marks can be put on either side of the passage in the main text, as in:

Hawkins claims in his book, "The childish side of the American character surfaced during the post-war period." He does not, however, go on to support this claim with evidence.

If you are using a longer quotation, you may indicate that someone else wrote it by indenting it to set it off from the main body of your writing, and giving the name of the author and the source.

> One encounter in particular threw these questions into focus. Each of the women's lives we have studied, including those in this book, gave us tentative answers—clues. But close to home we came to know a woman who expanded her own extraordinary insight into the relationship of class and struggle for identity. Through her we were able to tether our abstract theories to the actuality of two lives: a woman and her employer.
>
> Robert Coles and Jane Coles, *Women of Crisis*

Other uses of quotation marks. Writers often use quotation marks to set off words to which they want to call special attention. Sometimes they use the marks to indicate that they are using the word ironically, and sometimes they use them to indicate that the reader should pay special attention to that word.

IRONY: Presley's "friends" disappeared when he took bankruptcy.
SPECIAL ATTENTION: The overused jargon word "interface" comes from computer terminology.

Be careful, however, about putting quotation marks around words in an effort to disclaim responsibility for them. As William Strunk, Jr., and E. B. White say in *The Elements of Style:*

> If you use a colloquialism or a slang word or phrase, simply use it; do not draw attention to it by enclosing it in quotation marks. To do so is to put on airs, as though you were inviting the reader to join you in a select society of those who know better.

Many writers also use quotation marks around the titles of articles, short stories, or poems, but such usage is optional.

Other Punctuation with Quotation Marks

The rules about where quotation marks should go are not always logical, but probably you should try to observe them as much as possible. Briefly they are these:

1. Commas and periods are always placed *inside* quotation marks.

   "If Jerry leaves," he said, "that will be the last straw."

2. Colons and semicolons are placed *outside* quotation marks.

James Gould Cozzens writes about "the man of reason"; ironically his chief theme is that man is not reasonable.

3. Question marks and exclamation points may be placed inside or outside of quotation marks; if they belong to the quoted portion, they belong inside, but if they belong to the sentence as a whole they go outside. (Sometimes it is almost impossible to decide.)

The intruder cried, "Don't shoot!"
How can you have a discussion with people who are always "spaced out"?

Apostrophes /'

The apostrophe (') has two major uses and one minor use. Its first major use is to indicate the possessive form of nouns. It does this in two principal ways.

1. Use an apostrophe *plus* an *s* to make the possessive form of both single and plural nouns that do not end in *s:* Jack's apron, the men's soccer team.
2. Use an apostrophe *after* the *s* to form the possessive form of names, singular or plural, that end in an *s,* and of plural nouns that end in *s:* the Foxes' swimming pool, the girls' uniforms

You can also add an apostrophe plus an *s* to names ending in *s* if you prefer. Thus, the following forms are also acceptable: James's tractor, the Cousins's family tree.

Sometimes you may find that you have written what seems to be a double possessive in a sentence, but you think your phrasing should not be changed. For example, you might want to write, "These three books of Faulkner's have lasting value," and changing your phrasing to read "Faulkner's three books have lasting value" would alter your meaning. In such a case, it is quite acceptable to use the possessive form of nouns or pronouns in addition to the "of" construction.

That temper of hers will get her into trouble.
This plan of John's is insane.

Notice that possessive pronouns do *not* require an apostrophe after them; they are complete as they are: *my, mine, ours, his, hers, yours,* and so on.

The second major use of the apostrophe is to mark the omission of a letter in contractions, either of words or dates:

Family members *shouldn't* read each other's mail.
We're looking forward to an exciting conference.
The president *didn't* anticipate such hostility.
They'll regret having moved to the country.
Sally's scholarship began in the fall of *'79.*

Take care to put the apostrophe in place of the omitted letter or letters: thus the contraction of *would + not* is *"wouldn't,"* not *"would'nt,"* and *they + will* is *"they'll,"* not *"theyl'l."*

A minor use of the apostrophe is as an indicator of the plural form for individual letters and numbers.

Clark habitually slurs his r's.
Eunice writes her 7's with a bar across them.

Hyphens / -

Editors seem to be getting less prescriptive about the use of hyphens just as they are getting less prescriptive about commas. Nevertheless, you should know the guidelines for the four most common uses of the hyphen.

1. A hyphen is used as a mark for indicating where words should be divided when a separation occurs at the end of a line. (Even that use may disappear as modern automatic typesetters have built-in justifiers to take care of the problem.) Remember that there are standard and nonstandard ways to divide words, and when you are in doubt, you should check in the dictionary.
2. It is used as a separation mark in compound nouns: brother-in-law, court-martial, commander-in-chief, 17-year-old, lieutenant-governor.

Guidelines for hyphenating words like these are rather flexible; there is no sound reason for hyphenating mother-in-law and not hyphenating godfather or first lieutenant. If you have doubts about whether you should hyphenate a compound term, and can't find it in the dictionary, the safest course is to use hyphens.

3. A hyphen makes the division between parts of a compound modifier: a blow-by-blow description, a holier-than-thou attitude, his 13-year-old daughter, my end-of-the-semester slump.
4. It is also used as a marker between the prefix *ex* and the word it modifies, and as a marker after certain other prefixes when they come before capitalized words: ex-army officer, ex-wife, pro-Arab sentiments, anti-American.

Guideline Questions for Students
to Use in Evaluating Each Other's Papers

1. What do you think are the strong points of the paper?

2. What parts of the paper did you find particularly effective?

3. Does the writer make the purpose of the paper clear? What do you think it is? Does he or she fulfill this purpose?

4. Does the writer seem to have a specific audience in mind? Does he or she communicate successfully with that audience?

5. What promise or commitment does the writer make to his or her audience, or what expectation does he or she raise in the audience's mind?

6. Does the paper meet the commitment or expectation?

7. Are there places in the paper where the reader might get lost? Where are they?

8. Did you have to reread any parts of the paper to grasp the writer's ideas? Which parts?

9. Could the writer have expressed the ideas of the paper more economically? At what points, if any, could the paper be cut?

10. Does the paper seem unified? Are there places where the writer needed to show better connections or give clearer directions?

11. Are sentences constructed so the reader can follow them easily? Can you suggest specific improvements?

12. Has the writer used enough concrete and specific words? What words or phrases seem particularly effective?

13. Did the paper hold your attention to the end? Why or why not?

14. Is the writer convincing and informative? Remember, you should not focus on the beliefs or opinions expressed, but on the way in which they are presented.

15. Are there distracting mistakes in usage, spelling, or punctuation? To what matters does the writer need to pay particular attention?

A Glossary of Terms for Composition

Abstract language Language that refers to intangible concepts and qualities that one cannot perceive through the senses: *loyalty, friendship, evil.*

Active verb The form of a verb used when the subject of the sentence carries out the action expressed.

Adjective clause *See* Clause.

Adverb clause *See* Clause.

Agreement Correspondence in number and person between the subject and predicate of a sentence, and correspondence in person, number, and gender between a pronoun and its antecedent. See subject-verb agreement, pp. 251–53, and pronoun-antecedent agreement, pp. 255–56.

Ambiguity Possible multiple meanings in a sentence or passage of writing. "Einstein met Niels Bohr when he lived in Germany" is ambiguous because the reader cannot tell if "he" refers to Einstein or Bohr.

Antecedent The word or phrase for which a pronoun stands. In the sentence "Jason kept losing his fleece," "Jason" is the antecedent of "his."

Appositive A word, phrase, or clause that immediately follows a noun or pronoun and gives more information about it. In the sentence "Cerberus, *the watchdog at the gate of Hell,* kept an eye on him," the italicized portion is an appositive.

Article An indicator word used before a single noun. *A, an,* and *the* are articles.

Auxiliary verb A "helping" verb form that is joined with another verb to show tense, possibility, or obligation: "He *has* procrastinated until the game is over"; "She *could* stay with Jim"; "We *must* go immediately."

Balanced sentence A sentence in which all parts are constructed on the same pattern to give a balanced effect: "If nominated I will run, and if elected I will serve."

Case The forms of change in pronouns and nouns that indicate their function in a sentence. The three cases of pronouns are **subjective, objective,** and **possessive.**

Clause A group of words containing a subject and a predicate. Clauses are **independent** or **dependent (subordinate).** Independent clauses stand alone and function as sentences, but the meaning of dependent clauses partially depends on the independent clauses to which they are attached. Independent: *"He comes to our house frequently."* Dependent: *"Although John is not a good friend,* he comes to our house frequently."
An **adjective clause** is a subordinate clause that acts as an adjective modifier: "James is the man *whom I want to see."*
An **adverbial clause** is a subordinate clause that acts as an adverbial modifier: *"As Charles drove down the road,* he sang."
A **noun clause** is a clause that acts as a noun; it can serve as a subject, object, or complement: *"That skiing dominated his life* soon became evident"; "I heard *that skiing dominates his life."*

Comma splice, (Comma fault) A faulty sentence construction that uses a comma to join two independent clauses. See p. 247.

Complement A word or phrase that completes a linking verb and gives more information about the subject of the sentence. If the complement is a noun or noun phrase, it is called a **predicate noun;** if it is an adjective or adjective phrase, it is called a **predicate adjective.** Predicate noun: "Darby has become a *wrestler."* Predicate adjective: "Darby has become *famous."*

Complex sentence A sentence with one independent clause and one or more dependent clauses.

Compound sentence A sentence with two or more independent clauses joined by conjunctions or a semicolon.

Concrete language Language that refers to qualities or objects that can be perceived by the senses: *building, orange, slippery, gravel.*

Conjunction A word used to join the elements of a sentence: "I would have come, *but* I was not asked"; "He will be chosen today, *or* he will be passed over"; "Alexander was a dictator; *nevertheless* he ruled well."

Connotation The emotional associations that a word carries.

Coordination The balance of elements of equal value in a sentence in a construction that usually has independent clauses joined by a semicolon or coordinating conjunction.

Dangling modifier A modifying phrase, usually at the beginning of a sentence, that does not logically fit with the sentence element it seems to modify: *"Having left home,* money became a problem."

Declarative sentence A sentence that makes an assertion: "Lawrence is reputed to have Mafia connections."

Demonstrative pronoun A pronoun that refers specifically to a statement or concept already understood or previously expressed. *This, that, these,* and *those* are the demonstrative pronouns: "*That* is the reference I was looking for."

Denotation The limited and precise meaning of a word that is given in the dictionary.

Dependent clause *See* Clause.

Diction The choice of words, particularly as it affects the style of writing. Word choice largely determines whether the style of writing is high, middle, or low:

HIGH	MIDDLE	LOW (PLAIN)
disparate	*dissimilar*	*unlike,*
porcine	*obese,*	*fat,*
dessicated	*withered*	*dried-out*

Direct object A word that receives the action of the verb: "Adonis carried off the *prize.*"

Double negative A construction that includes two negating terms. Such usage is nonstandard in English: "The men at the office have *never* seen *no one* like her."

Ellipses A row of three or four dots inserted in a manuscript to indicate that material has been omitted.

Figurative language Metaphor, simile, personification, or synecdoche (having the part stand for the whole) used to make writing more vivid.

Gerund A noun form made by adding *-ing* to the verb stem. By itself, a gerund *cannot* function as a verb: "*Swimming* is wonderful exercise"; "Churchill loved *drinking.*"

Grammar A systematic account of the way in which a language works.

Imperative mood *See* Mood.

Indefinite pronoun Indefinite pronouns have no gender or case and do not refer to a specific person or thing. They are

all	*everybody*	*no one*
another	*everyone*	*one*
any	*everything*	*other*
anybody	*few*	*several*
anyone	*many*	*some*
anything	*most*	*somebody*
both		*someone*
	neither	*something*
each	*nobody*	*such*
either	*none*	

Notice that many of these words also act as adjectives.

Independent *See* Clause.
clause

Indicative *See* Mood.
mood

Infinitive The basic form of any verb, made by adding *to* to the verb stem: e.g., *to ride, to visit, to complete.* The infinitive frequently acts as a noun in a sentence: *"To serve* is his highest ambition"; "Cornelia loves *to ride."*

Interjection A word or phrase used by itself as an emphatic marker—e.g., *aha, alas, wow, all right, hey*—and frequently followed by an exclamation point.

Intransitive An active verb that expresses action or condition but does
verb not take an object. Intransitive verbs cannot be used in passive verb constructions: "Murrow *sleeps* through every meeting."

Irregular verb A verb whose past and past-participle forms do not follow the regular patterns of an -*ed* added to the stem. Typical irregular verbs are *go* (*went, gone*) and *swim* (*swam, swum*). If a verb is regular, the dictionary will give only the present tense; if it is irregular, the dictionary will give the present, past, and past participle forms.

Jargon (1) The specialized language of a trade or profession. (2) Inflated, pretentious, and sometimes evasive language that communicates poorly.

Linking verb A verb that joins the subject of a sentence to a noun or adjective complement. A linking verb expresses a condition, not an action. The most common one is *to be;* others are *seem, become, appear,* and *feel:* "I *feel* good"; "I *am* a poor golfer."

Modifier A word, phrase, or clause that gives additional information about another word or group of words.

Mood The attitude suggested by a sentence. The three grammatical moods are **imperative**—expressing commands: "Leave me alone!"; **indicative**—making statements: "Paris is the capital of France"; **subjunctive**—expressing desire or possibility (see p. 254): "I wish that I *were* more assertive."

Nonrestrictive A modifying phrase or clause that is not necessary to ex-
element pressing the basic sense of a statement (see nonessential modifier, p. 262): "The University of Texas owns a Gutenberg Bible, *the first printed book";* "Kingman, *president of our firm,* will open the meeting."

Noun clause *See* Clause.

Objective case The form of pronouns that indicates that the word designates the receiver of an action or an object, directly or indirectly: **direct object**—"The emperor dismissed *them* contemptuously"; **indirect object**—"Kostelanetz sent the message to *her* last week."

Parallelism The use of repetitive patterns of language in words, phrases, or clauses in a sentence: "It's a bird, it's a plane, it's Superman!"

Parenthetical element A group of words expressing something that is not essential to the main idea of a sentence, and thus can be marked off by commas, dashes, or parentheses: "Samson, by the way, is wearing his hair short."

Participle A word that comes from a verb but acts as an adjective: "*running* water," "*eroded* hills," "*cooking* school."

Passive verb The verb form used when the subject of a sentence receives the action of the verb: "Clements *was criticized* for his budget cuts"; "Rock stars *are idolized* in England."

Personal pronouns The pronouns used in the conjugation of verbs—e.g., *I* go, *you* go, *he* goes, *it* goes, and so on. This class of pronouns includes the **subjective, objective,** and **possessive** forms.

Phrase A group of words that does not have a predicate and is used in a sentence as if it were one word.

Possessive pronouns *See* section on pronouns, pp. 254–60.

Predicate The verb in any sentence or clause. **Simple predicate** designates only the verb or verbs; **complete predicate** designates the verb and all other elements in the sentence that are attached to it: simple predicate—"She *came* early and *helped* the ushers"; complete predicate—"He *arrived late and charmed the audience.*"

Predication *See* "The Grammar of Sentences," pp. 249–51.

Preposition A word used to show relationships or periods of duration. The most common are *in, by, among, between, for, at, after, around, with, about, to, near.*

Prepositional phrase A phrase that begins with a preposition and contains its object and any words that modify that object: "Jesse rewarded her *with grudging thanks*"; "Christina broke *into smiles.*" Note: when a prepositional phrase is followed by a pronoun, that pronoun should be in the objective case.

Reciprocal pronouns The pronouns that show reciprocal relationships: *each other, one another.*

Redundancy Unnecessary repetition of elements in writing. It may occur in phrases, sentences, or longer units. Redundant phrases: *refer back, consensus of opinion.*

Reflexive pronoun Pronoun forms including the term *self: myself, herself, themselves,* etc. For limitations see p. 259.

Relative pronoun The pronouns that come at the beginning of an identifying clause—e.g., *who, whom, whose, which, that.*

Restrictive element A modifying phrase or clause that is essential to the meaning of a statement. Since it is integral, not interrupting, in a sentence, it should not be set off with commas: "Any person driving *without a license* can be fined."

Rhetorical question A question used only for effect or emphasis. The framer of the question expects either no answer or an obvious answer: *"Can we call such a law just? No!"*

Run-on sentence *See "The Grammar of Sentences," p. 248.*

Sentence fragment *See chapter 7, pp. 145–48.*

Simple sentence A sentence containing only one independent clause. It may, however, have many modifying elements: "Coles struck oil"; "After years of frustration, Coles struck oil, the magic black gold."

Standard English The kind of English written and spoken by educated people in the United States. It is the language one finds in books, newspapers, public documents, and hears on radio and television. Also called Edited American English.

Subjective case *See Case.*

Subordinate clause *See Clause.*

Subordination Making one element of a sentence less important than another by expressing it in a dependent clause: *"Although Cassandra was always right,* nobody believed her."

Syntax The arrangement of words and sentence elements to show their relationship to one another.

Tense Time indicated by a verb.

Tone The mood and attitude that a piece of writing conveys to a reader.

Usage The patterns of syntax, diction, and mechanical conventions accepted by a substantial group of people. Patterns of usage change, and different patterns are accepted by different groups. The terms *usage* and *grammar* do not mean the same thing.

Verbal Used as a noun, the term identifies three kinds of words made from verbs, but that do not function as verbs: **gerunds, infinitives,** and **participles.**

Voice As used in referring to verbs, voice indicates whether the subject of a sentence is acting or being acted upon.

Index